Mexico and the
United States

Westview Special Studies

The concept of Westview Special Studies is a response to the continuing crisis in academic and informational publishing. Library budgets are being diverted from the purchase of books and used for data banks, computers, micromedia, and other methods of information retrieval. Interlibrary loan structures further reduce the edition sizes required to satisfy the needs of the scholarly community. Economic pressures on university presses and the few private scholarly publishing companies have greatly limited the capacity of the industry to properly serve the academic and research communities. As a result, many manuscripts dealing with important subjects, often representing the highest level of scholarship, are no longer economically viable publishing projects--or, if accepted for publication, are typically subject to lead times ranging from one to three years.

Westview Special Studies are our practical solution to the problem. As always, the selection criteria include the importance of the subject, the work's contribution to scholarship, its insight, originality of thought, and excellence of exposition. We accept manuscripts in camera-ready form, typed, set, or word processed according to specifications laid out in our comprehensive manual, which contains straightforward instructions and sample pages. The responsibility for editing and proofreading lies with the author or sponsoring institution, but our editorial staff is always available to answer questions and provide guidance.

The result is a book printed on acid-free paper and bound in sturdy, library-quality soft covers. We manufacture these books ourselves using equipment that does not require a lengthy make-ready process and that allows us to publish first editions of 300 to 1000 copies and to reprint even smaller quantities as needed. Thus, we can produce Special Studies quickly and can keep even very specialized books in print as long as there is a demand for them.

About the Book and Editor

The future of the Mexican economy is highly dependent on the health and vitality of its larger neighbor,
the United States. But the dependence is mutual:
Mexico is an important trade partner of the United States
and a vital link in its relations with other Latin
American countries. Contributors to this volume address
the key issues of economic interdependence between Mexico
and the United States, including problems of capital
flow and foreign dependence, the role of trade, the
impact of economic fluctuations and macro policies on
Mexico's economic development, and labor migration.
They highlight mutual approaches to solving joint problems and illustrate that U.S.-Mexico relations cannot be
understood in bilateral terms only but must be built
into the structure of a healthy world economy.

Dr. Peggy B. Musgrave is professor of economics at
the University of California, Santa Cruz. Her publica-
tions include Direct Investment Abroad and the Multi-
nationals: Effects on the U.S. Economy (1975) and Public
Finance in Theory and Practice (with R. A. Musgrave,
1983).

Mexico and the United States
Studies in Economic Interaction

edited by
Peggy B. Musgrave

Westview Press / Boulder and London

Westview Special Studies in International Economics

Copyright © 1985 by Westview Press, Inc.

Published in 1985 in the United States of America by Westview Press, Inc.;
Frederick A. Praeger, Publisher; 5500 Central Avenue, Boulder, Colorado 80301

Library of Congress Cataloging in Publication Data
Mexico and the United States.
    (Westview special studies in international economics)
    Bibliography: p.
    Includes index.
    1. Mexico--Foreign economic relations--United States.
2. United States--Foreign economic relations--Mexico.
3. Mexico--Economic policy--1970-   . 4. Mexicans--
United States. 5. Alien labor, Mexican--United States.
6. Mexicans--Employment--United States. I. Musgrave,
Peggy B.
HF1482.5.U5M5 1985   337.72073   85-3286
ISBN 0-8133-0242-0

Printed and bound in the United States of America

10 9 8 7 6 5 4 3 2 1

Contents

PART 5
GENERAL ASSESSMENT

Tables and Figures

FIGURES

Preface

  This volume explores major issues posed by the
interaction between the neighboring economies of the
United States and Mexico. The important problems that
are addressed include the key areas of Finance, Trade
and Industry, Economic Fluctuations and Growth, and
Labor Markets. In each of these areas the papers highlight elements of economic interdependence and examine
mutual approaches to the solution of joint problems.
The enormous weight of the U.S. economy and its close
proximity to Mexico render the future of the Mexican
economy highly dependent on the health and vitality of
the U.S. economy. But the interdependence is mutual;
Mexico is an important trading partner of the U.S. and
a vital factor in the economic life of the North
American continent.

  The papers were presented initially at a conference
held at the University of California, Santa Cruz,
jointly sponsored by the UCSC Seminar in Applied
Economics, the UC-MEXUS Consortium and the UCSC-MEXUS
Committee. It is hoped that this volume will make a
contribution to mutual understanding between Mexico and
the United States and to progress in seeking joint
solutions. We are grateful to our Mexican participants
for their contributions as well as to our American
colleagues, all of whom have greatly added to the
success of this endeavor.

Peggy B. Musgrave
Director of Seminar in
 Applied Economics

Part 1

Finance

1
Investment and Debt

Francisco Gil Díaz

INTRODUCTION

The topic of this book immediately suggests the problem of savings, since high levels of investment together with insufficient internal savings have led many countries, including Mexico, to their present situation of high external indebtedness. On the other hand, growth models have shown that no relationship exists between savings and growth. Changes in the savings ratio influence growth only temporarily as the economy glides from one steady state to another. But whatever growth models indicate, economists and concerned lay people have been preoccupied with the sufficiency of savings to generate or sustain growth. Perhaps this worry has its origins in the perception of the huge capital needs of a developing country to increase its infrastructure and to make its basic social investments.

The notion of insufficient savings ought perhaps not to exist. Compound economic growth provides some of the required savings and "reasonable" amounts of foreign capital should provide the rest; but often--and perhaps this is the root of most of the concern about the insufficiency of savings--the widespread involvement of the public sector in the economy will, through the prolonged and subsidized pricing of some government-supplied goods and services, continually build up their demand. The greater quantity demanded will require additional investment expenditures, since the government puts itself into the position of provider, in which it would find it politically difficult not to commit greater resources to satisfy the distorted levels of induced demand. Thus, savings are reduced and expenditure needs, however artificial, are raised.

The first and more general section of this chapter discusses Mexico's recent experience regarding its investment ratio and growth rate. It will be argued that the recent enormous rise in the investment ratio, associated with a slight decline in per capita growth, is

3

partly a statistical fallacy and that future growth
does not necessarily require the enormous amounts of
savings that might be inferred from these numbers, if
investment decisions are more carefully screened and
if the pricing of some government-provided services
follows an altogether different strategy.

The second section of the chapter follows through
on some of the ideas in the first part, using a case
study of water pricing in the Federal District. Its
purpose is to illustrate the chain of decisions involving subsidized pricing, lower savings, and higher
expenditures by the public sector. The section ends
with a numerical exercise on the overall budgetary
consequences of subsidized public prices.

In the third section, we show how the openness
of economies is affected by income generated in the
country and not consumed may be enough to finance
investment, if it were retained in the country. But
the greater the risk associated with a currency or the
country's economy, the less savings will be retained
and the more outside capital will be needed to maintain
investment. Since the greater risk is also perceived
by foreigners, the cost of these funds will rise,
especially if it comes in the form of debt. Economic
growth is retarded, the required return on capital is
missed, and unskilled labor income is depressed. It
will be shown how Mexico's rising indebtedness, due to
policies of this sort, has pushed the country into a
situation of financial openness or vulnerability, much
beyond what might be considered reasonable under a
normal functioning of international portfolio
selection.

MEXICO'S RECENT EXPERIENCE WITH INVESTMENT AND GROWTH

When growth rates are shifting from 8 percent in
1981 to perhaps -4 percent in 1983; when the immediate
prospect is at least a couple of years of relatively
low growth; and when the capital stock grew so rapidly
up to the previous 1981 peak, the usual steady-state
projection of output with nice, smooth growth rates in
productivity, labor force, and capital stock is no
longer immediately applicable. Nevertheless, a brief
look at the Mexican experience, which until 1981 had
been one of relatively uninterrupted growth, can be
informative. To do this, it will be useful to set out
the basic long-run trends and variables of the Mexican
economy.[1]

The basic data and assumptions concerning growth
in the Mexican economy are (a) a Divisia index of real
wage growth of 2.5 percent between 1939 and 1979; (b)
physical capital depreciating between 2 and 3 percent,
with a declining trend from 1939 to 1979, or between

TABLE 1
Savings Ratios Consistent with Balanced Growth of
Mexican Economy

Rate of Growth		
GDP	Labor	Gross Savings/GDP
0.0	-2.4	7.0
1.0	-1.5	9.8
2.0	-0.5	12.6
3.0	0.5	15.4
4.0	1.5	18.2
5.0	2.4	21.0
6.0	3.4	23.8
7.0	4.4	26.6
8.0	5.4	29.4
9.0	6.3	32.2

6.5 and 8.5 percent measured as a percentage of gross
domestic product (GDP); (c) a labor share of GDP of
about 45 percent; and (d) a labor-augmenting technological change between 1 and 1.3 percent. To pin down
the data, we shall assume that the capital-output ratio
is 2.8 (it has fluctuated between 2.8 and 3.3), technological change is 1.1 percent, and the depreciation
rate is 2.5 percent. With these data, the gross
savings-to-GDP ratio necessary to finance a steady-
state growth of 6 percent, with the labor force increasing at 3.4 percent per year, will be 23.8 percent.
These data are fairly consistent with our experience.
     When different assumptions about growth in GDP and
employment are combined, the resulting gross savings-
to-GDP ratios consistent with the parameters for the
Mexican economy in a steady-state growth are those
shown in Table 1. These figures fit reasonably well
into part of Mexico's recent experience. From 1956 to
1973, GDP growth was 6.8 percent per year whereas investment averaged 20.3 percent of GDP. Per capita
growth in the same period was 3.4 percent per year.
     Table 2 shows the figures for the gross fixed in-
vestment (GFI)/GDP ratio from 1956 to 1981. With the
exceptions of 1958 and 1959, the average investment
output ratio of 20.3 percent varies little in the 1956-
1973 period. The story is quite different from 1974
onward. Investment reaches an up-to-then unprecedented
26 percent of GDP and stays at high levels, reaching an
unheard-of 30 percent in 1981.
     Although higher investment ratios do not raise the
permanent growth rate of an economy, one would expect

TABLE 2
Ratio of Gross Fixed Investment to Gross Domestic
Product in Mexico, 1956-1981 (in percentages)

Year	GFI/GDP	Year	GFI/GDP
1956	21.5	1969	21.0
1957	20.0	1970	24.0
1958	17.6	1971	22.0
1959	16.9	1972	19.0
1960	20.0	1973	20.0
1961	19.0	1974	26.0
1962	18.0	1975	24.0
1963	20.0	1976	24.0
1964	20.0	1977	23.0
1965	22.0	1978	25.0
1966	21.0	1979	28.0
1967	22.0	1980	29.0
1968	21.0	1981	30.0

Source: Banco de México

a significant, if transitory, rise in total and per
capita output as a result of such a dramatic increase
in investment. But per capita yearly growth fell from
the 3.4 percent mentioned for the 1956-1973 period to
2.8 percent in the 1973-1982 period. Total output
growth went from 6.8 percent to 5.8 percent in the
respective periods.

Regarding the lower growth with higher investment
in the 1972-1982 period, it could be argued that the
buildup of plant, equipment, and infrastructure of slow
maturation will yield a greater output later. Although
that statement contains some truth, the bleak economic
situation faced by the country in 1972-1984 is not the
kind of outcome one could expect from an efficient
increase in the investment ratio. The raw aggregate
figures look worrisome, since one might conclude from
them that the Mexican economy needs to invest 28 to
30 percent of its GDP to achieve its former rate of
growth. As shown in column (i) of Table 3, this investment would amount to an increase of almost 50
percent in the internal savings rate.[2]

Although raising internal savings significantly
is quite a feat in any society, it simply does not
seem feasible in a situation in which real wages have
fallen, corporations are squeezed for cash, and the
government is barely able to finance its most urgent
current and capital expenditure needs. And yet
foreign credit has dried up to the point that the

TABLE 3
Mexico's Internal Savings Adjusted for Changes in the Terms of Trade, 1970-1982

	GDP (a)	Net Internal Savings (b)	Non-Factorial Exports (c)	Export Prices (d)	Import Prices (e)	Terms of Trade* (f)	Savings Rate* (h)	Adjusted Savings Rate* (i)
	(in billion pesos)							
1970	444,271	63,772	34,431	100.0	100.0	100.0	14.4	14.4
1971	490,011	62,648	37,438	104.6	104.5	100.1	12.8	12.8
1972	564,727	74,032	45,540	109.3	110.6	98.8	13.1	13.2
1973	690,891	96,053	58,127	122.7	124.3	98.7	13.9	14.0
1974	899,707	118,865	75,678	159.5	150.3	106.1	13.2	12.8
1975	1,100,050	154,733	75,839	175.4	166.5	105.3	14.1	13.8
1976	1,370,968	184,248	116,396	230.9	210.8	109.5	13.4	12.8
1977	1,849,263	278,373	190,800	330.1	327.9	100.7	15.1	15.0
1978	2,337,348	369,970	244,707	371.4	367.3	103.3	15.8	15.7
1979	3,067,526	506,142	343,284	474.6	418.7	113.4	16.5	15.4
1980	4,276,490	814,506	537,241	700.0	651.8	107.4	19.0	18.3
1981	5,874,386	1,085,540	701,553	860.8	781.4	110.2	18.5	17.6
1982	9,417,089	1,563,268	1,636,503	1,766.5	1,691.7	104.4	16.6	16.0

* $f = d/e$, $h = b/a$, $i = (fb + (1-f)c)/(fa + (1-f)c)$

Source: Secretariat of Programming and the Budget.

country has turned into a capital exporter for the
first time in many years, as shown by the surplus in
the current account in the balance of payments for 1983
and also quite likely for 1984. The short-run outlook
for the Mexican economy in 1983 is obviously one of
considerable difficulty, but do the facts just mentioned mean that it will continue to require huge savings and sacrifices to sustain growth even after the
current crisis has been superseded?

A future resumption of growth will certainly
require effort and an appropriate institutional framework, but it may not require a drastic rise in internal
savings much beyond what has already been achieved
through 1983 by the updating of the prices of many
services and goods provided by the public sector, because part of the rise in investment ratio from 1974 to
1981 was only apparent. In other words, many additions
to the public capital stock were wasted resources that
did not contribute to growth and that might more appro-
priately be classified as unenjoyed current expenditures.

It is beyond the scope of this chapter to make an
economic audit of public capital stock, but an unusable
seaport, a perennially fog-shrouded airport, and an unfinished and very expensive nuclear plant are only a
few of many proofs of the outcome from spending too
much, too fast. Although the amount of waste is
nothing to gloat about, the fact that it accounts for
what otherwise would seem to be a greater investment
requirement for growth is a comforting fact that
suggests that, under sound economic policy, the old
ratios should again work adequately. Following the
logic of the growth model implicit in the previously
given figures for required investment--given certain
growth rates in output, population, and productivity--
one might conclude that little, if any, net investment
will be needed through mid-1985, when output will
barely reach its 1981 level.

But this would certainly not be the case for
public investment because of so many glaring needs for
investing in infrastructure; and it might not be the
case either for private investment if the new exchange
rate is taken advantage of to implement some structural changes. If commercial policy is geared toward
efficiency and foreign markets; if the elimination of
waiting and red tape, and the adoption of a more
liberal attitude encourage investments in border industries; if international air fares are set at competitive world levels instead of those that produce a
profit for the national airlines; and if foreign investment is allowed and even encouraged in tourism--if
all these wonderful events combine, then a significant
amount of private investment will be needed despite the
apparent present level of excess capacity. Furthermore,

TABLE 4
Mexico: Public and Private Savings, 1970-1982

	GDP (1)	Net Internal Savings (in billion pesos)			Structure of Savings (%)		Savings Ratios to GDP (%)		
		Total (2)	Public (3)	Private (4)	Public	Private	Total	Public	Private
1970	444,271	63,772	15,052	48,720	23.6	76.4	14.4	3.4	11.0
1971	490,011	62,648	14,155	48,493	22.6	77.4	12.8	2.9	9.9
1972	564,727	74,032	13,161	60,871	17.8	82.2	13.1	2.3	10.8
1973	690,891	96,053	5,189	90,864	5.4	94.6	13.9	0.8	13.2
1974	899,707	118,865	2,326	116,539	2.0	98.0	13.2	0.3	13.0
1975	1,100,050	154,733	-8,212	162,945	-5.2	105.3	14.1	-0.7	14.8
1976	1,370,968	184,248	-1,196	185,444	-0.6	100.6	13.4	-0.1	13.5
1977	1,849,263	278,373	34,772	243,601	12.5	87.5	15.1	1.9	13.2
1978	2,337,348	369,970	68,824	301,146	18.6	81.4	15.8	2.9	12.9
1979	3,067,526	506,142	105,249	400,893	20.8	79.2	16.5	3.4	13.1
1980	4,276,490	814,506	118,253	696,253	14.5	85.5	19.0	2.8	16.1
1981	5,874,386	1,085,540	-24,285	1,109,825	-2.2	102.2	18.5	-0.4	18.9
1982	9,417,089	1,563,268	-539,536	2,102,804	-34.5	134.5	16.6	-5.7	22.3

Source: Secretariat of Programming and the Budget; Ministry of Finance.

if goods whose relative prices have suffered serious
deterioration because of price controls in recent years
acquire reasonable levels, new investments may also be
needed to expand their production. These goods are
mostly those defined as basic, an area in which investment has suffered serious deterioration. For the rest
of the economy--mostly goods and services not closely
linked to the international economy--there is, on the
average, ample capacity to satisfy rising demand to the
mid-1980s without significant new investments.

For the near future, greater political stability
and investors' confidence in the country ought to be
sufficient ingredients to ensure indigenous capital
that, together with small amounts of foreign capital,
will bring about an outward-looking reorientation of
the economy. For the longer run, if the public sector
is able to maintain the advances in savings achieved
in 1983, internal savings ought to be enough to resume
a balanced state of steady growth.

This reassuring conclusion is based on two facts.
First, after the adjustment period--say, at the beginning or middle of 1985--most of the internal debt will
have been paid up in real terms, and the pressure on
the government budget of interest expenditures will be
a fraction of what it has been in the last two years.
The other is the effect produced on savings by adequate public-sector prices. This theme is developed in
the second part of this chapter, but at this stage one
can point to the aggregate figures in Tables 3 and 4.
In Table 4, it can be seen that public savings have
fallen steadily as a proportion of GDP. The data in
Table 3 show that, even in the years when they appear
to recuperate--such as 1979, 1980, and 1981--an important part of the increase was due to improved terms
of trade.

THE ECONOMIC CONSEQUENCES OF SUBSIDIZED PRICING

The recent World Development Report put out by
the World Bank, dedicated to the development problems
of less developed countries, is interestingly more
concerned with problem areas like management, decentralization in decision-making, bureaucratic problems,
price distortions, project evaluation, and so on, while
devoting less than half a page to the role of domestic
savings. The emphasis is probably well-placed. Growth
has been more affected by the waste in resources
brought about by bad management, centralized decision-
making, and the huge triangles and rectangles of
welfare costs brought about by price distortions.

In the standard treatment of cost-benefit
analysis, the welfare cost attributed to prices,

distorted when set below the marginal cost of providing a good or a service, is represented by a triangle
generated by a linear approximation of the demand
schedule, combined with a constant cost supply function.
However, costs are rarely constant when the distorted
additional consumption is substantial, as often happens
when the price reductions are very important. Under
conditions of increasing cost, the resources involved
in provided the greater induced quantities demanded can
be huge. In some cases, externalities may add an additional important cost to the distortion.

Since price distortions are frequently dismissed
as second-order effects or small triangles that concern
only parket purists or fanatics, the numbers associated
with one such distortion should provide an eloquent
example of how far a market can go astray, wasting huge
amounts of resources and lowering the rate of economic
growth. One of the results of such waste is that more
and more savings are required to finance a lower rate
of growth.

A CASE STUDY IN WASTE: WATER USER CHARGES
IN MEXICO CITY

Water for family use in Mexico City is consumed up
to the satiation point. For families connected to the
municipal distribution system, water is practically
free. There is a nominal bimonthly fixed charge, un-
related to volume consumed, that fluctuates between
U.S. $2 and $3, but the marginal cost of water is zero.

One consequence of excessive demands for water by
the inhabitants of the Valley of Mexico is that the
amount extracted from the underground aquifers of the
valley--1.5 billion cubic meters per year--is twice the
recharge of the water table (700 million cubic meters
per year). Aside from rising pumping costs and pollu-
tion dangers, the city as a consequence of a drier sub-
soil has been continuously sinking for a number of
years--up to 9 meters (30 feet) in some places. A deep
drainage system needs to be built to prevent contaminated water from flooding the city[3] since a large part
of the urban area has sunk below the water level of the
Great Canal, the main conduit for sewage.

Many huge preventive expenditures have been
caused by this problem; the most important among them
is the Deep Drainage System, an engineering feat
started in 1967. At present, it has 90 kilometers
(56 miles) of underground tunnels, some as deep as 220
meters (721 feet), and it will eventually extend to
136 kilometers (81 miles). The cost of this project
up to 1983 has been U.S. $620 million, with a capital
at charge value[4] of $1.4 billion (see Table 6).

TABLE 5
Receipts from Water Services in the Federal District,
1967-1982

	Receipts (in millions of pesos)	Average Implicit Price[a] (in pesos)	Receipts (in millions of U.S. dollars)	Average Price (in U.S. dollars)
1967	133.1		10.66	
1968	143.6		11.50	
1969				
1970	154.1		12.34	
1971	166.2		13.31	
1972	161.1		12.90	
1973	274.6	0.2538	21.98	0.0203
1974	323.6	0.2819	25.91	0.0225
1975	538.9	0.4545	43.14	0.0363
1976	608.4	0.5050	39.39	0.0327
1977	624.0	0.5126	27.64	0.0227
1978	784.6	0.6513	34.46	0.0286
1979	948.4	0.7872	41.59	0.0345
1980	947.6	0.7724	41.29	0.0336
1981	1,119.0	0.8252	45.65	0.0336
1982	1,026.2	0.7567	17.86	0.0131

[a] per cubic meter

Source: Data from the D.D.F. (Mexico's federative
entity comparable to the District of Columbia).

Another consequence of the excessive water consumption induced by zero marginal cost pricing (except
in the poorest neighborhoods, where people pay large
amounts for truck-delivered water) is that more water
has had to be brought in from further away. At the
same time that sewage is sunk underground, clean water
has to be pumped up to the Federal District, with considerable energy costs. By 1985, water will be brought
from as far as 3,500 feet below the city level.

Beyond the engineering marvels of the Deep Drainage System are the costs associated with the consequences of subsidized pricing. It has been repeatedly
observed throughout the world that water pricing and
metering considerably reduce water consumption; in a
recent example of this relation, San Luis Potosí,
Mexico, water consumption was reduced by two-thirds.
Therefore, it is not far-fetched to assume that the
pricing and metering of home water consumption would

TABLE 6
Investment Costs of the Deep Drainage System in
Mexico City, 1967-1983

	Millions of Pesos	Millions of U.S. Dollars
1967-1975	5,400.0	432.33
1977	190.0	8.41
1978	109.1	4.79
1979	1,295.5	56.81
1980	1,320.9	57.55
1981	955.0	38.96
1982	692.2	12.05
1983	1,130.0	9.53

Source: Data from the Secretariat of Programming and
the Budget.

have made unnecessary the Deep Drainage System and
other marginal investments such as the Cutzamala project[5] to bring additional fresh water to the city.
Only some budgetary costs will be considered, ignoring
the benefits from consumer surplus gained from greater
demand; however, many other costs will be left out of
the picture as well. One of them never mentioned in
the Mexican literature is the opportunity cost of fore-
gone agricultural production.

The costs of the Cutzamala project have already
reached $429 million, with a capital at charge value[6]
of $537 million, and substantial amounts will still be
required (see Table 7). If one subtracts the investment expenditures on the Cutzamala project from the
total expenditures incurred on the provision of water
(column B in Table 8) and compares the result with the
revenue of the city government from water user charges,
the resulting figures (in Table 9) still show a deficit. The deficit appears lower for 1977 and 1978 only
because data for column B of Table 8 were not available
for those years. In any case, the figures show that
not even operating expenditures--let alone interest and
depreciation on investments--were covered by revenues.
But since these are average revenues, they do not contribute to reduce the quantities of water demanded, as
the marginal cost of water is nil.

Therefore, even the grossly underestimated capital
at charge values of the underground system, plus the
expenses for the Cutzamala project, look huge. Foreign
public debt might have been about $2 billion lower than

TABLE 7
Investment Costs of the Cutzamala Project, 1976-1982

	Millions of Pesos	Millions of U.S. Dollars
1976	13.00	0.84
1977	69.30	3.07
1978	160.90	7.07
1979	1,049.50	46.03
1980	2,232.50	97.27
1981	4,358.70	177.83
1982	5,574.40	97.01

Source: Data from the Water Commission of the Valley
of Mexico, Department of Agriculture and Water
Resources.

it is, if these investments financed with it had not
been induced through inappropriate pricing. This, of
course, is not the end of the story. Adequate pricing
would not only have made such investments unnecessary,
it would also have reduced considerably the maintenance
costs of water distribution and of the sewage system;
however, these will continue to be immense because of
the varying speeds at which different parts of the city
are sinking.

The overall city budget would have been better
financed with the additional revenues from higher water
charges. And one could go on and on. Correct marginal
cost pricing would have reduced part of the tremendous
inflow of people into urban areas, together with the
burdensome associated expenditures. The conclusion--as
pointed out at the beginning of the chapter--is that
the distortions provoked by subsidized prices not only
result in lost revenue, they also require huge amounts
of so-called investment expenditures to provide an induced need that in turn reduces the rate of growth and
erodes government savings.

This type of distortion, which has become increasingly prevalent, helps explain an important part of
Mexico's present economic difficulties. As a final
example of its effects, Table 10 lists in column A the
deficit of the public sector as a percentage of GDP
from 1965 to 1980, and column B shows the supposed
deficit if the price of petroleum products had been
equal to international prices,[7] and if the prices of
electricity and railways had covered costs, including
capital costs. The only savings on expenditures considered to recalculate the government budget are the

TABLE 8
Total Costs of Getting, Conducting, and Distributing
Water in the Valley of Mexico, 1977-1983

	Millions of Pesos			Millions of U.S. Dollars
	(A)	(B)	(A)+(B)	(A) + (B)
1977	997	n.a.	997	44
1978	1,014	n.a.	1,014	44
1979	1,851	3,533	5,384	236
1980	3,145	3,176	6,321	275
1981	6,209	6,093	12,302	502
1982	8,613	5,872	14,485	252
1983	11,795	n.a.	11,795	99

Source: (A) Data from the Department of Programming
and Budget with the exception of the first two
years as given by the Water Commission of the
Valley of Mexico. This column corresponds to
the expenditure incurred by the Water Commission. (B) Data from the Department of Federal
District and refer to expenditures incurred
for new projects and for maintaining the old
ones for distributing water in the Federal
District.

reduced interest expenses on a lower public debt.[8] The
government would have registered a surplus almost every
year as a result of only the interest savings, if just
three of its firms had kept constant their real 1965
prices. But even this dramatically different picture
is incomplete since many other subsidized goods and
services could be considered. Furthermore, budgetary
savings resulting from higher prices are not confined
to lower interest expenditures; investment expenditures
would also have been less (as suggested by the water
pricing exercise of this section).

INTERNATIONAL FINANCIAL INTERDEPENDENCE

Some interesting implications can be derived from
the Tobin-Markowitz portfolio model regarding the international financial interdependence of open economies.
An optimal world portfolio will by definition be
optimal and the same for everybody, which means that
the share a particular asset will have in the optimal
portfolio will be the same for investors in every
country. If assets issued by small economies appear

TABLE 9
Operating Deficit of Water Supply in the Federal
District, 1977-1982 (in millions of pesos)

	Receipts	Net Expenditures	Deficit
1977	624.0	927.7	-303.0
1978	784.6	853.1	-68.5
1979	948.4	4,355.0	-3,386.6
1980	947.6	4,089.0	-3,141.4
1981	1,119.0	7,944.0	-6,825.0
1982	1,026.2	10,127.0	-9,100.8

Source: Department of the Federal District.

in the optimal portfolio, they will, by necessity, be a
small share of the total world portfolio. And through
the same reasoning, the assets of large economies will
appear with significant shares in the world portfolio.
Since the shares will be the same and optimal for all
investors, any individual investor in any country--
large or small--will demand the same small percentage--
in relation to the world portfolio of assets--of assets
issued by small economies, and the same large percentage of assets issued by large economies.

This behavior has strong implications for global
financial interdependence. Assets issued by large
countries purchased by investors in small economies
will bear a disproportionate relationship to the size
of the small economies. By the same token, assets
purchased by foreigners--which will have the form of
foreign indebtedness and direct foreign investment--
will represent a relatively larger percentage of the
smaller economies than in large countries. What all
this means is that financial openness with regard to
GDP will be much greater in smaller than in larger
countries.

A numerical example, followed by an empirical esti-
mation of the hypothesis, will be used to illustrate
this argument. The empirical estimate will then be
used to calculate the degree to which Mexico's coefficient deviates from the "optimal." The latter is
interpreted to be the coefficient of financial interdependence predicted by the fitted curve, given Mexico's
relative standing in the sum of the GDP of the
countries included in the sample. Last, an attempt
will be made at interpreting the results.

TABLE 10
Mexican Public-Sector Deficit as Percentage of Gross
Domestic Product, 1965-1980

| | Actual | | | Hypothetical | |
	Deficit Including Subsidies[a] (A)	Deficit Excluding Subsidies[a] (B)		Deficit Including Subsidies[a] (A)	Deficit Excluding Subsidies[a] (B)
1965	1.0	-3.8	1973	4.9	-0.8
1966	1.3	-3.9	1974	4.9	-1.0
1967	2.2	-2.6	1975	8.0	2.7
1968	1.7	-3.3	1976	7.6	1.9
1969	1.6	-3.3	1977	5.0	-1.2
1970	2.2	-2.9	1978	5.1	-1.3
1971	1.8	-3.7	1979	5.5	-2.1
1972	3.6	-1.8	1980	5.8	-3.0

[a] Subsidies are those implicit in oil, electricity, and
railway pricing.

Source: See note 8 below.

A Numerical Example of an Optimal World
Portfolio and Financial Interdependence

Three countries are used in the numerical example;
their data appear in Table 11. The assets of country 1
are $100, and we assume that individuals wish to invest
50 percent of their portfolio in the assets of country
1. Country 2, in turn, participates with 30 percent in
the optimal portfolio, and country 3, with the remaining
20 percent. The percentages are, of course, completely
hypothetical. Country 1 distributes its wealth; it
places $50 within the country inself, $30 in country 2,
and $20 in country 3. These amounts are shown hori-
zontally in line 1'. Country 2, in turn, invests $15
in itself, $25 in country 1, and $10 in country 3.
Similarly, country 3 places its wealth of $10 in
countries 1, 2, and 3, using the same optimal proportions applied for countries 1 and 2. The respective
amounts of $5, $3, and $2 are shown in line 3'.
We can start by examining the amount of total
liabilities issued by each country. Country 1 issues
$50 places with its own residents, $25 placed with
residents of country 2, and $5 placed with residents
of country 3. The sum of the liabilities issued by
each country appears in line a', and their sum at the

TABLE 11
Numerical Example of International Portfolio Selection
(in U.S. dollars)

Assets / Liabilities	Countries 1	2	3	a Assets Owned by Nationals $(1+2+3)$	b Foreign Assets	c Net Foreign Assets$^\alpha$
Optimum proportion of assets	.5	.3	.2			
1'	50	30	20	100	50	20
2'	25	15	10	50	35	2
3'	5	3	2	10	8	-22
a' Total liabilities$^\beta$	80	48	32	160$^\gamma$		
b' Foreign liabilities	30	33	30		93	
c' Net foreign liabilities$^\delta$	-20	-2	22			0

$^\alpha$ Line $c = b - b'$

$^\beta$ Line $a' = 1' + 2' + 3'$

$^\gamma$ World assets

$^\delta$ Line $c' = b' - b$

intersection of line a' and column a adds up to $160,
which is equal to total world wealth, or what is equivalent, to the total assets owned by nationals of all
countries.
   The numbers can also be used to calculate the
amount that ends up abroad, the liabilities issued by
each country. Of the $80 issued by country 1, $50 is
purchased by its own nationals, so that $30 ends up in
foreign hands. The same accounting for country 2 shows
$33 = $48 - $15 held abroad. The result is similar for
country 3, where $32 is placed with residents abroad.
The numbers are shown in line b', totaling $93, which
is equal to the total foreign assets held by nationals
of each country, as shown in column b. Column b has
an entry of $50 for country 1 that is equal to the sum
of $30 + $20, the amounts of wealth by residents of

TABLE 12
Ratios to Measures of International Financial Openness

Country	Total liabilities / World assets	Assets owned by nationals / World Assets	Foreign Assets / Total liabilities	Foreign assets / Assets owned by nationals
1	50.0	62.5	62.5	50.0
2	30.0	31.2	72.9	70.0
3	20.0	6.3	25.0	80.0

Country	Foreign liabilities / Total liabilities	Foreign liabilities / Assets owned by nationals	Net foreign liabilities / Total liabilities	Net foreign liabilities / Assets owned by nationals
1	37.5	30.0	-25.0	-20.0
2	68.8	66.0	-4.2	-4.0
3	93.8	300.0	68.8	220.0

Country	Foreign assets plus foreign liabilities / Total liabilities	Foreign assets plus foreign liabilities / Assets owned by nationals
1	100.0	80.0
2	141.7	136.0
3	118.8	380.0

FIGURE 1
Numerical Relationship Between Size and Financial
Interdependence

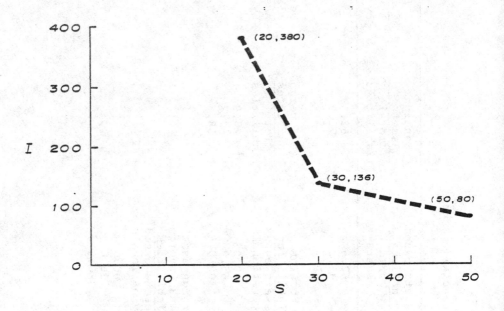

country 1 that are held in assets issued respectively by countries 2 and 3. The same explanation serves for the two other entries in column b.

These numbers already show the enormous degree of international financial linkages produced by the optimizing portfolio behavior of individual investors. For instance, country 2, which is half the size of country 1, has liabilities held by foreigners ($33) greater in an absolute amount than those issued by country 1 ($30). The case of country 3 is even more lopsided. Although one-tenth the size of country 1, it has issued liabilities held by foreigners equal in an absolute amount to those issued by country 1. In fact, country 3 has issued liabilities held by foreigners in an amount triple its own size. The last entry in Table 11 is in columns c and c', used respectively for net foreign assets and liabilities.

The information in Table 11 will now be used to calculate several ratios presented in Table 12. The first entry--total liabilities divided by world

assets--turns out to be the proportion of each country
in the total portfolio. Since there is an association
between a country's wealth and its GDP, the ratio can
be approximated by taking the participation of each
country's GDP in world GDP, if the product/capital
ratio is assumed not to differ substantially between
countries.

In the second column at the bottom of Table 12, it
can be seen how the selection by individual investors
of an optimal portfolio, under the assumptions stated
at the beginning of this section, will lead to an in-
verse relationship between international financial
dependence and the size of the economy. Smaller
countries, as a proportion of their size, will own and
owe more than larger countries simply as a result of a
normal portfolio adjustment. If the sum of the foreign
assets plus the foreign liabilities of a particular
country, divided by the assets owned by the nationals
of each country, is labeled as the international
financial dependence (I) of the particular country, and
this variable is plotted against the relative size (S)
of each country, the graph in Figure 1 results.

An Empirical Estimate of International Financial Interdependence

Data on the stock of foreign investment and
foreign debt are hard to obtain for a large sample of
countries. Data on the assets owned by nationals of a
particular country issued by other countries are
perhaps impossible to get, so to use consistent data
for all countries on both assets and liabilities, an
indirect test was devised, using something akin to a
perpetual inventory for debts and assets, accumulating
those items on the balance of payments that showed
gross inflows of capital for a number of years (1969-
1977) and adding the (absolute value of) errors and
omissions in the balance of payments for the same
period. An estimate of the stock of foreign debt plus
foreign assets was thus obtained.[9] The standard presentation by the International Monetary Fund (IMF) was
used, taking data for as many countries as were available for those ten years. Fifty-four countries were
included in the sample. Their data are presented in
Table 13, which includes all major market economies.
The data are also plotted on Figure 2, in which they
can be seen to follow a pattern resembling the curve
generated by the numerical example. The curve on this
chart is the graph of equation 3 from Table 14. This
curve is the one that had the closest statistical fit.

TABLE 13
Accumulated Flows of Assets Plus Liabilities on Capital Account of the Balance of Payments, 1969-1977 (in millions of SDRs)[a]

Country	Accumulated Flows of Assets and Liabilities 1969-1977		Gross Domestic Product 1977 (GDP)	AFAL/GDP (%)	AFAL*/GDP (%)	Country GDP Relative to Total GDP (%)
	(AFAL)	(AFAL*)				
1 Australia	14,644	17,875	81,261	18.0	22.0	1.759
2 Bolivia	1,246	1,478	2,834	44.0	52.2	0.061
3 Brazil	37,360	39,281	119,072	31.4	33.0	2.577
4 Canada	53,805	63,666	160,917	33.4	39.6	3.482
5 Chile	2,359	3,022	9,457	24.9	32.0	0.205
6 China R.	7,611	7,923	16,338	46.6	48.5	0.354
7 Colombia	2,438	3,175	15,519	15.7	20.5	0.336
8 Costa Rica	1,450	1,679	2,529	57.3	66.4	0.055
9 Cyprus	402	465	916	43.9	50.8	0.020
10 Denmark	13,797	15,266	39,658	34.8	38.5	0.858
11 Dominican R.	1,120	1,466	3,677	30.4	39.9	0.080
12 Ecuador	1,791	2,084	5,315	33.7	39.2	0.115
13 Egypt	4,044	4,651	15,444	26.2	30.1	0.334
14 El Salvador	705	825	2,344	30.1	35.2	0.051
15 Finland	9,469	10,474	26,035	36.4	40.2	0.563
16 France	163,542	178,705	328,107	49.8	54.5	7.101
17 Germany, F.R.	94,479	98,947	468,173	20.2	21.1	10.132
18 Greece	7,469	8,092	22,388	33.5	36.1	0.484
19 Guatemala	962	1,011	4,604	10.9	22.0	0.100
20 Guyana	255	304	360	70.8	84.4	0.008
21 Honduras	793	813	1,271	62.4	64.0	0.028
22 Iceland	574	601	1,508	35.7	39.9	0.033

23	Iran	19,368	22,727	63,001	30.7	36.1	1.363
24	Ireland	8,575	8,741	8,471	101.2	103.1	0.183
25	Israel	10,817	11,540	7,698	140.5	149.9	0.167
26	Italy	70,259	80,003	179,448	39.2	44.6	3.883
27	Jamaica	1,455	1,572	2,689	54.1	58.5	0.058
28	Japan	73,440	78,258	639,533	11.5	12.2	13.840
29	Jordan	399	549	1,234	32.3	44.5	0.027
30	Malta	293	368	500	58.6	73.6	0.011
31	Mexico	24,897	31,043	60,638	41.1	51.2	1.312
32	Morocco	2,146	2,259	8,908	24.1	25.4	0.193
33	Netherlands	66,321	6,800	94,749	70.0	7.2	2.050
34	New Zealand	1,469	1,869	12,857	11.1	14.5	0.278
35	Norway	17,659	18,830	30,501	57.9	61.7	0.660
36	Pakistan	4,262	4,460	12,428	34.3	35.9	0.269
37	Panama	1,950	2,611	1,773	110.0	147.3	0.038
38	Paraguay	546	594	1,722	31.7	34.5	0.037
39	Peru	5,232	6,037	6,643	78.8	90.9	0.144
40	Philippines	4,486	5,500	17,340	25.9	31.7	0.375
41	South Africa	2,289	4,056	32,979	6.9	12.3	0.714
42	Spain	21,232	22,603	92,609	22.9	24.4	2.004
43	Sri Lanka	554	597	1,677	33.0	35.6	0.036
44	Sweden	13,789	17,699	61,880	22.9	28.6	1.339
45	Switzerland	27,203	50,191	60,015	45.3	83.6	1.299
46	Thailand	3,159	3,491	15,458	20.4	22.6	0.335
47	Tunisia	1,819	1,874	4,269	42.6	43.9	0.092
48	Turkey	8,352	9,097	36,427	22.9	25.0	0.788
49	United Kingdom	83,186	92,093	223,016	37.3	41.3	4.826
50	United States	294,507	324,993	1,549,094	19.0	21.0	33.524
51	Uruguay	421	733	3,032	13.9	24.2	0.066
52	Venezuela	10,532	15,534	29,453	35.8	52.7	0.637
53	Yugoslavia	8,229	9,388	32,912	25.0	28.5	0.063
54	Zambia	1,043	1,614	218	478.4	755.5	0.005

(continued)

TABLE 13, continued

Notes

* This column includes accumulated flows in absolute
value of net errors and omissions in the balance
of payments.

a Special Drawing Rights (SDRs) are reserve assets
created by the International Monetary Fund.

Source: International Monetary Fund, Balance of
Payments Yearbook.

Interpreting the Results

It is remarkable--although perhaps common knowledge for those individual investors used to moving
their money around--that international financial
linkages behave in a predictable manner, despite all
the restrictions and obstacles often created by governments in capital movements. Perhaps the only working
restriction is the one placed on foreign direct investment, which apparently does not inhibit the degree of
dependence, except that claims on countries take the
form of debt instead of direct investment.

Interpreting the Results for Mexico

The statistical results seem reasonable considering the limitations of the data. The most serious of
these limitations is perhaps that the perpetual inventory assumption employed to calculate the stock of
foreign debt and foreign assets of the residents of
each country would need several more years of balance-
of-payments statistics to be fully acceptable. In
part because of data deficiencies and in part because
other variables perhaps ought to have been included
to reduce the dispersion of the data, the results are
inconclusive. They are, however, suggestive. They
show how relatively open financially small economies
are, and how careful authorities have to be to retain
savings, considering the strong magnetism of international portfolio selection.

The data for Mexico lie about 13 percentage
points of GDP above the financial interdependence
coefficient predicted by the equation. If more
private capital were retained in the country, or if

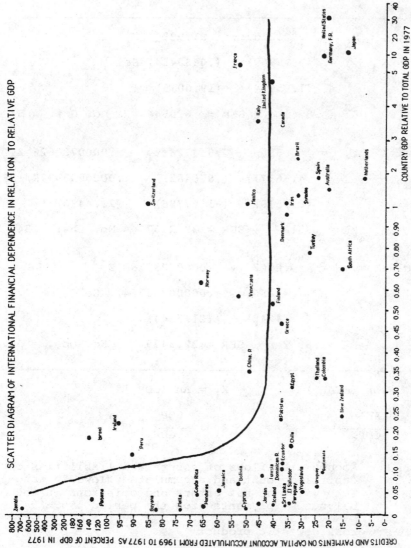

SCATTER DIAGRAM OF INTERNATIONAL FINANCIAL DEPENDENCE IN RELATION TO RELATIVE GDP

TABLE 14
Estimating Equations for Foreign Debt plus Foreign
Assets*

Eq. 1 $Y_i^* = .823028 + .817929 \ X_i$

$\qquad\qquad$ (.419969) $\quad$ (.0430454) Se

$\qquad\qquad$ (1.95974) $\quad$ (19.0015) $\quad$ t

$\qquad R^2 = .8741 \qquad SER = .620544 \qquad$ No. Obs. = 54

Eq. 2 $V_i^* = 42.6965 - .944726 \ z_i + .0000720626 \ z_i^{-3}$

$\qquad\qquad$ (4.76971) $\quad$ (.876482) $\qquad$ (.00000335972) SE

$\qquad\qquad$ (8.9510) $\quad$ (-1.07786) $\qquad$ (21.4490) t

$\qquad R^2 = .9014 \qquad SER = 32.2937 \qquad$ No. Obs. = 54

Eq. 3 $V_i^* = 40.8902 + .0000723026 \ z_i^{-3}$

$\qquad\qquad\cdot$ (4.47256) $\quad$ (.00000335754) $\quad$ Se

$\qquad\qquad$ (9.14246) $\quad$ (21.5344) $\quad$ t

$\qquad R^2 = .8992 \qquad SER = 32.3439 \qquad$ No. Obs. = 54

$Y_i^* = Ln \ (AFAL_i^*)$ $\qquad\qquad X_i = Ln \ (GDP_i)$

$V_i^* = \dfrac{AFAL_i^*}{GDP_i}$ $\qquad\qquad z_i = \dfrac{GDP_i}{\Sigma_i \, GDP_i}$

$AFAL_i^*$ = Accumulated flows of assets and liabilities on
capital account and accumulated flows in absolute value of net errors and omissions in the
balance of payments--for the period 1969-1977

GDP_i = gross domestic product

* For data see Table 13

less debt had been contracted, the observed point would lie closer to the estimated equation and internal financial intermediation might be greater. However, the countries above and below the estimated line do not follow a predictable behavior based, for instance, on economic and/or political risks, so further research is required in these areas.

NOTES

1. This part of the chapter uses results and data from a paper by Francisco Arreola (1982) on growth in the Mexican economy.

2. Table 3 refers to net savings. To make the figure comparable with gross investment depreciation has to be added. Depreciation as percentage of GDP is about 6 percent.

3. In the event of a disaster the historical center of the city would be covered by almost seven feet of sewage.

4. The capital at charge value is calculated at the end of 1973, using a 2.5 percent annual interest rate to reflate the $432 million figure up to 1975. From then on, a 10 percent interest rate is used.

5. Many other examples on a large scale can be provided. The lack of adequate marginal cost pricing to reflect the externalities produced by individual pumping in a common aquifer has been lowering the water table in Sonora to the point at which it is in danger of becoming contaminated with saline water.

6. The capital at charge value is calculated at the end of 1973 using a 10 percent rate of interest.

7. U.S. retail.

8. The data are taken from Gil Díaz (1983).

9. A more detailed explanation is offered in the Appendix.

10. International Monetary Fund, "Balance of Payments Yearbook," several volumes.

REFERENCES

Arreola, F., 1980. "Cálculo del Ahorro que la Economía
    Mexicana Requeriría para Financiar un Ritmo
    Deseado de Crecimiento." Working Paper, Dirección
    General de Política de Ingresos, SHCP.
International Monetary Fund (various years). Balance
    of Payments Yearbook.
Gil Díaz, F., 1983. "Mexico's Path from Stability to
    Inflation," in Arnold C. Harberger, ed., World
    Economic Growth, Institute for Contemporary
    Studies Press, San Francisco, 1984, p. 383.
Lessard, D., 1974. "Capital Market Strategies:
    National Versus International Integration."
    Paper presented at the First International
    Conference on Financial Development in Latin
    America and the Caribbean, Caraballeda, Venezuela,
    February 1979.

APPENDIX

METHODOLOGY FOR OBTAINING THE DATA USED
AND THE EMPIRICAL ESTIMATE OF THE MODEL

The flows of assets and liabilities abroad on
capital account were accumulated separately from the
standard presentation of the balance of payments
published by the IMF[10] during the 1969-1977 period for
each of the fifty-four countries in the sampling. The
period of study and the number of countries were determined by the availability of uniform information on the
balance of payments and GDP. The items considered in
the standard presentation shown of assets abroad in the
balance of payments published by the IMF were

Nonmonetary sectors
25. Direct investment abroad
27. Other private assets at long term
29. Other private assets at short term
31. Long-term government assets
33. Short-term government assets

Monetary sectors
34. Commercial banks: long-term assets
35. Commercial banks: short-term assets
36. Central banks: long-term assets
37. Central banks: short-term assets

The original information from the monetary sectors
is the net figure of liabilities minus assets. The
breakdown in assets and liabilities is presented only
for the most important items--34, 35, 36, and 37--
differing according to country. In those cases in
which a flow could not be explicitly identified as an
asset, the net figure was assumed to correspond to a
liability flow. All asset flows were accumulated with
the opposite sign to the one appearing in the balance
of payments.
The items considered, according to the same IMF
standard presentation of liabilities in the balance of
payments, were

Nonmonetary sectors
24. Direct foreign investment
26. Other private liabilities at long term
28. Other private liabilities at short term
30. Long-term government liabilities
32. Short-term government liabilities

Monetary sectors
34. Commercial banks: long-term liabilities
35. Commercial banks: short-term liabilities
36. Central banks: long-term liabilities
37. Central banks: short-term liabilities

Subsequently, the accumulated flows of both assets and liabilities were added up for the entire period of study and for each of the countries considered. The results appear in Table 13 in column AFAL, where the proportion these have with respect to the 1977 GDP of each country is also shown, as well as the ratio of such GDP to that of all countries.

The proportion of the accumulated flows of assets and liabilities with respect to GDP was used as a first approximation to an index for the financial openness of each country, just as the sum of imports and exports is taken in relation to GDP as an indicator of the openness of an economy to international trade. With these data, the following equations were estimated:

Eq. 1 $Y_i = .390333 + .850585\ X_i$

$\qquad\qquad$ (.413712) (.0424041) Se

$\qquad\qquad$ (.943491) (20.0590) t

$\quad R^2 = .8856 \qquad SER = .611299 \qquad No.\ Obs. = 54$

Eq. 2 $V_i = 38.7614 + .814028\ Z_i + .0000445959\ Z_1^{-3}$

$\qquad\qquad$ (3.84377) (.706332) (.000027075) Se

$\qquad\qquad$ (10.0842) (1.15247) (16.4712) t

$\quad R^2 = .8442 \qquad SER = 26.0246 \qquad No.\ Obs. = 54$

Eq. 3 $V_i = 37.2050 + .0000448027\ Z_1^{-3}$

$\qquad\qquad$ (3.61005) (.0000271) Se

$\qquad\qquad$ (10.3059) (16.5320) t

$\quad R^2 = .8402 \qquad SER = 26.1065 \qquad No.\ Obs. = 54$

where $Y_i = Ln\ (AFAL_i)$; $X_i = Ln\ (GDP_i)$; $V_i = \dfrac{AFAL_i}{GDP_i}$;
and $Z_i = \dfrac{GDP_i}{\Sigma_i GDP_i}$

All equations show an acceptable adjustment of the data
since the information comes from an international cross
section.

Using the coefficients of equation 1, we can see
that the elasticity of the estimated stock of assets and
liabilities the country has abroad with respect to the
GDP is sharply below one and statistically greater than
zero. In fact, a 95 percent confidence interval for
this elasticity places it between 0.77 and 0.94. This
result implies that the proportion represented by the
sum of the accumulated flows of assets and liabilities
abroad with respect to GDP diminishes as GDP increases.
This relation is congruent with the hypothesis that the
optimum portfolio that distributes assets among
countries is common to all countries, and implies that
the financial openness of the economies in proportion
to their size is greater the smaller their relative
size is.

Using the parameters of equation 1, which was adjusted with the data of 1977, the confidence intervals
of 95 percent and 50 percent were estimated for the
logarithm of the accumulated flows of assets and liabilities abroad that would correspond to Mexico's 1981
GDP. The result was that Mexico's external assets during the nine-year period under consideration are only
an approximation of the degree of financial openness--
not only because the initial stock of assets and liabilities is not included, but also because many flows
of assets and liabilities are not computed in the
capital account of the balance of payment, since they
form part of the errors and omissions item.

In tackling the second of these problems, an
alternate indicator was constructed of the degree of
financial openness, adding to the accumulated flow of
assets and liabilities abroad--as calculated previous-
ly--the accumulated flow from 1969 to 1977, of the
result in absolute value in the account of errors and
omissions of the balance of payments of each of the
countries considered in the sampling. This procedure
assumes first that errors and omissions in the balance
of payments only reflect movements of capital, and
second that the net result of errors and omissions
solely reflects the acquisition of external assets,
if their sign is minus, or only the acquisition of
external liabilities, if their sign is plus. The
results of this alternate indicator, which includes
the accumulated absolute flow of errors and omissions
in the balance of payments, appear in Table 13 in
column AFAL*. This information was used to obtain
alternate estimators. The adjusted estimating equations are

Eq. 4 $Y_i^* = .823028 + .817929 \quad X_i$

$\qquad\qquad (.419969) \quad (.0430454) \text{ Se}$

$\qquad\qquad (1.95974) \quad (19.0015) \quad \text{t}$

$\quad R^2 = .8741 \qquad \text{SER} = .620544 \qquad \text{No. Obs.} = 54$

Eq. 5 $V_i^* = 42.6965 - .944726 \quad Z_i + .0000720626 \ Z_i^{-3}$

$\qquad\qquad (4.76971) \quad (.876482) \qquad (.00000335972) \text{ Se}$

$\qquad\qquad (8.9510) \quad (-1.07786) \qquad (21.4490) \quad \text{t}$

$\quad R^2 = .9014 \qquad \text{SER} = 32.2937 \qquad \text{No. Obs.} = 54$

Eq. 6 $V_i^* = 40.8902 + .0000723026 \quad Z_i^{-3}$

$\qquad\qquad (4.47256) \quad (.00000335754) \text{ Se}$

$\qquad\qquad (9.14246) \quad (21.5344) \qquad \text{t}$

$\quad R^2 = .8992 \qquad \text{SER} = 32.3439 \qquad \text{No. Obs.} = 54$

where X_i and Z_i are defined as previously,

$$Y_i^* = \text{Ln} (AFAL_i^*), \quad \text{and} \quad V_i^* = \frac{AFAL_i^*}{PIB_i} \times 100$$

The results of these regressions, taking into account the accumulated absolute flows of errors and omissions in the balance of payments, are essentially equal to those we have already examined. A significant less-than-unitary elasticity of the accumulated flows of assets and liabilities abroad is maintained with respect to GDP.

2
Mexico's Foreign Financing

Thomas J. Trebat

INTRODUCTION

By mid-1982, Mexico's foreign exchange crisis had become fully apparent to the financial world. The closing of the foreign exchange market on August 5, 1982, followed two weeks later by the formal request for a partial moratorium on debt payments, marked a turning point in modern Mexican economic history. In retrospect, the crisis also put an end to a whole era of commercial bank financing of balance-of-payments deficits in developing countries. The Mexico "shock" spread quickly throughout the hemisphere, dealing a severe blow to development programs in almost every other Latin American country.

Much has happened since August 1982. Mexican authorities have distinguished themselves by their skillful management of the liquidity crisis and subsequent debr renegotiation discussions with bank creditors. An ambitious program of economic stabilization has been worked out with the International Monetary Fund (IMF) and implemented in a flexible but steadfast manner despite many obstacles. The debt crisis has also produced an extraordinary degree of cooperation between Mexico and foreign banks, governments, and multilateral institutions, particularly the IMF.

In the fall of 1983, the first signs appeared that the worst of Mexico's foreign exchange squeeze was coming to an end. An enormous trade surplus ($6.5 billion) was generated in the first six months of 1983, thanks to draconian cuts in the import bill. Authorities repaid on time an emergency bridge loan from the Bank for International Settlements and made all scheduled purchases under the IMF program, thus remaining eligible to draw additional tranches of the $5 billion new money facility arranged in late 1982 with the commercial banks. The foreign exchange cash position of the Bank of Mexico improved significantly in 1983, and all remaining payments arrears were cleared, including the final $560 million in private-sector interest payments accumulated in 1982.

In an atmosphere marked by cordiality, Mexico and the banks began signing a series of documents that reschedule public-sector debt amortizations maturing in 1983-1984 for a period of eight years. Finally, some banks, acting on independent credit judgments, were increasing loan exposures--cautiously and on a small scale--to Mexican borrowers, a sure sign of returning confidence.

Although increased optimism regarding Mexico's debt problem is warranted by the developments of 1983, formidable obstacles remain to be overcome over the next decade. The remarkable rebound in the balance of trade notwithstanding, the necessary move away from deflation in Mexico and the achievement of more satisfactory rates of growth will certainly require steady increases in foreign exchange inflows, including commercial bank debt, over the next decade. At the same time, the international financial world has changed: The era of massive commercial bank recycling of ample world liquidity and rapid expansion of international lending has ended. The growth prospects of the world economy are increasingly uncertain; the ability and/or willingness of commercial banks to increase their lending to the Latin American countries has unquestionably been reduced.

In this environment, what steps might Mexican authorities take to ensure an adequate and sustainable inflow of foreign capital in the later 1980s? In light of the new reality of international financial markets, and the legitimate demands of the Mexican people for a gradual end to their austerity, how should internal economic policy be reorganized and international borrowing strategy recast? From an external viewpoint, the challenge to policymakers is one of restoring the conditions for Mexico's creditworthiness outside the context of deflation in Mexico. In this regard, a perspective on how foreign banks might look at Mexico's future financing needs and creditworthiness over the next decade could be useful. The central argument is that the quality of future economic policy in Mexico will determine the country's ability to attract new capital from banks. Banks will closely monitor Mexico's progress toward real structural adjustment, meaning a set of basic economic policies that lead, over time, to an efficient substitution of imports and to the growth of exports.

BACKGROUND TO CRISIS: THE POLICY CYCLE

A careful analysis of the debt crisis in Latin
American countries would show that the crisis in each
country had its roots in a prolonged failure of domestic economic policy. By this interpretation, valid for
Mexico as well as for other Latin American countries,
balance-of-payments crises resulted from policymakers'
giving priority to their own internal, political goals
over the goals of sustainable growth of current account
deficits and external debt. Policymakers were encouraged in their behavior by their ability to gain access
to foreign bank inflows, especially the large Euro-
market syndicated credits that were the dominant form
of international lending to less developed countries
(LDCs) until very recently.[1]

The model implicit in this interpretation ascribes
today's debt dilemma to misperceptions by both princi-
pals--the borrowing government and the lending banks.
The borrowing government excessively trusted the ability
of international banks to make independent credit judgments, thereby mistaking abundant flows of foreign
financing for commercial bank acceptance and support for
economic policies of macroeconomic disequilibrium.
Initially, the banks financed and made possible the
disequilibrium in the balance of payments. In the
early stages of bank lending, banks concentrated more
intently on the ability to make money from large loans
to the different Latin American borrowers, tending to
overlook a deterioration in the standard indicators of
country creditworthiness. In the latter stages of the
crisis, when the deterioration in liquidity and creditworthiness was to clear to be ignored, banks tended to
assume that sooner or later the economic authorities
would take the right measures to correct the disequilibrium, to slow the rate of growth of debt, and to
improve the country's liquidity.

But the essence of the bank misperception was that
policymakers did not take, in most cases, the rational
economic measures necessary to control the disequilibrium and prevent the deficits from deteriorating into a
full-scale balance-of-payments crisis. Banks could not
understand why policymakers did not take "rational"
economic measures when they seemed to be in their
evident self-interest. The reason, of course, was the
influence of political factors, the internal political
objectives of policymakers that, from the very beginning, took precedence over the goal of maintaining
equilibrium in the balance of payments.

At times, the faith of banks in the will of policymakers to take the corrective economic measures seemed
to be well placed, e.g., the turnaround in Brazilian
economic policy toward austerity in early 1981. But
ultimately the availability of bank financing only

permitted policymakers to put off effective adjustment
or to slow down adjustment once adopted. Banks inad-
vertently permitted the problems to grow worse, realiz-
ing too late that policymakers would be unable to
stabilize the balance of payments. At this point, in
country after country a collective reaction appeared
to dominate calm, independent credit judgments, resulting in a sudden withdrawing of financing from Latin
American borrowers that had become dependent upon large
net inflows of credit. The sudden withdrawals of
credit precipitated the balance-of-payments crises in
many countries and touched off the present era of rescheduling.

Turning to the Mexican case, the beginning of the
most recent "policy cycle" can be traced to 1978, i.e.,
to the conclusion of the stabilization effort following
the 1976 devaluation. At that time, authorities repeatedly emphasized the need for Mexico to avoid the
"Venezuela syndrome," namely, the use of oil revenues
to support excessive fiscal spending by inefficient
public enterprises in unneeded, long-term development
projects. In its initial description of the intended
course of economic growth in Mexico, the administration
of José López Portillo had projected that its six-year
tenure would consist of two years of stabilization,
followed by two years of moderate economic growth to
consolidate the stabilization, and ended with two years
of growth close to Mexico's historical average of 6
percent or so. In fact, the oil windfall of 1979 un-
leashed tremendous political pressures in Mexico in
favor of much more rapid growth than policymakers had
initially thought sustainable. The Global Development
Plan of 1979 laid plans for spending that far exceeded
surplus oil revenues, especially after the decline in
world oil markets in 1981-1982, producing an enormous
disequilibrium in the balance of payments.

Victor Urquidi provided a concise characterization
of this post-1978 period of Mexican economic policy:

> After 1978, a spending spree ensued, based on
> oil. All pretense of scarcity and rationality
> in expenditure was thrown to the winds. Mexico,
> the President said publicly, was now going to
> manage abundance. Many optimists envisaged a
> surplus that would enable Mexico to repay its
> foreign debt which earlier had been judged to
> be rather high. Real investment by both the
> public and the private sector—the latter
> engaging in its own reckless expansion—was
> increasing by 15 to 20% per year. Aggregate
> real consumption was rising by 5 to 7% annually,
> also both public and private. Scarcities
> developed everywhere: skilled labor, executive

and technical personnel, building materials, transportation bottlenecks. In the end, the external debt had risen to close to $80 billion by the end of 1981 (of which $20 billion was due by private corporations in banks). Little effort was made to close the public sector financial gap by means of increased tax revenues, or elimination of subsidized prices of public utility services, oil products and the like. The public sector deficit had risen to 8% of GNP at the end of 1980 and to almost 17% at the end of 1981.[2]

Urquidi summarized as follows:

It is too easy as many have done in Mexico to blame the world economic crisis on the oil glut-- plus the voracious appetite for profit of the international banking system--for Mexico's recent and current economic and financial ills. The blame lies squarely on poor policy formulation and on overoptimistic expectations, with no contingency planning. This has fortunately been recognized by the present Mexican administration. It remains to be seen whether the new policies and their implementation are adequate to the real issues.[3]

The interaction of Mexican economic policy and patterns of bank lending is sketched in Tables 1 to 3. Selected indicators of economic policy in Table 1 tell the now familiar story: Mexican gross domestic product (GDP) after 1977 grew annually by rates of 8 to 9 percent until 1982. The rapid growth was led by an investment boom, particularly by the large state-owned enterprises (especially PEMEX and CFE), although the private sector also increased its investment spending rapidly in the boom period. The public-sector banking institutions were also prominent in channeling domestic and foreign resources to a large number of public and private investment projects.

The public deficit overwhelmed domestic savings, spilling over into inflation, which accelerated rapidly after 1980, and rapid increases of the current account deficit and external indebtedness. The boom in Mexico was further fueled by a loose monetary policy and by exchange rate policy, especially the rapid appreciation of the peso in real terms from 1977 through 1981. Domestic interest rate policy and exchange rate policy encouraged borrowing by the private sector abroad and, especially after 1980, significant capital flight.

Mexico after 1978 presented many clear signs of

TABLE 1
Mexico: Selected Indicators of Economic Policy, 1977-1982

	1977	1978	1979	1980	1981	1982 (est.)
GDP (real % change)	3.4	8.3	9.2	8.3	8.1	2.0
Investment (% of GDP)	22.8	23.6	25.9	28.1	28.6	23.0
Inflation (% change in CPI[a])	29.0	17.5	18.2	29.8	28.5	98.9
Index of Real Exchange Rate (1976-1981 = 100)	115.0	108.7	103.7	94.1	83.3	125.0
Money Growth (% change in M-1)	47.0	30.7	35.6	40.3	52.2	61.9
Public sector deficit (% of GDP)	-6.9	-6.2	-7.1	-7.5	-14.9	-16.5
Current account of the balance of payments (US$ billion)	-1.8	-3.2	-5.5	-7.5	-12.9	-2.7
Net international reserves (US$ billion)	1.4	2.0	2.9	3.7	4.9	.3

[a] Consumer price index

Source: International Financial Statistics and Bank of Mexico.

inadequate macroeconomic policy. The argument here is not to make explicit the political goals of the government in this period, but only to point out that these political goals apparently took preference over the goals of maintaining stability in the balance of payments. Mexican policymakers were able to get by with such policies for a long period of time because commercial banks were willing to provide most of the required external financing that public policy in Mexico made necessary.

In the early years of the policy cycle, commercial banks provided all the external credit that Mexico required. In this phase, commercial banks seemed to share the government's optimism about the future of oil revenues. Total external debt more than doubled between 1977 and 1981 (see Table 2). Banks were duly impressed by Mexico's adherence to the 1976 IMF program and by the country's progress in achieving stabilization. In addition, banks obviously were optimistic about the outlook for the Mexican oil sector and about the ability of the government to maintain control over Mexico's growing credit requirements. In fact, it even seemed possible for a time that oil wealth would soon convert Mexico from a chronic borrower into a capital-surplus economy providing liquidity to the rest of the world. In this environment, banks were obviously motivated by competitive pressures not to look too critically at the growing signs of internal and external instability. After all, a bank that refused to lend to Mexico for fear of growing instability would have found itself soon replaced by a bank with fewer concerns in this regard.

After 1977 bank lending to Mexico clearly took place despite a deterioration of some of the key debt service ratios (Table 2). For example, the debt service ratio, which measures the percent of total goods and service exports preempted by payments of amortization and interest, rose steadily after 1978. As an historical rule of thumb, banks engaged in international lending have been concerned when the debt service ratio increased beyond 20 to 25 percent. The debt service ratio in Mexico in 1977 stood at 63 percent, then <u>increased</u> to 81 percent in 1978, and remained at almost that level through 1979 as debt to banks increased by more than 50 percent. True, the traditional debt service ratio declined sharply in 1980 after the increase in oil prices, but it still remained in the 40 to 50 percent range and increased to 63 percent again in 1982.

Other standard indicators also suggested difficulties in Mexico in the 1977 to 1982 period. The net-debt to export ratio, which measures the number of years of exports necessary to repay the debt in its entirety, has traditionally been interpreted as being

TABLE 2

Mexico: Selected Indicators of External Debt and Debt Service Capacity, 1977-1982
(in billions of U.S. dollars unless indicated)

	1977	1978	1979	1980	1981	1982
Registered public debt	22.9	26.7	29.7	33.8	53.0	58.8
Debt of the banking system	1.8	2.0	2.6	5.1	7.0	8.0
Nonbank private sector debt (est.)	5.0	5.2	7.9	11.8	14.9	14.0
Total External Debt	29.7	33.9	40.2	50.7	74.9	80.0
Debt to banks[a] of which	20.3	23.3	30.9	42.5	57.1	62.9
short-term debt	3.4	4.6	6.4	4.8	22.7	16.7
Total amortization payments[b]	3.9	6.9	8.3	5.4	6.6	8.5
Interest payments	2.0	2.6	3.7	5.5	8.4	10.9
Debt service ratio (%)[c]	63.5	81.2	74.0	42.3	48.7	63.1
Net debt to export ratio (%)[d]	305	274	236	189	230	266
Short-term debt to imports ratio (%)[e]	.60	.59	.54	.62	.95	1.15
Interest payments coverage (%)[f]	544	-	-	-	-	133

a: Source: Bank for International Settlements
b: Excludes rollover of short-term debt
c: Short-term debt in percent of total merchandise imports
d: Total debt net of international reserves in percent of exports of goods and services
e: Defined as debt service payments (interest plus principal) in percent of total exports of goods and services
f: Total interest payments in percent of current account balance net of total interest. No entry indicates that the current account balance net of interest was negative.

in a safe range when the ratio has been less than 125
to 150 perce-t of exports. In Mexico, this ratio in
1977 stood at 305 percent of exports, and even with the
runup in oil prices, only declined to 189 percent in
1980 before rebounding to 230 percent in 1981.

A similar deterioration occurred in Mexico's volume
of short-term borrowing. Granted that the amount of
ohort term borrowing was difficult for banks to monitor
carefully because of data deficiencies, nonetheless
the Mexican case was consistently well in excess of the
rough rule of thumb that short-term debt should be at
most 50 percent of total merchandise imports, based on
the theory that trade flows alone justified short-term
debt and that most imports were financed on a 180-day
basis. In fact, in Mexico short-term debt was appoxi-
mately 50 percent of merchandise imports in 1979 but
grew to excessive levels after 1980, reaching 115
percent of merchandise imports in the first half of
1982.

Finally, Mexico's ability to cover interest payments to banks without recourse to more borrowing
weakened steadily after 1977. The ratio of interest
payment coverage, i.e., the ratio of total interest
payments to the current account surplus net of total
interest payments, could not even be calculated during
1978-1981 when no net surplus was obtained. In these
years, Mexico had to borrow from abroad the entire
amount of its interest bill to banks.[4] Even in 1982,
the interest burden was 133 percent of the current
account surplus as defined.

The pattern that emerged is one of very large
increases in bank lending to Mexico just as the traditional signs of creditworthiness deteriorated sharply,
and then the common realization of Mexico's debt
difficulties leading to a collective decision to halt
lending (see Table 3). The net inflow of bank credit
peaked in 1980 and 1981, then slowed sharply in the
first six months of 1982 with the traumatic developments touched off by rapid capital flight and the
February devaluation.

From 1979 through the end of 1981, Mexico had
experienced large positive net inflows from banks, even
after taking into account interest payments to banks.
This pattern changed dramatically after the end of 1981.
The net inflow of credit to Mexico, which had been
positive since 1977, turned to a negative $5 billion
in the second half of 1982. When added to payments of
interest due to banks during this period, Mexico
suffered a net outflow of payments to banks of almost
$10 billion in the last six months of 1982.[5]

A brief and therefore oversimplified explanation
of bank lending would go along the following lines.
Banks began to be seriously concerned about instability

TABLE 3
Bank Lending to Mexico, 1977-1982 (in billions of U.S. dollars)

	1979	1980	1981 I	1981 II	1982 I	1982 II
Changes in medium-term credit	4.8	3.9	1.0	4.8	2.8	1.4
Changes in short-term credit	2.8	8.0	3.1	5.8	4.5	-2.9
Changes in unused credit commitments[a]	1.5	.5	.6	.1	.3	-4.0
Net Inflow of new credit	9.1	12.4	4.7	10.7	7.6	-5.5
Interest payments to banks[b]	2.8	4.6	3.2	3.2	4.2	4.2
Net flow of funds from banks[c]	6.3	7.8	1.5	7.5	3.4	-9.7

[a] Includes unused portions of credit lines and committed but undisbursed term loans

[b] Estimated by author

[c] Equals net inflow of new bank credit minus interest payments to banks

Source: For credit data, Bank for International Settlements, as reported in AMEX Bank Review 10, no. 8/9 (September 15, 1983).

in Mexico in 1981, but their misgivings were easily put
to rest by the announced intentions of the López
Portillo administration in July of that year to begin
significant cuts in public-sector spending. Eventually,
this promised cut in spending did not occur, and
Mexico's public-sector deficit and current account
deficit continued to surge during 1981.

Banks were able to finance Mexico's requirements,
but they did so primarily by increasing short-term
credits, which they perceived as the best way to keep
portfolios liquid while waiting for an improvement in
the policy environment. Net bank inflows remained
positive in the first six months of 1982, despite all
the signs of debt service difficulties, again in large
part because of a willingness by banks to believe the
government's often repeated intentions to begin the
serious task of adjusting the economy. As the promised
cuts in public spending still did not appear to have a
material effect on overall borrowing requirements, and
as the flow of private capital from Mexico accelerated
during this period, banks reached a collective decision
in the second half of 1982 to withhold all new extensions of credit, thereby precipitating the August
crisis. Its international reserves depleted and without access to new bank credit, the Mexican government
was left no choice but to declare the partial moratorium of August.

FUTURE FOREIGN EXCHANGE REQUIREMENTS: A BASE CASE

The administration of Miguel de la Madrid made
remarkable progress in stabilizing the economy in a
relatively short period of time. With a revised set
of basic economic policies, Mexico was able to reduce
the public-sector deficit sharply and to satisfy the
key performance criteria of the IMF Extended Fund
Facility (EFF) with ample room to spare in early 1983.

The results in the Mexican balance of payments
were little less than dramatic. The stabilization of
international oil prices and the sharp decline in
domestic demand for imports produced a large trade
surplus. Mexico's current account position should have
been close to balance in 1983 and have stayed near
balance or even in surplus in 1984. This performance
contrasts very sharply with the large deficits recorded
through the first half of 1982 and the peak deficit of
$13 billion in 1981. The equilibrium in the current
account enabled Mexico to halt the growth of its
external debt, an achievement that caused Mexico to
stand out in Latin America. In all likelihood,
Mexico's requirements for new foreign financing in the
foreseeable future will be modest. The experience

stands in sharp contrast to that of other Latin American countries, notably Brazil, where large amounts of new financing still must be arranged to improve the foreign exchange position of the central bank.

Yet Mexico's debt will not be serviced through continued deflation; moreover, the recovery of the Mexican economy will lead to an increased demand for foreign financing of investment from the mid-1980s on. For illustration, projections have been made of one possible course of the Mexican balance-of-payments and borrowing requirements during this period. The only thing that can be said with certainty about these projections is that they will have to be revised, as new developments and economic cycles cause changes in some of the underlying parameters. However, a projection exercise can at least help define the outlines of Mexico's foreign financial requirements in the years ahead and to prod thinking about a strategy to ensure those requirements are satisfied.

Key assumptions in the balance-of-payments projections relate to the course of Mexican economy. In this exercise, Mexican policymakers are expected to pursue policies that lead to a rate of growth of about 2 percent in 1984, recovering to 5 to 6 percent in 1985-1986 and, with small fluctuations, remaining at or near the 6 percent mark through 1990. Imports recover strongly beginning in the second half of 1984 and in 1985 before settling down into a more normal pattern in line with annual rates of output growth. Mexican exchange rate policy and export promotion policies are assumed to stimulate the growth of nonpetroleum exports and to play a role in moderating import demand.

World oil prices are projected to decline in real terms in 1984-1985 and to remain stable thereafter. (World inflation is anticipated to remain in the 3 to 6 percent range throughout the projection period.) The oil price assumption is crucial to the projections exercise for Mexico, and various alternative scenarios for oil prices will also be tested. However, the base-case world for oil prices is one in which the Organization of Petroleum Exporting Countries (OPEC) discipline is maintained, no serious or prolonged instability occurs in the Middle East, and the gathering recovery of the world economy does not stimulate a rapid increase in demand for petroleum. These various assumptions suggest that nominal oil prices for Mexico will rise from about $26 in 1983 to $36 at the end of 1990.

Mexico's oil exports are expected to expand from 1.5 million barrels per day to more than 2 million barrels per day by the end of the 1980s. Other key assumptions in the projections exercise put the Organization for Economic Cooperation and Development (OECD) real growth, a key determinant of the demand for

Mexican exports, on the order of 3 percent and international interest rates at about 9 percent (i.e., 3 percent in real terms). No economic cycles are assumed to
occur over the period: The environment is surprise-
free, although surprises and shocks will occur. The
major export and import projections are reviewed in
Table 4. Both petroleum and nonpetroleum exports are
expected to expand at annual rates of more than 10 percent through the rest of the 1980s, i.e., a significant
increase in real terms. This expansion will produce a
doubling of Mexico's merchandise exports to $41 billion
by the end of the 1980s. In the surprise-free world of
the projections, Mexican import demand recovers in
1984-1985 then slows to a normal trend growth of 9 to
10 percent per year.

Commercial banks are likely to focus on Mexico's
trade surplus in the rest of the 1980s as an indicator
of the country's ability to manage its large interest
payments burden. The projections (see Table 4) suggest
that Mexico will be able to generate a significant
trade balance surplus through 1990. The trade surplus
should peak at $9 billion in 1983, but remain consis-
tently in a large surplus position. The annual trade
surplus will demonstrate to creditors Mexico's ability
to stabilize its external accounts. At the same time,
the trade results, although large in historical perspective, are based on export growth, and should be
consistent with a trend rate of growth in the Mexican
economy on the order of 5 to 6 percent and satisfactory
employment creation.

Mexico's current account position will be vastly
improved in 1983-1984, but beyond 1984, Mexico can be
expected to revert to its position of a net capital
importer, in large part because of the interest rate
assumptions. Annual interest payments have been on the
order of $10 billion to $11 billion in Mexico in recent
years and are not anticipated to decline significantly
in the foreseeable future even though the rate of increase in the external debt slows significantly.

In all, the current account should shift to a
small deficit position in 1985 and average about $3
billion in deficit through 1990. Although the current
account position would be a small percentage of GDP by
comparison to the recent past, the deficit calls attention to Mexico's need for access to new foreign financing in the future. Implicit in the current account
position is a growth in Mexico's external debt from $83
billion at the end of 1983 to $105 billion at the end
of 1990, a modest growth of 3.4 percent per annum, i.e.,
a decline in real terms and a sharp departure from the
18.9 percent annual growth of the debt during the 1977-
1983 period.

Mexico's gross foreign financial requirements take

TABLE 4
Mexico: Base-Case Projections for Current Account Balance, 1982-1990
(in billions of U.S. dollars, unless indicated)

	1982	1983	1984	1985	1986	1987	1988	1989	1990
Merchandise Exports	21.0	20.6	22.0	23.7	26.5	29.7	33.1	36.8	41.0
(% change)	8.2	-2.0	7.0	7.4	11.9	11.8	11.8	11.1	11.3
Petroleum exports	16.5	15.2	16.0	16.9	19.0	21.3	23.8	26.5	29.5
(% change)	13.1	-7.9	5.4	5.4	12.4	12.1	12.1	11.1	11.4
Nonpetroleum exports	4.5	5.4	6.0	6.8	7.5	8.4	9.3	10.3	11.5
(% change)	-6.6	19.2	11.4	12.8	10.8	11.1	11.1	11.1	11.1
Merchandise Imports	14.4	11.8	14.5	17.9	21.1	24.5	26.9	29.4	32.3
(% change)	-39.7	-18.0	22.5	23.4	18.3	15.7	10.1	9.1	10.0
Balance of Trade	6.6	8.8	7.5	5.8	5.4	5.2	6.2	7.4	8.7
Service Exports[a]	9.7	9.9	10.9	12.2	13.4	14.8	16.3	17.9	19.8
Service Imports[a]	19.0	17.7	17.8	18.9	21.0	23.3	25.3	27.2	29.2
Interest payments	10.9	10.4	9.6	8.8	9.1	9.5	10.0	10.5	10.8
Balance of Services	-9.3	-7.8	-6.9	-6.7	-7.6	-8.5	-9.0	-9.3	-9.4
Current Account Balance	-2.7	1.0	0.6	-0.9	-2.2	-3.3	-2.8	-1.9	-0.7
Key Assumptions									
Crude exports in 1000 bpd	1.5	1.5	1.5	1.6	1.7	1.8	1.9	2.0	2.1
Oil export price $/barrel	29.5	26.0	26.5	27.0	28.6	30.3	32.2	34.0	36.1
LIBOR rate, 6-mo. deposits	13.5	10.0	10.0	9.0	9.0	9.0	9.0	9.0	9.0
Mex. GDP, real % change	2.0	-4.0	2.0	5.0	6.5	6.0	5.0	5.0	6.0
OECD growth, real % change	0	2.0	3.0	4.0	3.0	3.0	3.0	3.0	3.0

TABLE 4, continued

Memo Items
Intl. reserves,

excluding gold[a][b]	0.8	2.4	2.9	3.6	4.2	4.9	5.4	5.9	6.5
Total external debt[c]	82.4	83.2	83.6	86.3	90.3	95.5	99.9	103.2	105.3

a Includes transfers

b Assumed to be 20 percent of merchandise imports, 1983–1990

c Derivation in Table 8

Source: Author's estimates.

TABLE 5
Mexico: Gross Foreign Financial Requirements Under Base-Case Projections, 1982-1990
(in billions of U.S. dollars)

	1982	1983	1984	1985	1986	1987	1988	1989	1990
Current account balance	-2.7	1.0	0.6	-0.9	-2.2	-3.3	-2.8	-1.9	-0.7
Amortization requirements	-30.5	-11.5	-11.1	-19.4	-18.2	-25.3	-26.2	-26.8	-26.4
Public sector debt[a]	-7.1	-1.5	-1.3	-9.6	-5.2	-12.3	-9.5	-8.3	-5.9
(owed to banks at end of 1982)		0	0	-8.7	-4.0	-11.1	-8.3	-7.7	-5.2
(owed to other creditors)		-1.5	-1.3	-0.9	-1.2	-1.2	-1.2	-0.6	-0.7
Private sector debt[b]	-1.4	-0.2	0	0	-3.2	-3.2	-3.2	-3.2	-3.2
Amortization of post-1982 debt[c]	0	0	0	0	-1.2	-2.2	-2.7	-3.5	-4.4
Rollover of short-term debt[d]	-22.0	-9.8	-9.8	-9.8	-9.8	-9.8	-10.8	-11.8	-12.9
Increase in international reserves[e]	3.2	-1.5	-0.5	-0.7	-0.7	-0.7	-0.5	-0.5	-0.6
Gross financial requirements[f]	-30.0	-12.0	-11.0	-21.0	-21.1	-29.3	-29.5	-29.2	-27.7
Gross financial requirements (excl. rollover of short-term debt)	-8.0	-2.2	-1.2	-11.2	-11.3	-19.5	-18.7	-17.4	-14.8

TABLE 5 notes:

a After rescheduling 1983–1984 maturities.

b Existing private-sector debt at end-1982 assumed to be rescheduled at eight years, three years grace. Includes debt of nationalized banks.

c Author's estimate. Terms assumed: eight years, three years grace.

d Level of June 1983 assumed to remain unchanged through 1987. Thereafter, short-term debt assumed stable at 40 percent of merchandise imports.

e See assumption in Table 4.

f Sum of current account balance, amortization, reserve increase.

Source: Author's estimates.

into account requirements for financing the current account balance and rolling over the maturing debt (see Table 5). Amortization requirements include repayments of public-sector debt outstanding at the end of 1982, eventual repayments on remaining public-sector debt (including debt of the nationalized banking system), and amortization of any new debt contracted after 1982. Mexico will also need to roll back its remaining large short-term debt (here estimated to range from $10 billion to $12 billion through the projection period) and to add to international reserves to maintain these at prudent levels.

Mexico has large built-in demands for credit created by the need to refinance a large volume of outstanding external debt, to contract minimal amounts of new trade and project financing, and to maintain a minimum level of international reserves (Table 5). Even assuming that short-term, trade-related debt is always rolled over and not reduced, Mexico's gross financial requirements will begin to increase sharply after 1984, when large amortization payments are once again due on the maturing portions of the external debt. Gross financial requirements in 1985 are anticipated to reach $11 billion, rising to almost $20 billion per year toward the end of the 1980s. It is important to point out that these rough estimates of gross financial requirements do not allow much room for inevitable slippage, e.g., for miscellaneous short-term capital outflows that would increase borrowing requirements, or occasional diffi-culties in rolling over the short-term debt, or a worsened current account position for any of a number of reasons.

What are the sources of these gross financial

TABLE 6
Mexico: Residual Foreign Financial Requirements Under Base-Case Projections, 1982-1990 (in billions of U.S. dollars)

	1982	1983	1984	1985	1986	1987	1988	1989	1990
Gross financial require-ments[a]	8.0	2.2	1.2	11.2	11.3	19.5	18.7	17.4	14.8
Sources of financing									
Official sources[b]	1.8	2.1	3.0	3.25	2.3	2.6	2.9	3.0	3.2
Official disbursements	1.5	2.8	1.7	1.9	2.0	2.2	2.4	2.5	2.7
Supplier credits	0.1	0.1	0.2	0.25	0.3	0.4	0.5	0.5	0.5
Reserve-related inflows									
International Monetary Fund	0.2	1.1	1.1	1.1	0	0	0	0	0
Bank for International Settlements, U.S. Treasury, others	0	-1.9	0	0	0	0	0	0	0
Direct private investment	1.0	0.5	0.7	0.8	0.8	0.9	1.0	1.0	1.1
Total identified sources	2.8	2.6	3.7	4.05	3.1	3.5	3.9	4.0	4.3
Residual for financing[c]	5.2	-0.4	-2.5	7.15	8.2	16.0	14.8	13.4	10.5
Amortization payments to commercial banks[d]		0	0	8.7	4.0	11.1	8.3	7.7	5.2
Residual net of amortization payments to commercial banks		-0.4	-2.5	-1.55	4.2	4.9	6.5	5.7	5.3

TABLE 6 notes:

[a] Derived from Table 5. Excludes rollover of short-term debt.

[b] Includes World Bank, Inter-American Development Bank, Commercial Credit Corporation, and other bilateral disbursements.

[c] Equals gross financial requirements minus identified sources.

[d] Scheduled amortizations on public-sector debt (after rescheduling) owed to commercial banks on December 12, 1982

requirements? In Table 6, the gross financial requirements (excluding rollover to short-term debt) are contrasted with two identified sources of balance-of-payments financing: disbursements of official credits (including the World Bank and the International Development Bank) and direct private investment. Official disbursements have played only a minor role recently in meeting Mexico's foreign financing requirements and these inflows are not projected to increase dramatically during the remainder of the 1980s. No further emergency, reserve-related inflows, such as those provided by the Bank for International Settlements and the U.S. Treasury in 1982, are projected to occur in the future, and no further IMF disbursements are anticipated after the expiration of the present EFF in 1985. Foreign direct investment has declined sharply in the crisis years of 1982-1983, and is here projected to recover only very slowly through the end of the 1980s. The assumption is that it will take time for both the market in Mexico and the confidence of foreign enterprises to recover so that for the balance of the 1980s, foreign equity inflows will be less than the peaks recorded in recent years.

No other relatively secure sources of capital inflows are assumed.[6] The comparison of identified sources of financing with gross financial requirements results in a relatively large residual for financing (see Table 6). The financing "gap" is modest in 1984, but increases sharply to average almost $14 billion a year by 1990. Even if the highly questionable assumption were made that commercial banks would agree voluntarily to refinance all amortization payments on medium-term public-sector debt in the rest of the 1980s, the residual gap for financing would remain in the $4 to $7 billion range each year in the second half of the 1980s.

The implications of Mexico's balance-of-payments performance and financial requirements on external debt

TABLE 7
Mexico: Total External Debt, Debt to Banks, and Major Debt Service Indicators Under Base-Case Projections, 1982-1990 (in billions of U.S. dollars and percentages)

	1982	1983	1984	1985	1986	1987	1988	1989	1990
Total external debt[a]	82.4	83.2	83.6	86.3	90.3	95.5	99.0	103.2	105.3
Debt to international commercial banks[b]	62.9	67.9	71.9	74.2	77.7	82.1	85.9	88.8	90.6
Change in debt to banks	5.8	5.0	4.0	2.3	3.4	4.5	3.8	2.8	1.8
Change in bank exposure (%)	10.1	7.9	5.9	3.2	4.6	5.8	4.6	3.3	2.0
Major Debt Service Indicators									
Net debt as % of exports of goods and services[c]	265.6	264.6	243.9	229.1	213.4	201.3	188.6	175.4	161.2
Interest and amortization as % of exports of goods and services	63.1	39.5	32.9	51.4	46.4	60.9	51.2	46.4	39.8
Interest payments coverage (%)[d]	132.7	91.4	93.5	112.4	133.7	156.0	139.5	120.9	107.7
Net bank flows[e]	-2.5	-3.5	-4.3	-5.3	-4.4	-3.7	-4.8	-6.2	-7.5

TABLE 7 notes:

[a] Increase in external debt assumed given by current
account deficit plus change in reserves net of direct
private investment inflows.

[b] For 1984-1990, commercial bank share of total Mexican
external debt is assumed to remain constant at 86
percent.

[c] Total debt net of international reserves.

[d] Total interest payments in percent of current account
balance net of total interest payments.

[e] Change in debt to banks minus approximate annual
interest payments to bank creditors.

Source: Author's estimates.

and the key debt service indicators are seen in Table 7.
We assume, for illustration only, that the world has not
changed and that commercial banks continue not only to
refinance maturing debt but to add to exposure as well.
On past patterns, the commercial bank portion of Mexico's
debt would expand from about $67 billion at the end of
1983 to more than $90 billion by the end of 1990. In
retrospect, the required exposure increase appears
relatively modest: 4 percent per annum over the rest
of the 1980s compared to 22 percent during 1977-1983.
Later, the argument will be made that even exposure
increases of this magnitude could be large relative to
the supply of bank financing.
     The debt service indicators (see Table 7) suggest
a very slow return to creditworthiness as traditionally
measured. For example, the net-debt to export ratio,
under the base-case projections, is not expected to fall
below 160 percent of exports of goods and services before
the end of the 1980s. The traditional debt service
ratio (debt payments in percent of exports) will decline
to the 30 to 40 percent range in 1983-1984, but increase
to 40 to 60 percent through the end of the 1980s. The
interest payments coverage ratio indicates that Mexico's
surpluses on trade will generally not be sufficient to
meet all interest payments without recourse to additional borrowing. Finally, in contrast to the boom
period, net financial flows to the international
financial community with be substantially negative
through the balance of the 1980s as interest payments
can be anticipated to exceed by a considerable margin
the hypothetical net increases in bank borrowing
(compare data in Table 7 with those in Table 3).

54

TABLE 8
Mexico: Impact of Alternative Scenarios on Key
Performance Indicators, 1984-1990 (in billions
of U.S. dollars and percentages)

	1984	1986	1988	1990
Current account deficit				
Base case	0.6	-2.2	-2.8	-0.7
Oil price increase	2.1	-0.1	0.2	3.3
Oil price decrease	-0.9	-3.7	-3.6	-2.2
Interest rate decline	2.3	-0.8	-1.4	0.6
Interest rate rise	-1.0	-4.4	-5.2	-3.6
Gross financial requirements[a]				
Base case	1.2	11.3	18.7	14.8
Oil price increase	0	9.7	14.3	8.5
Oil price decrease	2.1	13.2	18.1	14.2
Interest rate decline	0	10.4	16.0	11.2
Interest rate rise	2.3	13.8	19.8	15.4
Total external debt				
Base case	83.6	90.3	99.9	105.3
Oil price increase	81.9	84.7	89.7	90.3
Oil price decrease	84.9	93.8	105.2	113.9
Interest rate decline	81.8	85.0	91.4	94.4
Interest rate rise	85.0	94.9	108.7	119.8
Net debt to export ratio (%)				
Base case	243.9	213.4	188.6	161.2
Oil price increase	229.4	191.8	159.5	125.2
Oil price decrease	260.9	235.1	208.6	185.3
Interest rate decline	251.0	211.9	179.8	151.8
Interest rate rise	261.2	237.8	215.8	195.6
Debt service ratio (%)				
Base case	32.9	46.4	51.2	39.8
Oil price increase	31.6	44.6	47.6	35.7
Oil price decrease	34.6	49.3	52.4	40.3
Interest rate decline	29.3	44.7	48.2	36.5
Interest rate rise	39.9	54.0	56.6	44.1

[a] Excludes rollover of short-term debt

Scenario description

1. Oil price increase: oil prices each year 10 per-
    cent higher than base case
2. Oil price decrease: oil prices each year 10 per-
    cent lower than vase case
3. Interest rate decline: LIBOR each year 2 percent
    lower than base case
4. Interest rate rise: LIBOR each year 2 percent
    higher than base case

ALTERNATIVES TO THE BASE CASE

To examine the sensitivity of the key results of
the exercise, alternative assumptions have been made
for the future paths of oil prices and interest rates
(Table 8). Changes could also have been made in the
growth parameters set for the Mexican economy and the
world, but changes only in oil prices or interest rates
demonstrate sufficiently the direction of changes in
such projection results as the current account deficit,
gross financial requirements, total external debt, and
the major debt service indicators. This scenario
exercise is artificial because parameters are assumed
to occur in isolation; e.g., changes in the oil price
are not anticipated to occur simultaneously with
changes in world economic activity or interest rates.
    The major conclusions from the alternative
scenarios can be summarized as follows:

1. If oil prices average 10 percent higher than
    the base case the current account surplus be-
    comes positive by the end of the 1980s. This
    leads to zero growth of external debt, though
    no reduction in the debt occurs. By the same
    token, an oil price decrease averaging 10 per-
    cent per year by comparison to the base case
    would lead to a faster annual rate of growth
    of external debt: 5 percent versus 3 percent
    in the base case.
2. Base-case projections are sensitive to assump-
    tions regarding international interest rates,
    with each percentage point change in the LIBOR
    rate affecting $700 million in current interest
    payments. Assuming that interest rates in the
    balance of the decade averaged 2 percent
    higher in each year than the base case would
    lead to a 5 percent annual rate of increase in
    the external debt through 1990. A 2 percent
    decline in LIBOR rates would benefit the
    Mexican current account and external debt
    positions in much the same way as the increase
    in oil prices.
3. Even under optimistic assumptions regarding
    oil prices and interest rates, the nominal
    value of Mexico's external debt continues to
    increase through the end of the 1980s. More-
    over, the major debt service ratios show very
    little improvement by comparison to the base
    case. For example, in the case of an oil
    price increase the net debt to export ratio
    only declines to 125 percent by 1990. The
    debt service ratio only declines to about 35
    percent of exports.

4. Thus, even with optimistic assumptions, Mexico
    will require <u>net</u> new inflows of foreign capital
    in the 1980s <u>and</u> some of the closely watched,
    traditional indicators of the debt service
    burden will indicate external vulnerability.
    With more pessimistic assumptions, Mexico's
    gross financial requirements and external debt
    increase significantly by comparison to the
    base case.

FUTURE OF BANK FINANCING: LESSONS FROM THE PAST

How should policymakers in Mexico react to the
challenge of ensuring adequate access to financing
from the mid-1970s to the mid-1980s? What will be the
role of international commercial banks that up until
now have been Mexico's major source of financing?
Answers to such questions require a perspective on how
banks are likely to read the lessons of the past. The
principal argument here is that the crisis in Latin
America has fundamentally altered the nature of international lending by banks, and Mexican strategy will
have to be reformulated in the 1980s to adapt to this
new reality.

The first conclusion that banks are likely to draw is
that debt levels in Latin American countries, including
Mexico, are excessive and that a prolonged period of
adjustment is required before increases in debt levels
are feasible. In the case of Mexico, the growth of
external debt far exceeded the growth of Mexican exports
for years prior to the 1983 crisis (see Table 7). Many
banks are likely to be extremely cautious in extending
new credit until export growth reduces the relative
burden of the debt. The projections exercise suggests
that the reduction of the debt burden will take years
to become fully apparent.

The past pattern of bank lending to Latin American
countries gives additional grounds for skepticism concerning the future volume of bank lending to the region.
Although detailed breakdowns of bank exposures by
country of nationality are not available, most credit
to Mexico has been provided by a relatively small
number of very large banks. The largest nine U.S.
banks accounted for more than 20 percent of total bank
lending to Mexico at the end of 1982 (see Table 9).
Each of these banks increased relative exposure to
Mexico from 1973 to 1982 as new lending far exceeded
the growth of bank capital. Credits to Mexico now
represent almost 50 percent of the combined capital
of these nine largest banks; exposures to Brazil are
equally high on average.[7] Even if the region were not
in crisis, prudent banking practice would suggest that

TABLE 9
Concentration of Bank Lending to Brazil and Mexico at the End of 1982
(in billions of U.S. dollars and percentages)

	Brazil		Mexico	
	Exposure ($ billion)	% of Total Bank Debt	Exposure ($ billion)	% of Total Bank Debt
U.S. banks				
Nine largest banks	13.3	22.0	12.9	20.5
Next fifteen largest banks	3.9	6.5	5.1	8.1
Subtotal of twenty-four largest banks	17.2	28.5	18.0	28.6
All other U.S. banks	3.3	5.5	6.4	10.2
Total	20.4	34.0	24.4	38.8
Non-U.S. banks	40.7	66.0	38.5	61.2
Total banks	60.5	100.0	62.9	100.0

Source: Federal Financial Institutions Examination Council, Country Exposure Lending
Survey, December 1982.

loans to Mexico in the 1980s would be limited by capital growth, which can roughly be projected at 5 to 10 percent per year. With uncertainties still clouding Latin America's financial future, a safer assumption would be a reduction in the relative exposure of Mexico's largest bank creditors.

Other factors also point to a reduced financing role for major creditors. Changes in banking regulations in the United States now require banks to maintain minimum levels of capital relative to total loan portfolios. The 5 percent minimum capital requirement will affect primarily the large U.S. banks that were able to expand Latin American loans in the past by running down the ratio of capital to total loan assets. Furthermore, many of the largest U.S. banks in the 1970s moved aggressively into international lending in that decade, and international loans commonly represent 50 percent of the loan assets in these banks. Portfolio balance considerations will suggest a relative slowdown in the growth of all international lending in the 1980s, including loans to Mexico and other Latin American borrowers.

Almost 20 percent of Mexico's loans from U.S. banks were provided by smaller, regional U.S. institutions. Many of these, it is reasonable to surmise, are reevaluating their international strategy in the light of recent developments in Latin America. Some of these banks will opt to improve their monitoring abilities and to stay actively involved in international lending. However, many others will probably decide that the importance of their international business does not justify considerable expense for monitoring and business development and will seek to reduce their portfolios. Many regional banks entered international lending either as participants in large syndicated loans organized by larger international banks, or to engage in short-term lending, both trade and nontrade related. The syndicated market will certainly be a much less important factor during the 1980s; short-term working capital credits have been rescheduled in Mexico and elsewhere into eight-year assets, making such loans less attractive; and a very active competition can be expected in the future with larger U.S. banks to provide high quality trade-related credits to Mexico.

Some of the same factors are likely to constrict the future lending of non-U.S. banks that account for almost 60 percent of total bank lending to Mexico and were particularly active in lending to Mexico after the late 1970s. Without a long tradition of lending, European and Japanese banks are less well situated to follow developments in Mexico in the future. Many of these banks will probably defer decisions to extend new credit until the recovery process is well under way in Mexico. Finally, international banks have come through

a very difficult period in Latin America over the last
twelve to eighteen months with further difficulties yet
to be overcome. Many banks (though not all) have incurred losses from loans to the private sector in Latin
America, especially in Mexico. Loans to borrowers in
Brazil, Argentina, Venezuela, and elsewhere have moved
to nonperforming status on the books of many banks,
though it is hoped that these problems will soon be
overcome. But until the consequences of the 1982-1983
bank crisis become clearer, it is not reasonable to
assume that these institutions will soon return to a
business-as-usual expansion of credit to Mexico or other
Latin American borrowers. Just as its August 1982
moratorium affected an entire region, Mexico will be
affected by developments in Brazil and elsewhere: Some
period of time will have to go by before banks begin
adequately to differentiate Mexico from other less
developed countries (LDCs) that will have more difficulty implementing stabilization programs.

If adequate amounts of "voluntary" commercial bank
financing may not be assumed, can the "involuntary"
provisions of refinancing and "new money" that have
characterized the first round of rescheduling in Latin
America simply be repeated at annual intervals in the
future?[8] These emergency financings, involving large
numbers of bank creditors working in tandem with the
IMF, have worked reasonably well in 1983 to provide
Latin American countries with net new lending from banks
ranging from 5 to 12 percent. They have served the
short-term interests of Latin American governments and
creditor banks.

Several considerations suggest that these emergency
schemes are not workable beyond the immediate crisis
period. Such schemes are ultimately dependent on the
willingness of individual banks to cooperate for the
common good with a master financing plan worked out in
closed negotiating sessions between a small group of
very large banks and country authorities. In fact, many
banks have refused to participate in these bailout
schemes. Most of these have been smaller banks, and
larger banks have been able to compensate for the attrition. For example, only 172 of Brazil's more than 800
bank creditors participated in the new money facility
of February 1983. Furthermore, some very large international banks refused to participate in important
aspects of the Brazilian refinancing, notably the provision of "money market" lines to the foreign branches
of Brazilian banks. Considerable pressure brought to
bear on "recalcitrant" banks by central banks the world
over was not successful in most cases.

The Mexican scheme, possibly because it was the
first such exercise, was more successful in obtaining
cooperation from creditors. Not all banks, however,
took up their "fair share," and the lesson for the

future is the same. Some banks will see the pursuit
of the common good as harmful to their individual interests and either refuse to participate or exercise
whatever discretion is available to reduce their
exposure. Other banks will decide that they do not
wish to see secular increases in their international
lending and will drop out. Still others will decide
that the mandatory aspect of the refinancings only
means more "good money after bad." In fact, news reports suggest that some large European banks have already begun to write off their existing loans to
Brazil.[9]

For these reasons, one must assume that banks in
the future increasingly will make independent credit
judgments and that the attrition rate of participating
banks will only mount the longer the pattern of involuntary lending is prolonged. For Mexico's largest
international creditors that will continue to support
such schemes, the consequences of attrition are clear:
They will be forced to shoulder a relatively larger
share of new money requirements and to compensate for
eventual exposure reductions by "recalcitrants."
Although these larger banks undoubtedly believe in
Mexico's long-term prospects, they may well be reluc-
tant to increase their already high exposures relative
to capital. It is also doubtful that individual regulatory agencies in the lending countries will be enthusiastic about this process of LDC loan concentration in
the largest banks.

The era of recycling has ended and banks probably
cannot be forced indefinitely to lend to Latin American
countries. Where does this leave a country such as
Mexico that has legitimate demands for incremental
foreign financing? The choice of action seems clear:
A strategy must be developed to attract adequate inflows from banks in the 1980s. A possible strategy for
Mexico in that decade is blocked out in the following
section.

TOWARD A STRATEGY FOR THE 1980S

During the 1980s banks will engage in much more
careful monitoring of the economic policy framework in
Mexico. In retrospect, they probably will conclude
that they failed to understand properly the role of
political considerations in economic policymaking in
Mexico and elsewhere in Latin America. As a result,
banks were too willing in the past to share in a
government's optimistic view of the future while over-
looking the present, unmistakable signs of instability
in the economy. In the future, banks are likely to
look for clear progress in a number of critical policy
areas related to development and stabilization,

focusing on select policy issues that permit easy
monitoring from abroad. Obviously, banks do not have
the legitimacy or the capability to become involved
in policymaking as such. However, they do have the
responsibility to justify their own lending decisions.

The focus here is the best strategy for Mexico to
follow to attract additional inflows of private bank
capital in the 1980s. Obviously, many other developments
will be necessary during the decade that reach well
beyond the control of the Mexican authorities. Two of
these developments are improvement in world economic
activities, including improved macromanagement in the
United States, and more flexible support from the IMF
and other official lenders.

The strategy recommended is one of structural
adjustment in Mexico, and the specific issues discussed
rest on a bedrock of rational economic policies of
special concern to banks. Most of these are already
defined as policy objectives of the Mexican government
in the IMF program. They include an exchange rate
policy that avoids a real appreciation of the peso,
interest rate policy consistent with rates that are
positive in real terms, and a set of policies consistent with a secular deficit of the public sector of
no more than 3 to 4 percent of GDP.

But I wish here to be more specific about the
areas of structural adjustment that seem to be of most
concern to banks. These are areas in which a whole set
of economic policies will have come to bear to produce
results that can be monitored unambiguously from
abroad.

Macroprogramming of Public-Sector Investment

Although commercial banks in the future may prefer
to provide relatively safe, collateralized, short-term
trade financing (PEMEX export credits come immediately
to mind), Mexico will also require longer term funds from
banks to support investment. Barring a rapid restoration of Mexican private-sector confidence and creditworthiness, most of the country's long-term foreign
financing will have to be raised through public-sector
borrowing.

But important changes will have to be made in the
ways in which the public sector borrows abroad. Banks
have learned to be wary of the massive balance-of-
payments financings that characterized the era of the
voluntary bank lending to Mexico before 1982. They
have come to realize that such loans basically provide
budget support to the government, even if, on the face
of it, the loans are tied to high-priority investment
projects of such companies as PEMEX, CFE, or NAFINSA.

No matter what the stated purpose of a loan, banks understand that their loans replace allocations the government would otherwise need to make from its budget and hence facilitate disequilibrium government spending.

Commercial banks in the 1980s and beyond will turn much more attention to the nature of the deficit that underlies the foreign borrowing request of the government, i.e., to exactly why the government is borrowing. In consequence, public-sector borrowing in the decade will have to be much more clearly focused on the investment projects of the governments as these provide the only legitimate rationale for medium-term commercial bank borrowing. A fundamental priority of the Mexican government must be to develop a rational public-sector investment program, one that sets clear investment priorities among competing projects and involves payoff periods consistent with the use of commercial bank financing rather than longer term, more concessional financing, such as that provided by the World Bank and IADB.

A possible approach to macroeconomic planning of this sort might be to establish annual targets for the scale of net external borrowing by the public sector of Mexico, particularly the scale of its net borrowing on international financial markets.[10] Mexico's total borrowing needs, carefully designed to be consistent with overall macroeconomic equilibrium, could then be presented for the consideration and support of the international financial community.

It must be emphasized that this scheme does not involve a return to project lending whereby commercial bank loan disbursements and repayments are tied to the progress of a specific project. Although project lending (including cofinancing with the World Bank) may become more important in the future, this type of lending is too inflexible for Mexico's foreign exchange cash needs and is cumbersome for banks to administer. Without tying lending to specific projects, but within the strict ceilings of the investment budget, banks would then compete to provide Mexico with the needed financing. Obviously, it is crucially important to the credibility of the exercise not to exceed the borrowing targets set at the beginning of the planning exercise.

Bank monitoring of the medium-term, macroeconomic consistency of the public-sector investment program presents another challenge. With Mexico in crisis and closely monitored by the International Monetary Fund, it is not difficult to convince banks that Mexico's medium-term economic program is an equilibrium program and that rational economic policy is being followed. Beyond the expiry of the Extended Fund Facility in 1985, communication of higher quality than that in the past will be necessary between the government and its creditors. Banks will need better information of a general macroeconomic nature along with specific information on the shape and progress of the investment program. Information will also be needed on the amount of foreign public-sector borrowing that has taken place by comparison to the amounts projected at the beginning of the planning period. The important point is that banks in the 1980s will be looking much more closely at the underlying rationale for government borrowing than they have in the past.

Prior to the crisis, a large proportion of total gross fixed investment in Mexico was carried out by state companies, particularly in the energy and petrochemical sectors, but also in steel, agriculture, and transportation infrastructure. A large number of projects were in the start-up stage in early 1982. Now that the crisis is easing, the government faces many difficult decisions about which of these projects to continue and which to cancel or postpone. Presumably, those projects selected as priority would benefit from access to commercial bank financing.

Banks can be expected to react more positively to such requests to the extent that the economic rationale of the individual projects is made clear. In this regard, efforts now under way in the Secretariat of National Patrimony to improve public investment allocation through tighter central controls on state-owned enterprises are certainly a step in the right direction. In general, those projects that result directly (e.g., oilfield development) or indirectly (e.g., port construction) in increased exports would be the most suitable for foreign commercial bank financing.

Export Promotion

The debt crisis in Latin America can be managed in the very short-run through deflationary domestic policies, but in the longer run the real burden of the debt will only be reduced through increased export growth. In the future, foreign commercial banks will be very sensitive to the quality of economic policy as it affects export potential and to a country's success in export growth and diversification.

In the case of Mexico, banks are likely to focus on the rationality and consistency of trade and exchange rate policy. Exchange rate policy is undoubtedly the most critical issue and for a long time to come banks will be concerned by any prolonged real appreciation in the value of the peso. The debt crisis has brought with it a series of emergency policies with possibly harmful long-term effects on export growth, including the dual exchange rate system and the system

of import controls and licenses. Beyond the gradual
elimination of these emergency policies, authorities
may wish to review the underlying structure of protection (including production subsidies and tariffs) in
Mexico. The system has resulted in very high rates of
effective protection and thus an anti-export bias for
intermediate and manufactured goods (especially consumer durables).

In all these policy areas, banks are likely to see
rational measures as leading to improved export prospects. A matter of concern since the mid-1970s has
been Mexico's growing dependence on petroleum for the
bulk of its export earnings. Pervasive export pessi-
mism in Mexico (and elsewhere in Latin America) notwithstanding, the record indicates that Mexico has
excellent potential as an exporter of diversified manufactured products. The volume of these exports grew
very rapidly after the 1976 devaluation and could once
again become a dynamic factor as the world recovery
consolidates.

Banks will probably look to the volume and composition of manufactured exports as a key indicator of
structural adjustment in Mexico in the second half of
the 1980s. Given the size of the domestic economy and
the improving level of technology, Mexico should be
able to compete more successfully in foreign markets in
general and in the U.S. markets in particular. Mexican
private firms (those making automobiles and chemical
products, for example) have been successful in such
efforts in the past and have the capacity to become
more successful in the future. The key will be the
adequacy of economic policy and the government's
specific efforts to promote non-oil exports.

Relations with the Private Sector

The priority issues--greater rationality in public-
sector investment and export promotion efforts--tie in
with an improvement in the economic relations between
the Mexican government and the private sector. Foreign
banks will almost certainly be concerned with the
future of their private-sector clients and the economy
would seem well served by policies that strengthen the
private sector--both domestic and foreign companies.

Despite its sharp decline in relative importance,
foreign direct investment really can be an important
source of foreign capital inflows in the future. The
attendant burden of external servicing of foreign
equity is directly correlated with economic conditions
in the country rather than inversely correlated as is
the case with foreign loan capital. Improved policy
can be an important means to rebuild equity inflows

quickly to the high levels recorded in years before the
1982 crisis. In this regard, Mexico's more flexible
interpretation of foreign ownership rules and recent
changes regarding regulations for in-bond industries
are encouraging steps in the right direction.

The point of encouraging the private sector to play
a greater role in Mexico's investment needs in the
1900s is by no means limited to multinational enterprise;
it extends as well to domestic private enterprise.
From afar, the past relations between the government
and the private sector appear to have given way to
much uncertainty that has adversely affected private
investment and increased the propensity of the corporate sector to engage in destabilizing capital outflows. Indeed, a return to more satisfactory rates
of growth in Mexico in the future will certainly require a strong recovery of private-sector confidence
and investment.

Encouraging the private sector would begin by
recognizing the adverse impact of present deflationary
policies under the IMF program. These policies include high real rates of interest, the rapid pace of
devaluation, the system of import and price controls,
public-sector procurement, and other policies meant to
bring about a rapid adjustment of the public sector,
but which deal heavy blows to the domestic private
sector. The FICORCA scheme has been an important step
by the government that shows it recognizes the difficulties faced by private-sector companies with severe
mismatches between foreign currency liabilities and
the currency structure of their earnings. Other ways
must be found to reduce financial pressures on the
private sector.

The growth of the private sector is essential to
increasing the volume of national savings, investment,
and crucially, exports in the 1980s without recourse to
large sovereign borrowings abroad and large government
budget deficits. The policy of stimulating the private
sector includes a review of present regulation in
Mexico to encourage increased competition and lower
barriers to entry, a thorough review of protectionist
legislation that seems to have encouraged the growth of
profitable but inefficient and inward-looking corporations, and a very careful monitoring of lending
policies of the nationalized banks to prevent the
emergence of rigid credit allocation schemes that would
stifle the flow of credit to the private sector. In
general, the government may wish to review nationalized
bank policies to determine the possible roles for
private financial institutions that would be consistent
with the longer term commitment to public ownership of
the major commercial banks. An active private presence
in the banking system might prove a valuable means of

stimulating competitive practices in the state-owned banks.

The encouragement and promotion of the private sector can be directly related in several ways to Mexico's foreign financing requirements. Increased inflows of multinational risk capital obviously will reduce the residual balance-of-payments financing gap in the future and keep in check the growth of bank debt. Furthermore, multinational investment in Mexico will provide a natural export platform for Mexico's major market for manufactured exports, the United States. Although not without considerable government prodding, the foreign-owned automobile companies have shown the usefulness of outward-oriented foreign investment.

The Mexican private sector can also be very valuable in raising foreign loan capital. Public-sector borrowing, the dominant pattern of Mexico's external debt in the 1970s, resulted in no meaningful distinction for banks between the credit risk of any given loan and the transfer or sovereign risk. By permitting the private sector to engage in foreign borrowing, the state will be able to shift at least the credit risk involved in such borrowing onto the foreign private banks. This shift alone is a strong argument for permitting (although not actively encouraging) the growth of private-sector borrowing abroad, despite the legacy left by the bankruptcy of the Alfa group. Public-sector guidelines might be needed to prevent or to discourage private-sector contracting of external debt in cases in which private-sector companies do not have access to foreign currency earnings.

One lesson learned by foreign banks in the Latin American debt crisis is not necessarily the best approach for efficient allocation of resources in the future. The lesson is that it is safer to deal with sovereign lenders and government guarantees than with unsecured credits to the private sector. Borrowing by some private-sector companies was excessive in Mexico (and elsewhere in the hemisphere), but relatively large Mexican companies, especially those engaged in foreign trade and with access to foreign currency earnings, have been and will remain attractive customers for foreign lenders. Mexican debt strategists in the 1980s would do well to recognize this fact. This scale of net foreign lending to the Mexican private sector will be quite modest until banks can fully assess the impact of the crisis on their existing portfolios. But a healthy private sector able to finance viable export-oriented investment projects abroad clearly seems in the best interests of Mexico and its foreign bank creditors.

The Role of the International Community

The task of ensuring adequate flows of foreign financing to Mexico in future years does not belong exclusively to the Mexican authorities. Other participants in international financing--governments, multilateral institutions, foreign banks--will have to adapt their own behavior to the new realities of international financing.

The Government Agenda. Mexico has a right to expect better economic policies in the United States that will lead to a consolidation of the present world recovery and a reduction in interest rates. The impact of interest rates on Mexico's financing requirements and the growth rate of world trade are critical. Another key issue that must be addressed by the U.S. and other governments is combatting the protectionism that flies in the face of Mexico's need to boost non-oil exports. An increased share of Mexico's foreign financing requirements will have to come from bilateral sources until foreign bank confidence recovers and the real burden of Mexico's debt is reduced. Trade credits from the U.S. Commercial Credit Corporation and the Export-Import Bank have been important in 1982-1983; more bilateral credits of this sort will be crucial in boosting the volume of Mexican trade. Finally, Mexico has a right to expect a much more supportive stance by the United States in such issues as the proposed increases in IMF quotas and capital of the World Bank as well as specific backing when Mexico approaches these agencies in the future.

Agenda for Banks. Many banks will withdraw permanently from lending anywhere in Latin America or seek to reduce their relative exposures. Little can be done to change this fact. At the same time, the larger banks (not just those in the United States) have an historical commitment to Mexico and very large loan portfolios that will require management in the future. The attitudes of these banks are critical in influencing the behavior of smaller lenders.

The major bank lenders, taken as a group, will recognize that their role in the policy cycle was not always helpful and that, in particular, bank lending to Latin American countries proved unstable: Periods of excessive lending were followed immediately by no lending at all. This instability suggests that bank credit decisions were too often influenced by marketing considerations and the behavior of the competition and not often enough by independent assessments of country creditworthiness. Although common patterns of bank lending behavior can be anticipated in the future, Mexico can expect foreign bank creditors to improve their systems for processing economic and financial

information on the country and to react positively to
concrete evidence that rational economic policies are
leading to the type of structural adjustment described
earlier in this chapter.

Agenda for the IMF. The IMF has recommended the
standard fund medicine to Mexico, and the deflationary
policies followed over the last year seem to have produced the desired results. But the future relevance of
the IMF to Mexico will also have to be seen in the
light of the need for structural adjustment. The
nominal aim of Mexico's Extended Fund Facility (EFF) is
precisely to promote structural adjustment, but neither
the meaning of this objective nor the means to obtain
it have ever been made clear--in Mexico or in other EFF
programs in Latin America. On the surface, the EFF in
Mexico promises to be no more than a series of one-year
standby programs strung together by a chain of quarterly performance targets.

In the light of the arguments already given, the
program of the International Monetary Fund should be
recast to emphasize more rational investment allocation
in the public sector, export promotion, and support for
the private sector. All these objectives are probably
given lip service in the present agreement (e.g., the
reduction of the credit requirements of the public
sector is supposed to increase credit availability to
the private sector), but more is needed.

As a start, the horizon of the Fund program could
be stretched from three years to five, or even more if
necessary, recognizing that structural adjustment
efforts will take time. Methods could be examined
whereby the general structural adjustment targets could
be expressed in the form of specific government programs that the Fund staff could use in fashioning a
realistic public-sector investment program to be presented to the international banking community.
Specific programs to promote export growth could be set
up and the volume of non-oil exports established as a
type of performance indicator.

The sense of these suggestions is that actively
promoting recovery in Mexico should be just as much a
function of the Fund in the future as achieving short-
run stabilization of prices and the balance of payments
is today. As recovery proceeds in Mexico, the volume
of Fund resources could diminish to be replaced by
increased inflows of voluntary lending from the
commerical banks, but an important oversight or monitoring role for the Fund could be preserved.

SUMMARY AND CONCLUSIONS

The central argument of this chapter is that the external debt crisis in Mexico was the result of a prolonged failure of economic policy made possible by the availability of ample external financing. A review of Mexico's foreign financing requirements in the balance of the 1980s and beyond suggests that the needs for gross borrowing from abroad will continue to be substantial even as Mexican authorities revamp economic policies in the direction of greater rationality.

The need for additional borrowing comes up against a fundamental constraint imposed by the debt crisis: The era of massive recycling by international commercial banks has come to an end. In the future, far fewer banks will be actively involved in international lending and those that do participate will be under pressure to reduce their relative exposure not only to Mexico, but to other Latin American countries as well. Thus, we cannot safely assume any voluntary expansion of commercial bank lending to Latin American countries in the absence of specific strategies on a country-by-country basis to attract new inflows. To assume otherwise is to wish the problem away. Furthermore, beyond the immediate crisis period no practical way is available to compel banks to lend if this conflicts with their independent credit judgments.

A strategy to attract inflows of voluntary commercial bank lending has been considered for the case of Mexico. The essence of the strategy is a program of structural adjustment, one that will convince commercial bank lenders of Mexico's future creditworthiness even as it sets the foundations for higher rates of growth of output and employment in Mexico. The three key elements of the strategy are macroprogramming of public-sector investment, export promotion, and support for the private sector in Mexico. Banks will need to see monitorable progress in each of these areas before reaching independent decisions regarding the extensions of new credit. Banks have little willingness or ability, let alone legitimacy, for becoming involved in the policymaking progress in Latin America. However, they do have an obligation to make clear the longer term justification for their lending decisions. Ultimately, only credible programs of structural adjustment will provide this justification.

Mexico is in a unique position among Latin American borrowers to begin this process of structural adjustment and a new era of relations with the international banking community. Political stability, close financial and political relations with the United States, oil, and the demonstrated competence of economic managers--these are the factors that allow

Mexico to stand out. These factors will certainly make
it easier, but no less imperative, that needed reforms
be made that will assure adequate access to foreign
financing in the decade ahead.

NOTES

1. The concept of the policy cycle was more fully
developed in Lawrence J. Brainard and Thomas J. Trebat,
"The Role of Commercial Banks in Balance of Payments
Crises: The Cases of Peru and Poland," presented in
the International Conference of Multinational Corporations in Latin America and Eastern Europe, Bloomington,
Indiana, March 5-8, 1981.
2. Victor L. Urquidi, "The Domestic Causes of the
Mexican Crisis," Xeroxed (April 1983), paragraph 12.
3. Ibid., paragraph 22.
4. Debt service indicators for this period for a
broad cross-section of developing countries are reported in the Morgan Guaranty Trust Company's World
Financial Markets, June 1983.
5. For more details on Mexico and other borrowing
countries see AMEX Bank Review 10, no. 8/9 (September
15, 1983).
6. For example, no assumption has been made that
flight capital will be repatriated in response to an
improvement in economic conditions in Mexico.
7. Source: Institute of International Economics,
using data compiled by Prudential-Bache.
8. For more on this topic, see William Cline,
International Debt and the Stability of the World
Economy, Institute of International Economics, Washington, D.C., September 1983, pp. 73-78.
9. Reuters, October 14, 1983.
10. A strategy along these lines was recommended
some years ago to LDCs in Walter Robichek, "Official
Borrowing Abroad: Some Reflections," Finance and
Development, World Bank, March 1980.

Comments

Kenneth Flamm

Francisco Gil Díaz and Thomas J. Trebat are to be congratulated for presenting two thoughtful and often complementary analyses of the future requirements of Mexican economic development. Gil Díaz is concerned mainly with what usually appears in models as the savings gap, whereas Trebat considers Mexico's future foreign exchange requirements. Given the exigencies of the current crisis, Trebat's concerns are more immediate in nature; Gil Díaz addresses issues of long-run growth.

Perhaps not very surprisingly, both discussions share a common point of departure. Gil Díaz, concentrating on whether Mexico is likely to be generating sufficient internal savings to meet the investment requirements associated with its traditionally high rates of growth, focuses on the failures of Mexican investment policy and argues that without an inefficient subsidy policy and plenty of flat-out waste, there would be little need to raise levels of domestic savings. Trebat, concerned with the foreign exchange gap, also looks to macroprogramming of public-sector investment to rationalize and reduce foreign exchange inputs.

The two chapters share a common thread in an indictment of public-sector management of investment programs, yet they diverge sharply on what the consequences of these poorly conceived investments for the future of the Mexican economy will be. Gil Díaz is not worried about savings and maintains that traditional savings rates will more than cover future investment requirements once inefficiencies are eliminated. Trebat, in contrast, is clearly very worried about the future and thinks that even in the best case, the availability of foreign exchange will prove to be a serious and recurrent problem for the remainder of the 1980s.

Specific issues raised by both authors deserve a moment's thought, and I would like to raise them before outlining what I believe are the central themes

71

underlying the two chapters. One point made by Trebat
(and also by Gil Díaz)--that specific policy failures
are responsible for Mexico's predicament--is a worthy
place to start. On this point, the two authors seem to
share what appears to be a widely held consensus among
economists: that serious errors and waste of resources
were associated with Mexican economic policies going
into the 1983 crisis.

However, the same is also said of the policies of
Brazil, Venezuela, Argentina, the Philippines, and any
other of the debtor economies currently preoccupying
the international financial community. One is then
forced to explain why all these economies got into
trouble at precisely the same moment. Surely some
systemic failure must play a role in a dispassionate
analysis of the origins of this international crisis.
After all, investment policies not enormously different
from those described in both chapters have been
followed in Mexico (and other developing countries) for
decades without leading to collapse. Although self-
improvement is a laudable goal, a certain amount of
self-flagellation is also currently taking place. In
truth, the problems were not entirely of Mexico's own
making, and movements in interest rates and oil prices,
quite far from Mexican control, played a major role in
the demise of the oil-led growth model.

Trebat argues that rational measures were not
adopted by both public and private sectors in Mexico
during the years of expansion. The public sector, he
observes, did not control the deficit in the balance of
payments, and the private sector engaged in a wild investment spree that (after the balloon was pricked by
recession) left Mexico with production capacity that
far exceeded its current needs. These developments are
not so erratic when seen from the perspective of the
years in which these decisions were made. Mexican
policymakers were quite aware that the decisions to invest in petroleum depended on projections of future
interest rates and oil prices. In the late 1970s, some
expert predictions forecast continued gradual rises in
the real price of oil and relatively low interest rates.

In fact, some of the contributors to this book
were working with complicated optimal control models
that took projected paths for oil prices and interest
rates and cranked out optimal policies that, broadly
interpreted, were similar to some of the decisions
actually made. Basing policy on these projections was,
in a sense, a giant gamble that failed. Real interest
rates skyrocketed from close to zero to historic highs,
and the bottom fell out in the world oil market.
Similar stories could be told in other third world
nations, where governments borrowed short term to invest in long-term development projects. It was a

maturity mismatch of historic proportions, with the countries involved exposed to most of the risk.

The public sector was not alone in this gamble. In Mexico, much of the enormous investment undertaken by the private sector must certainly have depended directly on the vision of oil-led expansion that gripped the nation. And the vision was not even exclusively Mexican: Foreign investors plowed in new investments in record amounts, and after a decade of very sluggish growth, direct foreign investment soared. So if the expansion of the late 1970s was an irrational delusion, it was based on a dream that was very widely shared--by the Mexican government, the Mexican private sector, the foreign business community, and the international financial system. Therefore, the proposition that Mexican irrationality (public or private) was exclusively at fault is difficult to accept. A much more reasonable stand is that the lack of contingency planning for the worst-case scenarios and perhaps the refusal to accept the unpleasant facts as they unfolded were Mexico's main contribution to its current economic problems. Preparing for pessimistic contingencies is not a particularly rewarding task for planner or bureaucrat.

Trebat goes on to warn that yet another crunch may be expected after 1984 (under what seem to be reasonable and fairly realistic, in the best case, assumptions), and that continued deflation of the Mexican economy will have little long-run utility in helping the Mexicans to service their debt. Here the analysis is right on target. Ultimately, a solution to the debt problem must involve growth in the developing world, since precious little austerity can be imposed without leading to extraordinary suffering and political upheaval. What government--democratic, authoritarian, or totalitarian--can long impose malnutrition, increased mortality rates, and dashed expectations on its populace to service foreign debts? Surely a solution to Mexico's problems must be part of some global package of debt relief, sharing the burden and losses of the disappointed optimism of the late 1970s in an equitable fashion among all parties involved. Although this book necessarily focuses on Mexico, perhaps we should be talking about constructing some socially acceptable way of writing down international debts as a significant component of any approach to Mexico's problems. These problems are not entirely dissimilar from those of the wartime debt in the 1920s, of which John Maynard Keynes wrote; we lack, however, the vision and leadership of Keynes.

Trebat concludes by suggesting some strategies for Mexican economic policy. They are clearly sensible and include better macroprogramming of investment, export promotion, forging of a social compact between government and private industry, creation of a more conducive environment for direct foreign investment, and increased awareness in the United States of the impact of its interest rates on the financial burdens of the developing world, as well as increased support for the international financial institutions charged with easing these strains. I would add to this list further import substitution policies and increased participation in regional integration arrangements, which at least for the moment promise to have a positive impact on pressing foreign exchange constraints.

Gil Díaz sets his sights on Mexican savings and develops an interesting analysis of changes in internal savings. He argues that the balanced-growth savings requirements of Mexico are really quite modest and that resumption of the high growth rates of past decades should not require a much higher savings rate than the historical standard. My principal difficulty with this analysis is that it ignores the demands on savings that continued debt service will make. Gil Díaz deals with Mexico as if it has a closed economy from the standpoint of savings. This perhaps may have been a tolerable assumption in the late 1970s, but is very far from reality by 1983. Mexico is currently a net exporter of capital, which will have an effect on the savings required to finance domestic capital accumulation.

Gil Díaz devotes some of the most fascinating pages of his analysis to the economic history of the Mexico City water system. His extremely interesting description illustrates the importance of investment in public infrastructure and the problems associated with planning and evaluating these investments. He concludes that much of the investment in these projects has been economically wasteful, serving only to disguise more fundamental problems in the pricing of public services. He is quite convincing on these points.

Nonetheless, it is not immediately clear how much of Mexico's current problems, evident in 1983, can be blamed on such inefficiencies. For one thing, as the history of the various water projects illustrates, such boondoggles have been going on for some time in Mexico without causing the sort of crisis currently seen. Also, a very reasonable argument for subsidy of public services exists, when large fixed costs are in their provision, and marginal cost pricing will not permit the recovery of these costs. Finally, much of the public investment in recent years must have gone into the petroleum sector, and a similar analysis of these projects would be essential in conclusively making the case that unproductive investment projects exhausted savings and ran up foreign indebtedness.

In the last part of his chapter, Gil Díaz argues
that in a small economy, outflows of capital into
foreign financial assets naturally are larger relative
to the size of the economy than in a large economy.
This argument is based on the observation that in a
world of perfect capital markets, all investors would
hold the same portfolio of risky investments. When
extended internationally, this standard result of the
capital asset pricing model implies that, since
national assets may be assumed to be roughly propor-
tional to the size of the national economy, large
countries' assets would be a much larger portion of
this standard international portfolio than those of
small countries. Therefore, nationals of a small
country would have a much smaller portion of their
wealth in their own national assets than citizens of
large countries. The implication is that smaller
economies, like Mexico's, might expect to be much more
open financially than large countries as a consequence
of the efficient operation of capital markets.

This insight is useful, but the underlying assumptions are patently unrealistic. It presupposes what
might be called a "world federalist" view of capital
markets--a world in which the nationality of the investor and the physical location of the asset make no
difference in the evaluation of the risk and return
characteristics of an asset. These assumptions are
clearly not true--I would not realistically expect a
Ruritanian court and jury, no matter how the laws are
written, to treat me on equal footing with a Ruritanian.
The costs of acquiring information and adjusting portfolios probably vary substantially across national
boundaries; some preference for assets denominated in
the home currency might be expected; and, of course,
real world capital markets have myriad imperfections
too numerous to mention.

In short, Mexicans might be expected to prefer
relatively more Mexican assets in their portfolios, and
Frenchmen relatively more French assets. Nevertheless,
the argument does make the important point that smaller
economies probably can be expected to be more open
financially than large economies. This difference
raises problems when any sorts of controls on international transactions in financial assets are contem-
plated and is perhaps one reason such controls have
rarely been imposed very effectively in small developing countries.

I would like to conclude by expanding on a theme
found in both chapters. The authors are relatively
optimistic about the role of foreign investment in
easing the foreign exchange constraint on the Mexican
economy. It seems to me unlikely that much help will
be coming from this quarter. The vast bulk of direct

investment in Mexico is oriented toward local markets;
more than 90 percent of sales are national. Foreign
investors at the moment are holding excess capacity
built up to service an oil-drenched internal market
that never quite materialized; little new investment
will take place until the domestic market is well on
the way to recovery.

The 10 percent of sales that are exports are
almost entirely confined to offshore assembly in
maquiladora firms. Here the outlook is relatively
bright since the various devaluations have left wages
at levels comparable to those in Southeast Asia. But
significant barriers to very great expansion are also
found here: The low dollar wages are not politically
sustainable in the long run (I believe); the array of
products in which offshore assembly is a cost-effective
production technology is limited (mainly electronics
and apparel) and shrinking with the effects of inci-
pient automation; and resurgent protectionism in the
United States, the primary market, continues to grow.

The contribution that foreign investment can make
to renewed growth in Mexico probably lies in somewhat
different areas. A key role of direct investment has
been in the transfer of technology to Mexican industry
(this role is implicitly recognized in numerous Mexican
policies affecting foreign investment). By making such
transfer attractive (perhaps in exchange for the
promise of access to the Mexican market at a more
profitable future date), Mexican authorities can encourage import substitution in more technically complex
products, where the greatest promise of further import
substitution lies. Since roughly 60 percent of Mexican
imports (in 1977 for which year figures are available)
were shipped by U.S. multinational firms, some
mechanisms providing an incentive for such firms to
arrange trade credit for Mexican imports might also be
constructed to ease Mexico's current exchange shortages.

Part 2

Trade and Industry

3
Trade and Structural Change

Sidney Weintraub

INTRODUCTION

The United States in the 1980s is going through a flirtation with protectionism that is more serious than any since an earlier love affair led to the Smoot-Hawley tariff in 1930. Actual protection today is not even remotely on the same scale as that adopted more than fifty years ago, since lessons have been learned, but the flinging around of words like fair trade and reciprocity, in the sense of trade-contracting rather than trade-liberalizing action, and support for domestic content legislation to protect the U.S. automotive industry are symptoms of the times. The state of Ohio recently enacted "buy-Ohio" legislation, and more than fifteen states now give preference for official procurement to firms located in the state. There are even trade wars between states reminiscent of trade wars between countries during the 1930s; North Dakota retaliated against buy-Minnesota legislation, and a state senator from Minnesota recommended on national television that Minnesota should relatiate against Ohio.[1]

The unconditional most-favored-nation clause (MFN), the principle set forth in Article I of the General Agreement on Tariffs and Trade (GATT), was discarded in the establishment of codes in the Tokyo round of multilateral trade negotiations. Key nontariff barrier codes, such as that on subsidies and countervailing duties and on government procurement, are based on the conditional form of MFN; that is, equal treatment is not accorded to all other GATT contracting parties but only to those who sign the codes and grant equal treatment in return. The proliferation of nontariff measures, such as "voluntary" export restraints (the language is again being despoiled), "orderly" marketing agreements, and a rash of dumping and countervailing duty cases have been amply discussed in the general and specialized media in the United States.

79

The impression has gained hold that the provisions of the GATT are now irrelevant and that the most important trade actions being taken by governments are <u>ultra vires</u>.[2] The escape clause of the GATT, which permits import restrictions under limiting conditions and with the requirement that compensation should be made if a bound duty is abrogated, has fallen into disuse. The United States and other industrialized countries are generally not prepared to honor the limits developed under this article before imposing import restrictions, to use tariff measures to restrict as the GATT recommends, or to grant compensation for import restrictions imposed. The contracting parties to the GATT have been unable to agree on a new safeguard clause or code precisely because it is impossible to agree on limits prior to permissible imposition of import restrictions or on compensation, or on whether import restrictions should be generalized when imposed, as the MFN clause of the GATT would require, or should discriminate against the most competitive exporters and thus further scrap the MFN clause.[3] In recent years there has been official speculation about the need for more bilateralism in trade relations, relegating to subsidiary status the commitment to multilateralism adopted as the end of World War II.[4] The Europeans embarked on this preferential route some time ago; the United States recently did so for countries in the Caribbean Basin.

This list of symptoms of trade-policy unease is formidable. Substantial trade-restrictive action has been taken by the United States (on such products as textiles, apparel, steel, automobiles, television sets, shoes, agricultural products), but the action is still less severe than the talk.[5] The concept that threatens to make the post-World War II trade rules irrelevant once and for all centers around what is called an industrial policy for the United States. Such a policy is hard to define, but it must relate to official governmental action to foster through tax, financing, and even protective measures, particular sectors, either those believed to be on the frontier of development or those older U.S. industries that are not thriving. The difference between the new industrial policy talk and what now exists is that the former would be thoroughgoing (as is the case today for agriculture and the arms industry), whereas existing policy is sporadic (an import restriction here and a state subsidy there). Countries would be hard put to permit reasonably unrestricted trade in an industry or sector when they are investing substantial resources to develop all aspects of that industry and sector. This approach is evident in U.S. treatment of agriculture and arms production and procurement or in Mexican automotive trade, which has been the object of the country's industrial policy for decades.

I do not wish to single out the United States as the sole country in which this combined issue of industrial policy/trade protection has moved to center stage in the national economic debate. A similar debate is taking place in Europe. Japan, which has emerged from its intense protective phase, is now the most consistent advocate of free trade among the major industrial countries, but Japan hardly comes to the debate with an unsullied record. Developing countries rarely have played by the rules set forth in the GATT and instead have argued that their underdevelopment provides a rationale for protectionism and an industrial policy that fosters infant industries into maturity. This argument does not apply to all developing areas-- certainly not to Hong Kong, not to Singapore, and in varying degrees less to countries in Asia than those in Latin America--but the characterization is not unfair. Part IV of the GATT, the demand for "special and differential" treatment, the existence of general and some special systems of preferences for exports from developing to industrialized countries, and the clamor raised by many developing countries when suggestions are made that some of them might "graduate" from this special treatment--all are illustrations of this different set of rules for developing countries compared with the written rules for industrialized countries. Mexico has never joined the GATT and can thus devise its own trade policy without having to explain why it is not conforming to GATT provisions.

Mexico is also going through a period of major transformation in its trade and industrial policies. Past Mexican trade and industrial policy can fairly be described as one of subsidizing domestic industrialization, using an import substitution model, and providing as much protection from imports as necessary to ensure the survival of the domestic industry. The protection largely took the form of prior import licenses, which were granted or refused on an arbitrary basis. Even some Mexican economists who supported the import substitution concept voiced considerable criticism of the pervasiveness of the domestic protection.[6] Some shift from reliance on import licenses to tariffs occurred early in the administration of José López Portillo, but the experiment was disbanded when the country ran into balance-of-payments difficulties. Probably after Mexico emerges from its current economic crisis, another effort at trade liberalization will be made.[7]

The effort will not be an easy one to carry out. Subsidies are rife throughout the Mexican economic structure, and the authorities may not be willing to face this inherently inconsistent combination of government subsidization of domestic industry and

competing imports. Import competition also implies
that some firms or even industries may not survive,
or may survive only if subsidies are increased; and
Mexico in the past was loath to accept the logic of
competition.

The backdrop to the discussion in this chapter is
that both countries, Mexico and the United States, are
going through intense internal debates about short-
comings of their economic policies as these affect
their industrial structures and the trade consequences
of these structures. The debate in the United States
is about whether the government has played too small a
role in fostering structural change on an industry-by-
industry basis and in Mexico whether the government has
played too large a role in this respect. Mexico is
likely to experiment again with import liberalization,
once the economic crisis is past, and the United States
may embark on a policy of greater import restrictions
to make valid a new industrial policy.

This chapter will look in turn at current U.S. and
Mexican trade and structural policies and at the content of the current debates on these issues in the two
countries; at the changing structure of their trade;
and at how industrial policies in three sectors (automotive, textiles and clothing, and steel) are affecting
the two countries. The final section will discuss
policy options for the future.

TRADE/STRUCTURAL POLICY DEBATE

I do not wish to go too deeply into the industrial
policy debate but rather to provide enough background
to facilitate discussion of U.S.-Mexican trade and industrial relations. The terms of the current trade/
structural policy debate in the United States are not
easy to define because the discussion is largely self
serving. According to one strand of the argument, the
United States is losing its industries to other
countries that use fiscal incentives and import restrictions to develop competitive home industries,
which then displace U.S. exports in world markets.
First, simple industries, like shoes, textiles and
apparel were affected; then more complex industries,
like steel, office equipment, automobiles. The pattern
is increasingly often being played out in the very industries in which the United States should have a comparative advantage--those involving innovation, such as
computers and software, telecommunications, robots,
complex chemicals and petrochemicals, and biotechnology.
According to another strand, through the workings of
the international trading system the United States
(which is depicted as being the last of the free

traders) is being forced to deindustrialize by not only
losing export markets but the U.S. market itself. This
rationale is used to explain the domestic content legislation for automobiles: Other countries subsidize,
restrict imports, impose their own variety of domestic
content legislation, and even insist on export performance requirements whereas the United States preaches
the virtues of free trade.[8] Let's do unto others as
they do unto us--let's have reciprocity.

To deal with the deindustrialization problem, the
suggested solution from those who believe the foregoing
description about how other countries behave is to have
an industrial policy that provides incentives to
specific industries. The phrase "picking the winners"
is pejorative, but this is what is intended. If not,
why name industries? "Targeting" is the current jargon
for this practice. The solution to the problem of
protectionism by others is to discard free trade and
emulate the practices of other countries. The GATT is
dead anyhow. Its rules were devised for a different
time when the market was expected to rule, but in fact
what rules are companies trading among their own affi-
liates and governments trading on their own account.[9]

One way to define the current debate is as follows:
Advocates of an industrial policy for the United States
believe that organized targeting of industries for incentives (and perhaps for protection against imports)
is apt to be more effective than the ad hoc policies
that now prevail.[10] By ad hoc industrial policy, these
partisans mean actions such as the trigger price
mechanism for steel, forcing Japan to restrain its
automobile exports for a year or two at a stretch, and
the drive for domestic content legislation for automobiles.[11] In place of this partial industrial policy
that responds to self-interested pressure, they propose
using planned encouragement of certain types of industries. Such an industrial policy works at the microeconomic level: It encourages specific industries and
sectors. It requires detailed government involvement
in the planning since only government can give fiscal
incentives and grant import protection.

The contrary argument is that an organized policy
exists, at least in concept--namely, the search for
maximum liberalization of international trade--but
there will be some backsliding. Raymond Vernon has
described U.S. trade policy as demonstrating a long-
term commitment to open markets, but at the same time
a tendency to stray in individual cases.[12] Those who
are uneasy with the idea of industrial policy are
especially fearful about its micro aspect. They argue
that if U.S. policy were correctly managed instead, the
appearance of deindustrialization of the United States
would dissipate.[13]

Those who argue that the GATT is becoming increasingly irrelevant obviously have much evidence on their side. The nondiscrimination principle has become persistently less universal over the past twenty-five years, not only because of the formation of the European Economic Community and the European Free Trade Association, but the granting of tariff preferences by these two groups to each other and to scores of other nations. Mention was hardly made in the U.S. literature when the United States modified more than fifty years of practice and granted special tariff preferences to beneficiary nations in the Caribbean Basin. The toying with the idea of sector agreements between the United States and each of its neighbors, Canada and Mexico, again illustrates that the most-favored-nation principle no longer is as important in U.S. thinking (or in the thinking of other countries) as it once was.

The critical issue, it seems to me, is not whether the GATT still plays as significant a role as it once did (since it is self-evident that it does not), but whether discarding it in favor of a system under which each country decides for itself what forms of protection and incentives it will use, for industries of its own choosing, would lead to something better. The effect on the rest of the world must be radically different when a country like Mexico pursues such a policy (which it does) from what it would be if the United States did so. Other nations producing automobiles hardly retaliate when Mexico imposes domestic content legislation, but they could not refrain from retaliating if the United States did so. A thoroughgoing U.S. industrial policy would mean jettisoning the central features of the multilateral GATT structure, and the United States cannot take such a step lightly.

Those who argue that the United States is deindustrializing because of the trade consequences of industrial-policy measures taken by other countries have not provided evidence to prove the assertion. Robert Z. Lawrence looked at the evidence of U.S. deindustrialization from trade in the 1973-1980 period and found precisely the opposite to be true.[14] His data, using input-output analysis, showed the volume of U.S. manufactured exports increasing more than imports and employment increasing because of trade in thirty-one of the fifty-two industrial sectors he examined. He also found that international trade was not the cause of the employment decline in most of the other sectors. The automobile industry was virtually the only industry in which he found an employment decline resulting from international trade, but even in that industry the employment decline had many causes. The steel industry, he said, would have had a difficult time in the years he examined regardless of imports.

Lawrence's final point is a macroeconomic one--that the
erosion of the U.S. trade position from 1980 through
1982 was largely the consequence of the appreciation of
the U.S. dollar.

Philip H. Trezise, in an examination of Japanese
industrial policy, made the following comments: "The
impressive economic growth and social stability of postwar Japan are not owing in any decisive degree to the
microeconomic decision making that is often held up as
a source of Japanese accomplishments." He also made the
point that the "visions" of the Japanese Ministry of
International Trade and Industry did not provide resources and that not many resources were provided from
elsewhere in the Japanese government for a micro-
economic-based industrial policy.[15]

The U.S. government does affect specific industries
by a thoroughgoing "industrial" policy in agriculture
and by sporadic protectionism, regulation and disregu-
lation, environmental standards, and tax measures. However, the major influence of the government in the United
States, for better and for worse, is the mix of macroeconomic policies. Advocates of an industrial policy
would alter this by introducing more, and more systematic, microeconomic judgments, backed by resources.[16]

The situation in Mexico has been very different
in the modern era. As did many other Latin American
countries after World War II, Mexico adopted an industrial policy based on import substitution. This policy
required not only setting up industries to replace goods
previously imported, but also protecting them against
competition from imports. Certain sectors were reserved
for the state (for example, petroleum and basic petrochemicals) because they were believed to be critical to
the economic development of the country. The state
acquired many other industries out of less lofty
motives, frequently to keep them from failing, but often
further state aid was required to continue operating
these industries under state control. Other industries
were provided with substantial assistance from the
budget, without necessarily reserving the activity to
the state, because they were believed to provide employment and production benefits directly and through a
ripple effect on companies supplying intermediate products to them and on companies for which the industry
provided intermediate products. The automotive and
parts industries were particularly important examples
of this form of industrial policy; subsidization of
these industries has been substantial for decades. In
addition to fiscal subsidization, the state decreed that
the production and assembly of automobiles must have
rising proportions of domestic content (of goods and services), and in theory imports of automotive vehicles and
parts were prohibited unless the importer exported an

equivalent value of automotive products. I use the
words in theory because these performance requirements
did not eliminate Mexico's import surplus in this
sector.

This elaborate import substitution model of industrialization inevitably required planning and targeting.[17] Mexico tried to pick the winners--the automotive industry, basic petrochemicals, steel, cement,
capital goods--sometimes with reasonable (but costly)
success, sometimes without. The need to pick the
winners was made necessary not only because of the
development model, but also because for much of the
period since World War II the Mexican peso was overvalued. This overvaluation made restrictions against
imports even more imperative and also made necessary
export subsidies on a case-by-case basis to make
Mexican goods more competitive in export markets.

Mexico's import substitution model came under fire
from Mexican economists beginning in the 1960s. Whatever the model's initial success in helping to establish an industrial base in Mexico, many (most) of these
industries clearly were inefficient and survived at
home only because of restrictions against imports (that
is, the infants were not growing up to stand on their
own), and could not compete in world markets. Also in
practice import substitution did not mean doing without
imports, but rather substituting one kind of imports
(usually consumer goods) for other kinds (intermediate
goods for the newly established industries and capital
goods, which Mexico had not efficiently developed).[18]
Mexican economists also were learning from the
experience of other developing countries, particularly
those in Asia, about the importance of promoting
exports in the development process.

The issue is not import substitution or export
promotion, but the balance between the two. From time
to time, therefore, efforts were made to shift away
from the extreme import substitution policy in favor of
more import openness and incentives for export. An
attempt was made during the López Portillo administration to shift import protection from nontariff measures
(import licenses) to tariffs in order to introduce a
degree of price competition. The effort halted during
the balance-of-payments crisis of that administration.
The liberalization effort received a further blow when
Mexico negotiated for membership in the GATT but then
at the last moment decided not to join. The decision
reflected, among other influences, the unwillingness of
Mexican industrialists, particularly those running
small and medium-sized enterprises, to face potential
competition from imports.

Future Mexican structural and trade policy is as
uncertain as that in the United States. The issue of

future policy must be held in abeyance until economic
stabilization is achieved, probably beginning in the
mid-1980s. Imports are being drastically limited not
necessarily out of motives of protection but to
strengthen the balance of payments. Planning for the
postausterity period is taking place, but the new plan
is mostly silent about how much import liberalization
will be permitted or how far Mexico will stray from its
microeconomic emphasis in industrial and trade policy.
The most recent plan talks of the need to diversify
export products and markets and of the introduction of
an "efficient" system of import substitution, but this
plan hardly differs from what has been said for almost
fifty years.[19]

The mid-1980s are a particularly fascinating time
to observe industrial and trade policy developments in
the two countries. The United States was questioning
its adherence to a liberal trading system and reliance
on macroeconomic policy as the major determinant of its
industrial structure. Mexico was questioning the
wisdom of its extreme import restrictiveness and its
great reliance on microeconomic decisions made necessary by its overall economic policy framework as a
major determinant of its industrial and agricultural
structure. Although there was no assurance that the
two countries would come together somewhere in the
middle, it is a distinct possibility.

THE CHANGING TRADE STRUCTURE

The mid-1980s, however, are also an uncertain time
to be analyzing the trade structure of either the
United States or Mexico or the two of them with each
other. The United States was experiencing dramatic
increases in its merchandise trade deficit (projected
for 1984 at about $100 billion) and in the current
account of its balance of payments as well (projected
for 1984 at $60 billion).[20] The Organization for
Economic Cooperation and Development ascribed this
deterioration to the relative economic bouyancy of the
United States and the weak competitive position stem-
ming from the strong dollar.[21] Mexico, on the other
hand, under its austerity program, turned around what
had been a steadily growing merchandise trade deficit
into a surplus of $12.5 billion in 1983. The Mexican
current account, which had been in deficit by $12.5
billion in 1981, was projected to be in surplus by
about $3.5 billion in 1984.[22] Table 1 shows the
Mexican merchandise trade picture since 1979.

The import decline in the first half of 1983 as
compared with the first half of 1982 came from a 55.8
percent decrease in volume and a 9.5 percent decrease

TABLE 1
Mexico: Foreign Trade, 1979-1983
(in billions of U.S. dollars)

	Exports (fob)	Imports (fob)	Balance
Jan.-Dec.			
1979	8.8	12.0	-3.2
1980	15.1	18.8	-3.7
1981	19.4	23.9	-4.5
1982	21.0	14.4	6.6
Jan.-June			
1981	10.5	12.1	-1.6
1982	9.4	9.2	0.2
1983	10.1	3.7	6.4

Source: El Mercado de Valores, Sept. 19, 1983, pp. 972-3.

in prices.[23]   The value of all categories of imports
decreased with the exception of food and feedstuffs,
particularly corn, sorghum, and soybeans.   This last
point is significant in the Mexican economic structure
since it reflects the long-standing problem of increasing
agricultural production sufficiently to meet domestic
needs.   The 8.2 percent increase in exports in the first
half of 1983 as compared with the first half of 1982
resulted from the combination of a 20.2 percent increase
in volume and a 10 percent decrease in export prices.
When disaggregated, the export performance in the first
six months of 1983 shows striking differences among
sectors. Earnings from petroleum increased even as price
decreased.   The same was true for manufactures.   The
value of primary product exports decreased.   Mexico's
competitive exchange rate during this period explains
much of the increase in the volume of manufactures.
This relation points to another significant policy
issue, namely, the need for Mexico to have a competitive
exchange rate to diversify its exports away from petroleum.   The government of President Miguel de la Madrid
has reiterated at each opportunity that the exchange
rate will not be used as a tool of trade and economic
policy and that the maintenance of a given rate will
not be the objective of policy.   This has not always
been the case in Mexico.   An overvalued peso has been
the norm since World War II, and devaluation has tended
to come when the overvaluation exploded in the form of
capital flight and the exhaustion of reserves.
      It is impossible to state what the trade pattern
of either country will be in the future.   If one
accepts that the large U.S. merchandise trade deficit

since 1981 is in substantial part the result of an
overvalued dollar, then any projection must be based
primarily on what will happen to the dollar. This, in
turn, is undoubtedly a partial function of the mix of
U.S. fiscal and monetary policy, and resultant interest
rates, and my crystal ball is cloudy with regard to all
these variables. What I believe I can predict with
some assurance is that to the extent the dollar remains
strong and weakens the competitive position of U.S.
manufactured goods in international trade, then the
more likely the United States is to adopt a form of
industrial policy focusing on specific industries combined with a protectionist trade policy.

Predicting the trade and industrial policy that
Mexico will pursue in the years ahead is just as hard.
The recent drastic reduction in imports must be adversely affecting industries that depend on imported
spare parts and intermediate goods since it is unlikely
that the domestic supply could have responded so
quickly to meet these needs. One suspects, from the
drastic nature of the import decline, that the official
figures must understate imports and that goods are
entering Mexico without being recorded by the customs
officials. Whether this is accurate or not, Mexico is
in no position to continue for very long to provide
resources to the rest of the world, which the current
account surplus reflects. The situation that exists in
the two countries is not what the textbooks tell us
should be happening: At present, the richer country is
importing resources from the rest of the world and the
poorer country is exporting resources to the rest of
the world.

Before the onset of the current economic crisis,
some interesting structural changes were taking place
in the trade between the two countries. Tables 2
through 5 give data on shifts in the shares of manufactures (defined as Standard International Trade Classification categories 5 through 8) moving in each direction. Only a few comments are needed to highlight
significant points from this shift-share analysis.
Table 2 shows the rising share of manufactured goods in
U.S. imports from Mexico, although by 1981 petroleum
had overtaken manufactured products as the main U.S.
import. Table 4 adds some light to the data of Table
2. The big gainers in the U.S. share of imports from
Mexico were mainly products likely to be produced in
the maquiladora (assembly plants), most of which are
near Mexico's border with the United States. The point
is significant: In 1981, U.S. imports from Mexico
under tariff items 806.30 and 807.00 (mostly 807; these
are the tariff provisions under which assembly-plant
products pay duty on entry into the United States only
on the value added in Mexico and not on the materials

TABLE 2
U.S. Imports from Mexico, Selected Years, 1962-1981*

	1962	1970	1977	1981
	in millions of dollars			
Total imports	539	1,219	4,689	14,007
(of which SITC 3[a])		.	(876)	(701)
SITC 5[b]	16	25	114	1,170
SITC 6[c]	64	120	584	2,547
SITC 7[d]	1	154	1,060	787
SITC 8[e]	8	99	435	248
Total SITC 5-8[f]	89	398	2,193	4,752
	in percentages			
Total imports	100.0	100.0	100.0	100.0
(of which SITC 3)			(18.7)	(50.0)
SITC 5	3.0	2.0	2.4	8.4
SITC 6	12.0	9.9	12.5	18.2
SITC 7	0.0	12.6	22.6	5.6
SITC 8	1.5	8.2	9.3	1.8
Total SITC 5-8	16.6	32.7	46.8	33.9
(if oil excluded)			(57.5)	(68.0)

* Professor Robert Green of the Business School of the University of Texas at Austin provided the data for this table.

a Standard International Trade Classification 3 comprises mineral fuels, lubricants, and related materials.

b SITC 5: chemicals and related products, nspf (not specially provided for)

c SITC 6: manufactured goods classified chiefly by material

d SITC 7: machinery and transport equipment

e SITC 8: miscellaneous manufactured articles

f Totals may not add because of rounding.

Source: U.N., Direction of International Trade

TABLE 3
U.S. Exports to Mexico, Selected Years, 1962-1981[a]

	1962	1970	1977	1981
	in millions of dollars			
Total Exports	739	1,674	4,733	17,296
SITC 5	118	171	555	1,697
SITC 6	77	171	507	2,498
SITC 7	307	801	2,151	8,402
SITC 8	43	123	340	1,035
Total SITC 5-8	544	1,265	3,554	13,632
	in percentages			
Total Exports	100.0	100.0	100.0	100.0
SITC 5	15.9	10.2	11.7	9.8
SITC 6	10.4	10.2	10.7	14.4
SITC 7	41.5	47.9	45.5	48.6
SITC 8	5.8	7.3	6.4	6.0
Total SITC 5-8	73.7	75.6	74.1	78.8

[a] Professor Robert Green of the Business School of the University of Texas at Austin provided the data for this table.

Source: U.N., Direction of International Trade

sent from the United States to Mexico for further processing or elaboration) were $2.7 billion or 57 percent of all U.S. imports of manufactured goods from Mexico. Of this value, $1.3 billion or 47 percent represented value added in Mexico.[24]

Mexico's gains in exports of manufactured goods, in other words, came largely from initiatives by U.S. entrepreneurs and only marginally altered the structure of Mexican production. The maquiladora provide jobs (more than 100,000 in 1981 and about 160,000 in 1985)[25] but they are predominantly enclave operations that have a modest impact on the rest of the Mexican productive sector. If Mexico wishes to have an export diversification that permeates production through its economy, as its current plan states as the objective, it must increase its competitiveness in the manufacturing sector outside the maquiladora. This fact highlights the importance of greater attention to export promotion, as opposed to import substitution strategy, and of maintaining the peso at a real competitive level.[26]

Table 3 shows the relative stability of the shares of U.S. manufactured exports to Mexico, at least until

TABLE 4
Shifts in U.S. Imports from Mexico, 1962 and 1981[a]

SITC no.	Category	Total Net Shift (1)	1962 Share (2)	1981 Share (3)
6556	Cordage & manufactures	-24.9	22.0	0.7
6851	Lead, alloys, unwrought	-15.9	14.1	0.5
6821	Copper, alloys, unwrought	-12.4	11.4	0.8
5140	Other inorganic chemicals	-3.9	3.6	0.3
5417	Medicaments	-3.8	3.5	0.2
5511	Essential oils, resinoids	-3.2	3.0	0.2
6624	Brick, etc., nonrefractory	-3.0	3.3	0.7
5135	Metallic oxide for paint	-2.7	2.8	0.4
6861	Zinc, alloys, unwrought	-2.7	2.6	0.3
6328	Other wood manufactures	-2.1	1.9	0.1
7249	Telecommunications equipment, nes	17.9	-b	15.7
8960	Works of art, etc.	9.7	0.6	9.1
7231	Insulated wire, cable	5.9	-	5.1
7222	Switchgear, etc.	5.7	-	4.9
6811	Silver, unwrkd., partly wrkd.	5.0	-	4.4
7328	Motor vehicle parts, nes	4.9	-	4.3
7221	Electric power machinery	4.7	-	4.1
7293	Transistors, valves, etc.	4.2	-	3.7
7299	Other electrical machinery	3.3	-	2.9
8411	Textile clothes, not knit	2.8	0.2	2.6

[a] Professor Robert Green of the Business School at the University of Texas at Austin was helpful in securing data for this table. The upper part shows manufactured imports losing share. Column 1 shows the loss of share as a percentage of total losses. Columns 2 and 3 show the shares of the four-digit items cited as a percentage of all manufactured imports (defined as SITC categories 5-8) in the two years shown. The lower part of the table shows the main items gaining shares.

[b] Means share was less than 0.1

Source: U.N., Direction of International Trade.

TABLE 5
Shifts in U.S. Exports to Mexico, 1962 and 1981[a]

SITC no.	Category	Total Net Shift (1)	1962 Share (2)	1981 Share (3)
7323	Lorries, trucks	-13.4	6.8	0.6
7321	Passenger motor vehicles, except buses	-10.9	5.3	0.2
7111	Steam boilers	-7.2	3.4	-[b]
5413	Antibiotics	-5.5	2.5	-
7313	Locos, not steam, not electric	-4.3	2.3	0.3
7125	Tractors, nonroad	-4.2	3.5	1.4
5999	Chemical products, preps, nes	-3.2	2.6	1.0
5992	Pesticides, disinfectants	-3.0	1.6	0.2
5997	Organic chemical products, nes	-2.7	1.7	0.4
5417	Medicaments	-2.4	1.3	0.2
7328	Motor vehicle parts, nes	14.1	5.3	10.6
7341	Aircraft heavier than air	7.0	2.0	4.7
5120	Organic chemicals	5.0	2.5	4.4
7184	Construction, mining machinery, nes	4.1	2.5	4.0
6911	Structures, parts, iron, steel	3.7	0.2	1.7
7116	Gas turbines, nonaircraft	3.4	0.0	1.4
7293	Transistors, valves, etc.	2.6	0.4	1.4
5812	Products of polymerizing, etc.	2.5	1.0	2.0
6291	Rubber tires, tubes	2.3	0.3	1.2
7149	Office machines, nes	2.1	0.3	1.1

[a] Professor Robert Green was helpful in securing the data for this table. The upper part shows manufactured imports losing share. Column 1 shows the loss of share as a percentage of total losses. Columns 2 and 3 show the shares of the four-digit items cited as a percentage of all manufactured imports (defined as SITC categories 5-8) in the two years shown. The lower part of the table shows the main items gaining shares.

[b] means share was less than 0.1.

Source: U.N. Direction of International Trade.

the stabilization program was instituted in 1982.
Table 5 shows that Mexico increased its own truck production between 1962 and 1981 but also had to rely
increasingly on parts from the United States for its
motor vehicle production.

SOME INDUSTRY ISSUES

I propose in this section to touch briefly on
three industries that have been targets of industrial
policy either in Mexico or internationally--the automotive industry, textiles and apparel, and steel. I
wish here to repeat a point (and then to drop it): In
practice industrial policy has meant trade restriction.
In theory, perhaps, this relation need not be true; one
can conceive of production incentives that would lead
only to trade expansion without any need for restriction. This conception, however, has not happened:
Industrial policy, as it has been practiced, has been
protectionist.[27]

Automotive Industry

A most revealing decree was issued by the Mexican
president in September 1983 dealing with the "rationalization" of the automotive industry. The decree makes
important changes in Mexican policy in this sector, the
most significant of which may be the intention to
"eliminate unnecessary and socially unjustifiable subsidies." The quoted phrase is not further defined.
Mexico has issued many decrees to promote the automotive industry: The most important ones were in 1962
and 1977. The purpose of the decrees was to establish
a viable industry, force it to use increasing amounts
of domestic labor and intermediate products in production, and promote sufficient exports so that the sector
as a whole would be self-sufficient in the use of
foreign exchange. Over the years, government subsidization of the automotive industry was heavy, probably
more than to any other industry.
Much was accomplished, although not without some
subsequent deterioration. Employment in the industry
rose to 160,000 in 1981, declining to 130,000 in 1982.
Employment probably declined further in 1983 because of
the sharp drop in production. Much foreign investment
was attracted as companies found they had to invest in
production in Mexico in order not to lose the market,
actual and potential. Exports of parts from these
plants did increase, but not enough to cover the cost
of imports. Despite the provision in the 1977 decree
that the industry as a whole was to achieve a no-net-

import position (that is, any import was to be matched by an export of comparable value from the sector), the trade deficit in 1981 was $2.6 billion or 58 percent of the total trade deficit for that year. Domestic content provisions were not met. Mexican vehicles were substantially more costly than equivalent models assembled elsewhere, frequently by as much as 100 percent.

It is not easy to assess the success or failure of such an industrial policy. An automotive industry does exist, and it may be possible to rationalize it. It has provided employment for many people, directly and indirectly. On the other hand, the opportunity cost was high. The new decree repeats many of the earlier goals (increasing domestic content, achieving a no-net-import position, limiting the number of models, and reducing prices so that vehicles are competitive internationally), and it remains to be seen whether they will be reached.

I do not wish to add unnecessarily to the literature on the U.S. automotive industry.[28] The major U.S. companies operate in Mexico, and the United States has a surplus in its automotive (parts) trade with Mexico. One must assume that in the future the Mexican market for vehicles will become as important as (or more important than) the U.S. market itself since the Mexican market is still undeveloped whereas in the U.S. market consumers largely replace existing vehicles. The U.S. government has complained perennially about Mexican domestic content and performance requirements, but these complaints have not hampered Mexico in its resolve to have an automotive industrial policy and they have not prevented U.S. companies from investing in Mexico.[29]

Textiles and Clothing Industry

An international industrial policy for textiles and clothing has been in existence since 1961.[30] Although the policy was precipitated by U.S. protectionism, the United States was joined by other industrial countries. This industrial policy is recorded in the multilateral multifiber arrangement (MFA) and the many bilateral agreements between industrial and developing countries controlling textile and clothing trade. The GATT has a standing mechanism for supervising the operations of the MFA. As with the automotive sector, a large body of academic and official literature has been written about international trade in textiles and clothing, and I do not wish to repeat here what is stated more extensively there. My interest, rather, is to look at the U.S.-Mexican relationship in this sector.

Mexico has developed a significant textile and clothing industry. In 1981 reported employment was 255,000 and value added in the industry contributed 1.7 percent of GDP.[31] In looking at the structure of the industry, I will use 1981 trade data to be consistent with other data used in this chapter and because 1981 was the last more or less "normal" year before the onset of the economic crisis and the austerity program. In 1981 Mexico's exports of textiles and apparel to all destinations were $149 million.[32] Using U.S. data (which are not comparable to Mexican data), the value of textile and clothing imports from the maquiladora in Mexico (under U.S. tariff item 807) was $198 million; $62 million of this represented value added in Mexico.[33] This last figure is reasonably close to what Mexican data would show for textile and clothing exports from the maquiladora; that is, the data exclude from Mexican exports the intermediate products that were originally imported into Mexico from the United States.

What the figures demonstrate is that the U.S.-owned portion of the clothing and textile industry in Mexico (the maquiladora) is geared for exports and can compete in the U.S. market, but that the Mexican-owned portion (the nonmaquiladora) is geared mostly for internal sale and may not be able to compete in the U.S. market. The restrictive U.S. trade policy in this sector affects the maquiladora and hardly matters to the remainder of the industry in Mexico. The worldwide restrictive industrial policy represented by the MFA has little effect in restricting Mexico's textile and clothing trade, again, except for the maquiladora. A convincing argument can be made that the way textile and clothing import restrictions developed in the industrial countries, particularly in the United States--namely, on a product-by-product basis for each country--benefited Mexico by limiting the exports of more competitive producers, especially those in Asia. The Mexican policy was designed to protect a domestic industry producing for domestic consumption. This was achieved. But this was about all that was achieved.

The United States, it can be argued, has had the elements of an industrial policy in the textile and clothing industry. It is primarily a trade-restrictive policy, but it has been accompanied by significant structural adjustment. In addition to competition from imports, the industry had to adjust to the substitution of synthetic fibers for cotton and wool and to a change in consumer tastes to easier care fabrics. The protectionism provided time to adjust. And adjust the industry did. The industry increased its capital investment and by 1980 was one of the most productive textile industries in the world and one of the most competitive in those textiles on which it concentrated.[34]

The clothing and textile industries in the two countries have similarities. In both, producers have sought protection from imports, and the emphasis has been on securing the domestic market. The difference between the two industries is that a concerned effort was made in the United States to bring about structural change whereas the structural adjustment was less pronounced in the Mexican industry.

Steel Industry

Steel is another industry in which the U.S. and Mexican governments have been deeply involved. However, unlike in the textile and clothing industry, Mexican policy was more forthright in facing the structural changes needed in the steel industry, whereas the United States supported the steel industry by protection against imports and only very recently acknowledged the need for such changes. I will not repeat here the information available in the extensive literature on the steel industry, but will instead provide a few thoughts about the industrial policies of the two countries and how they might affect trade between them.

As they have to the automotive industry, the Mexican authorities have devoted substantial resources to increasing steel production. Three of the five vertically integrated steel companies in Mexico are wholly government owned. The steel industry has faced severe management and production problems in Mexico, particularly since 1981, when production fell because of the economic slowdown in Mexico. The decline, however, was less severe than for segments of the automotive industry. For example, in June 1983 billet steel production was 85 percent of the 1981 monthly average whereas car engine production was only 48 percent of the 1981 monthly average.[35] The Mexican steel industry is more modern than that of the United States and faces lower wage costs. At present its production is primarily for internal use but over time it is apt to be in a position to compete with U.S. production.

In the United States the response to the internationalization of the home market was less one of technological modernization than it was to lobby for protection. As one author put it, the response to the import challenge was "political."[36] I argue that only in 1977 did the major producers begin to make fundamental changes in strategy by abandoning obsolete installations, discontinuing unprofitable product lines, and even hiring Japanese technical consultants.

U.S. and Mexican Industrial Policies

The purpose of this brief foray into industrial
policy was to demonstrate how the government involved
itself in each country in three important industries.
The initial motivations were not the same in each
country. In Mexico, the motive was to foster a domestic industry by providing whatever protection was
needed against imports and, in two cases (automotive
and steel) by devoting substantial resources to the
industry. This involvement was part of an overall
plan, or structural program, based on the philosophy
that the development of these industries was important
to the overall national development of Mexico. They
were not the only industries in which the Mexican
government was involved or to which it devoted
resources--the petroleum and petrochemical industry is
another striking example--but they represented a large
amount of government subsidization of industry. It is
difficult to say whether government involvement was
beneficial for the country as a whole. I would guess
that most Mexicans believe it was--the policy was
costly and even inefficiently managed, but industries
that might not have existed otherwise (steel and automotive) are in place and may well thrive in the
future. In the United States, government involvement
was mostly protectionist and did not involve the direct
expenditure of fiscal resources. (Such an expenditure
might have been required if the U.S. government had had
to meet guarantees on Chrysler loans.) The consumers
were allowed to bear the burden directly.[37]
How have the two policies affected trade between
the two countries? Again, the question is difficult to
answer. In the automotive sector, the Mexican intent
was to achieve zero net imports, an aim that thus far
has been unsuccessful. What U.S. automotive exports to
Mexico might have been without the pressure on U.S.
companies to invest is impossible to determine; the
bulk of the Mexican market might have been lost to
U.S. companies if other foreign companies had invested.
As it is, the United States has a large surplus in
automotive trade with Mexico driven by related-party
trade between affiliated companies in the two countries.
Over time, the bilateral trade position in this sector
may shift in Mexico's favor--but this is speculation.
In the steel industry, the policies of the two
countries probably had little effect on bilateral
trade. The U.S. industry was losing its export competitiveness in any event and its short-term strategy was
to protect the home market. And the Mexican industry
has been unable to meet its home-market demand in most
of the good years in recent decades. Again, the future
seems more promising for the Mexican than for the U.S.

industry.

Finally, in the clothing and textile industry, substantial trade has been generated primarily by U.S. companies taking advantage of Mexico's proximity to the United States and its cheaper labor. In this industry, the trade reflects what theory would predict--that Mexico is exporting a product that embodies its relatively abundant labor factor--but it took U.S. entrepreneurs to make the theory operational. For its part, the U.S. textile industry invested heavily in capital improvement while simultaneously protecting its position by import protection and structural adjustment. In this industry as well, the future is more promising in Mexico because of its wage advantages coupled with the relative ease of transfer of the relevant technology.

LOOKING AHEAD

Each country has separate options for its future trade and structural policies, and it has options on how it will interact economically with the other. That what happens in each country profoundly affects the other has become so self-evident that it hardly needs elaboration.

The decline in Mexico's imports--$9.5 billion from 1981 to 1982 and another $6 billion more from 1982 to 1983--has meant a loss of U.S. exports of more than $10 billion over two years, because the expectation was for export growth. The number of U.S. jobs lost from this decline in exports, particularly at a time of less than full employment when the slack cannot be compensated elsewhere, must be more than 200,000. The effect on the border economy in the United States from the precipitous fall in the value of the peso in 1982 was devastating, for a while at least. A survey by a Mexican bank in seven U.S. border towns (San Isidro, Chula Vista, and Calexico, California; Nogales, Arizona; and El Paso, McAllen, Laredo, and Brownsville, Texas) showed a decline in retail sales of 50 percent in the first half of 1983 compared with the first half of 1982. For consumer durables, such as domestic appliances, furniture, and jewelry, the decline was 70 percent.[38] Unemployment along the U.S. border, particularly in Texas, exceeds the national average; in 1983 it was 27 percent in Laredo, the highest for any city in the nation. Apprehensions in the United States of the migration of undocumented aliens from Mexico increased sharply following the Mexican devaluation. The increase in these illicit border crossings comes at a particularly difficult time because of the high rate of unemployment in the United States.

Mexico has been adversely affected by the recession in the United States. Exports undoubtedly would have been far more buoyant if U.S. growth in 1981 and 1982 had been consistently positive. High U.S. interest rates are adding to Mexico's debt-service burden. Every fraction of a percentage point increase in the nominal interest rate is significant for Mexico because of its external debt, which exceeds $80 billion.

The policy choices for the United States deal with macroeconomics, particular industries, and trade. Each area of options is related to the others. If macroeconomic policy leads to sustained economic growth, much of the pressure for trade protectionism will abate--much, but not all, since even with overall growth, some industries will not recover. If macroeconomic policy leads to lower interest rates and a diminution of interest-induced capital inflows, much of the pressure for an industrial policy is also likely to diminish. This is one group of options: to focus on getting macroeconomic policies right for the fostering of growth and employment and not to deal with industrial policy on an industry-by-industry basis.

The second group of options is to encourage a variety of industries about which there is some consensus that the United States is apt to have a future comparative advantage. These presumably would be industries heavily dependent on research and innovation. The encouragement could take a variety of forms--tax incentives, loans on favorable terms, writeoffs for research and development, and others. In addition to encouraging these research- and innovation-intensive industries, the government under this option could provide resources for the rationalization (to use the word in the Mexican automotive decree) of basic industries now in trouble, such as steel and automobiles.

This option is hard to define since the United States has had less experience with this kind of industrial policy than with macroeconomic policy. The United States does know something about industrial policy: The government knew how to encourage the building of merchant ships during World War II; it put a man on the moon in ten years; and it knows how to develop an arms industry. But the government does not know how to replicate these accomplishments in many other industries or sectors with a reasonable outlay of resources. The government easily chose merchant shipping as a priority sector when it meant national survival but not when it is just one more industry competing for scarce resources.

Finally, the United States has choices in trade policy. U.S. protectionism has always been selective, even during the liberal trading era since World War II, and this approach is expected to continue. The policy choice deals with the extent of microprotectionism even as the government professes a belief in a liberal world trading system. The governmental tendency in the 1980s has been to charge other countries with predatory protectionism, use this as the basis for emulation, and then argue that this defensive protectionism will provide a bargaining chip to achieve worldwide trade liberalism. It is hard to know how far down the protectionist road this logic will take the country.

Mexico's starting point is very different. Government incentives to particular industries have been substantial, and the question for Mexico is not whether these should be increased—which is the question being debated in the United States—but by how much they should be decreased. In trade policy, the issue is not whether to increase protection, but when, by how much, and by what techniques, protectionism can be reduced.

The third level of options has to do with what the countries can do jointly. At this level, there are essentially two choices:

1. The two countries can continue their interaction more or less as it has been pursued since the 1970s. This has involved the establishment of joint committees to discuss industrial and trade issues. When U.S. countervailing duties became frequent, negotiations were opened for a possible bilateral agreement similar to the subsidy/countervailing duty code of the GATT. The discussions thus far have come to nothing (and the issue itself seems less urgent because the current Mexican exchange rate obviates the need for many export subsidies, and the budget austerity under which Mexico is operating reduces the resources available for subsidies). When problems flare up in trade in particular products (tomatoes, for example), the two governments keep in close touch. Each complains about the practices of the other—e.g., the United States about Mexico's performance requirements in the automotive sector and Mexico about U.S. removal of preferences when this is not required under the U.S. law, as was the case for Mexican beer—usually without tangible result. Most countries interact bilaterally in this way. The difference between Mexico and most other major U.S. trading partners is that bilateral trade is not conducted under an overall legal framework as it is among GATT members; and the proximity of the countries means that actions in each have a pervasive impact on the other.

2. The countries can look toward eventual free trade to provide a framework under which individual investors and the governments themselves can make industrial and structural adjustment decisions. This framework would involve more profound consultation than

now exists because the two countries would consult knowing that ten or twenty years later tariff and non-tariff barriers would have been substantially removed. Industrial policy in either country could not take the same form it now takes if there were a probability close to certainty that protection against imports from the other country would disappear. Each of the three industries discussed--automotive, textiles and clothing, and steel--would be approached differently in each country under prospective free trade from what takes place under protection.

The United States and Mexico are finding their economies increasingly interrelated. The growth of this relationship is inevitable if each is to attain the maximum national welfare. This general assertion does not require that there be a particular framework under which the countries pursue their trade and development strategies--bilateral free trade is no more inevitable than is the continuation of stringent protectionism in Mexico or the growth of protectionism in the United States--but it does lead to the conclusion that a great effort should be made by each to take into account the effect on the other of new policy measures. Even this modest step would constitute an advance. But aspirations need not be this modest, as the free-trade option illustrates.

NOTES

1. "MacNeil/Lehrer Report," October 10, 1983.
2. See op-ed column by U.S. Senator Robert Dole entitled, "Reciprocating in Trade," New York Times, January 22, 1982.
3. Rodney de C. Grey, Trade Policy in the 1980s: An Agenda for Canadian-U.S. Relations (Montreal: C. D. Howe Institute, 1981). Grey saw much scope for U.S.-Canadian bilateralism in dealing with nontariff barriers. Raymond Vernon in "International Trade Policy in the 1980s," International Studies Quarterly 26, no. 4 (December 1982): 483-510, noted with concern the tendency to consider trade policies that are less than global.
4. This was the sense of Section 1104 of the Trade Agreements Act of 1979 asking the president to "study the desirability of entering into trade agreements with countries in the northern portion of the western hemisphere."
5. A discussion of trade restrictions on these and other products by the United States and other industrial countries can be found in S. J. Anjaria,

Z. Iqbal, L. L. Perez, and W. S. Tseng, Trade Policy
Developments in Industrial Countries, Occasional Paper
no. 5 (Washington, D.C.: International Monetary Fund,
1981).

6. One example is Gerardo Bueno, "The Structure
of Protection in Mexico," in Bela Balassa, ed., The
Structure of Protection in Developing Countries
(Baltimore: Johns Hopkins University Press, 1971), pp.
169-202.

7. This is the implication of Mexico's current
development plan. Poder Ejecutivo Federal, Plan
Nacional de Desarrollo 1983-1988 (Mexico, D.F.:
Secretaria de Programacion y Presupuesto, 1983),
p. 195.

8. Lane Kirkland, president of the AFL-CIO, used
satire to mock free traders by proposing a "Free Trade
Anti-Protectionism and Anti-Hypocrisy Act of 1983"
under which a person making a free-trade speech "shall
have his tongue extracted by heated tongs." Quoted by
Leonard Silk, in the New York Times, April 13, 1983.

9. Robert B. Reich, "Beyond Free Trade," Foreign
Affairs 61, no. 4 (Spring 1983): 773-804.

10. William Diebold, Jr., Industrial Policy as an
International Issue (New York: McGraw-Hill for the
Council on Foreign Relations, 1980).

11. Ira C. Magaziner and Robert B. Reich in
Minding America's Business: The Decline and Rise of
the American Economy (New York: Vintage Books, 1982),
cited ad hoc import restrictions as examples of the
current ineffective U.S. industrial policy.

12. Vernon, "International Trade Policy in the
1980s."

13. Charles L. Schultze, "Industrial Policy: A
Dissent," Brookings Review 2, no. 1 (Fall 1983): 3-13.

14. Robert Z. Lawrence, "Is Trade Deindustrializing America? A Medium-Term Perspective," Brookings
Papers on Economic Activity 1 (1983): 129-161.

15. Philip H. Trezise, "Industrial Policy Is Not
the Major Reason for Japan's Success," Brookings Review
2, no. 3 (Spring 1983): 13-18.

16. Robert B. Reich, The Next American Frontier
(New York: Times Books, 1983).

17. Gerardo M. Bueno, "Economic Interdependence:
Perspectives from Latin America," paper presented at a
conference on Economic Interdependence: Perspectives
from Developing Countries, organized by the International Economic Association and the Federation of ASEAN
Economic Associations, Manila, May 23-27, 1983.

18. Fernando Clavijo and Susana Valdivieso, "El
comercio exterior y su efecto en la ocupacion, 1950-
1980," paper presented to a conference on United
States-Mexico Trade and Financial Interdependence,
Stanford University, September 15-17, 1983.

19. _Plan Nacional de Desarrollo_, 1983-1988, p. 192.

20. Estimate by Morgan Guaranty Trust Company of New York, _World Financial Markets_, February 1984, p. 2.

21. Organization for Economic Cooperation and Development, _OECD Economic Outlook_, no. 33, July 1983 (Paris: OECD), p. 61.

22. Estimate by American Chamber of Commerce of Mexico, _Business Mexico_ 1, no. 2 (February 1984): pp. 38-39.

23. Data in this paragraph are from Nacional Financiera, "Comercio exterior en el primer semestre de 1983," _El Mercado de Valores_ 43, no. 38 (September 19, 1983): 971-973.

24. U.S. International Trade Commission (ITC), Statistical Services Division, "Tariff Items 807.00 and 806.30: U.S. Imports for Consumption, for Specified Years, 1966-1981," Washington, D.C., March 1983, pp. 18 and 51.

25. Dennis P. Hodak, "Mexico's In-Bond Industry: Crucial Job Source and Dollar Earner," _Business Mexico_ 1, no. 2 (February 1984): 62.

26. A more detailed discussion of this issue was given in Sidney Weintraub, "U.S.-Mexican Trade: Situation and Outlook," in Richard D. Erb and Stanley R. Ross, eds., _United States Relations with Mexico: Context and Content_ (Washington, D.C.: American Enterprise Institute, 1981), pp. 179-194.

27. Diebold in _Industrial Policy as an International Issue_, p. 80, also makes this point.

28. Norman S. Fieleke in "The Automobile Industry," _Annals of the American Academy of Political and Social Science_ 460 (March 1982): 83-91, gave a summary of recent developments in the U.S. industry.

29. An overview of the position of the U.S. industry on this score can be found in the statement of the Motor Vehicle Manufacturers Association of the United States for the ITC on "The Impact of Foreign Trade-Related Performance Requirements on U.S. Industry and Foreign Investment Abroad," August 19, 1982.

30. Diebold, _Industrial Policy as an International Issue_, pp. 95-106.

31. Nacional Financiera, "Informe de la camara nacional de la industria textil," _El Mercado de Valores_ 41, no. 32 (August 10, 1981): 836.

32. _Comercio Exterior_ 32, no. 4 (April 1982): 475.

33. ITC, "Tariff Items 807.00 and 806.30," p. 17.

34. Joseph Pelzman, "The Textile Industry," _Annals of the American Academy of Political and Social Science_ 460 (March 1982): 92-100.

35. Banamex, _Review of the Economic Situation of Mexico_ 59, no. 693 (August 1983): 236.

36. Hans G. Mueller, "The Steel Industry," Annals of the American Academy of Political and Social Science 460 (March 1982): 75.

37. On this point, see Robert W. Crandall, The U.S. Steel Industry in Recurrent Crisis: Policy Options in a Competitive World (Washington, D.C.: Brookings Institution, 1981), pp. 129-139.

38. Banamex, Review of the Economic Situation of Mexico, p. 252.

REFERENCES

Anjaria, S. J., Z. Iqbal, L. L. Perez, and W. S. Tseng. 1981. Trade Policy Developments in Industrial Countries. Occasional Paper no. 5. Washington, D.C.: International Monetary Fund.

Banco Nacional de México (Banamex). 1983. Review of the Economic Situation of Mexico 59, no. 693 (August 1983).

Bluestone, Barry, and Bennett Harrison. 1982. The Deindustrialization of America. New York: Basic Books.

Bueno, Gerardo. 1971. "The Structure of Protection in Mexico." In The Structure of Protection in Developing Countries, ed. Bela Balassa, pp. 169-202. Baltimore: Johns Hopkins University Press.

Bueno, Gerardo M. 1983. "Economic Interdependence: Perspectives from Latin America." Paper presented at a conference organized by the International Economic Association and the Federation of ASEAN Economic Associations on Economic Interdependence: Perspectives from Developing Countries, May 23-27, 1983, Manila.

Business Mexico 1, no. 2 (February 1984): 38-39.

Clavijo, Fernando, and Susana Valdivieso. 1983. "El comercio exterior y su efecto en la ocupacion, 1950-1980." Paper presented to a conference on United States-Mexico Trade and Financial Interdependence, Stanford University, September 15-17, 1983.

Comercio Exterior 32, no. 4 (April 1982): 475.

Crandall, Robert W. 1981. The U.S. Steel Industry in Recurrent Crisis: Policy Options in a Competitive World. Washington, D.C.: Brookings Institution.

Diebold, William, Jr. 1982. "Past and Future Industrial Policy in the United States." In National Industrial Strategies and the World Economy, ed. John Pinder, pp. 158-205. London: Croom Helm and Totowa; N.J.: Allanheld, Osmun.

Diebold, William, Jr. 1980. Industrial Policy as an International Issue. New York: McGraw-Hill for

106

the Council on Foreign Relations.

Dole, Robert. 1982. "Reciprocity in Trade." Op-ed
column, New York Times, January 22, 1982.

Fieleke, Norman S. 1982. "The Automobile Industry."
Annals of the American Academy of Political and
Social Science 460 (March 1982): 83-91.

Grey, Rodney de C. 1981. Trade Policy in the 1980s:
An Agenda for Canadian-U.S. Relations. Montreal:
C. D. Howe Institute.

Hodak, Dennis P. 1984. "Mexico's In-Bond Industry:
Crucial Job Source and Dollar Earner." Business
Mexico 1, no. 2 (February 1984): 62-69.

Lawrence, Robert Z. 1983. "Is Trade Deindustrializing
America? A Medium-Term Perspective." Brookings
Papers on Economic Activity 1: 129-161.

Magaziner, Ira C., and Robert B. Reich. 1982. Minding
America's Business: The Decline and Rise of the
American Economy. New York: Vintage Books.

Morgan Guaranty Trust Company of New York. 1983.
World Financial Markets, July 1983.

Morgan Guaranty Trust Company of New York. 1983.
World Financial Markets, September 1983.

Morgan Guaranty Trust Company of New York. 1984.
World Financial Markets, February 1984.

Motor Vehicle Manufacturers Association of the United
States. 1982. Statement before the U.S. Inter-
national Trade Commission on "The Impact of
Foreign Trade-Related Performance Requirements on
U.S. Industry and Foreign Investment Abroad,"
August 19, 1982.

Mueller, Hans G. 1982. "The Steel Industry." Annals
of the American Academy of Political and Social
Science 460 (March 1982): 73-82.

Nacional Financiera. 1981. "Informe de la camara
nacional de la industria textile." El Mercado de
Valores 41, no. 32 (August 10, 1981): 836-837.

Nacional Financiera. 1983. "Racionalizacion de la
industria automotriz." El Mercado de Valores 43,
no. 38 (September 19, 1983): 961-970.

Nacional Financiera. 1983. "Comercio exterior en el
primer semestre de 1983." El Mercado de Valores
43, no. 38 (September 19, 1983): 971-973.

Organization for Economic Cooperation and Development.
1983. OECD Economic Outlook, no. 33, July 1983.
Paris: OECD.

Pelzman, Joseph. 1982. "The Textile Industry."
Annals of the American Academy of Political and
Social Science 460 (March 1982): 92-100.

Pinder, John, ed. 1982. National Industrial Strategies and the World Economy. London: Croom Helm
and Totowa; N.J.: Allanheld, Osmun.

Poder Ejecutivo Federal (of Mexico). 1983. Plan
Nacional de Desarollo 1983-1988. Mexico, D.F.:

Secretaria de Programacion y Presupuesto.

Reich, Robert B. 1983. The Next American Frontier. New York: Times Books.

Reich, Robert B. 1983. "Beyond Free Trade." Foreign Affairs 61, no. 4 (Spring 1983): 773-804.

Schultze, Charles L. 1983. "Industrial Policy: A Dissent." Brookings Review 2, no. 1 (Fall 1983): 3-13.

Stein, Herbert, and Lester Thurow. 1983. Conversation on "Do Modern Times Call for an Industrial Policy?" Public Opinion 6, no. 4 (August/ September 1983): 2-7, 58-59.

Trezise, Philip H. 1983. "Industrial Policy Is Not the Major Reason for Japan's Success." Brookings Review 1, no. 3 (Spring 1983): 13-18.

U.S. International Trade Commission, Statistical Services Division. 1983. "Tariff Items 807.00 and 806.30: U.S. Imports for Consumption, for Specified Years, 1966-1981." Washington, D.C., March 1983.

Vernon, Raymond. 1982. "International Trade Policy in the 1980s." International Studies Quarterly 26, no. 4 (December 1982): 483-510.

Weintraub, Sidney. 1981. "U.S.-Mexican Trade: Situation and Outlook." In United States Relations with Mexico: Context and Content, ed. Richard D. Erb and Stanley R. Ross, pp. 179-194. Washington, D.C.: American Enterprise Institute.

Comments

Santiago Levy

Sidney Weintraub's chapter raises a number of
interesting issues concerning economic relationships
between Mexico and the United States derived from trade
and energy-related problems. In these short comments I
would like to mention some additional issues related to
these two topics and to conclude by mentioning an un-
solved, but important, problem that was not discussed.

PROBLEMS OF TRADE POLICY

The context of trade relations between Mexico and
the United States was aptly described in Chapter 3.
Nevertheless, the essential facts are worth repeating.
For some years we have been observing that world trade
is increasingly ruled by a series of ad hoc unilateral
actions and bilateral agreements between countries,
with the General Agreement on Tariffs and Trade (GATT)
playing a consequently diminished role. The United
States, at the same time, is being pressured internally
to implement a so-called industrial policy, which would
most likely be translated into increasing protectionism.
Mexico, on the other hand, is going through its worst
economic crisis in half a century, one symptom of which
is the acute shortage of foreign exchange.
A good starting point for discussion is to look at
the problem from Mexico's viewpoint. The situation is
well known (see, for example, Chapter 5 by Lance
Taylor) so that we can be brief. In essence, Mexico
must quickly and substantially increase its export
earnings. Although the trade balance did improve
during 1983, this clearly was brought about by the
substantial drop in the level of output. Even with
this very low level of economic activity, most oil
earnings are being used to service the foreign debt,
with very little foreign exchange left for complementary intermediate inputs. The recession, of course,

109

cannot be sustained for very long;[1] as soon as growth resumes, the balance-of-trade situation will change substantially. However, contracting additional foreign debt to cover the deficit is not a viable solution.

It can therefore be concluded, almost without exaggeration, that a fundamental prerequisite for steady growth is for Mexico to go through a definite structural change and develop an export promotion strategy. Mexico's record on this front is rather poor: Although there has been much talk, the actual policies taken with regard to exchange rate and tariff policy show that export promotion and the development of an export mentality have not been on the economic agenda of policymakers. Excluding 1983, trade and macrolevel policy in Mexico have been consistently biased against exports.

To circumvent this longstanding anti-export bias, Mexico will have to carry out some drastic changes in its trade policies. In particular, it will not only have to use a battery of policies that will keep a "realistic" (i.e., not overvalued) exchange rate but will also have to implement export subsidies and other mechanisms. The export issue, I believe, will stay in the forefront of Mexican economic policymaking during much of the 1980s unless, of course, a drastic change occurs to the price of oil or world interest rates.

Recent developments in U.S. trade policy, however, show clearly that Mexico and the United States have plenty of room for conflict on the issue of trade. Mexico cannot realistically be expected in the short run to both increase and diversify its manufactured exports; for the time being an increase in Mexican exports is almost equivalent to an increase in exports from Mexico to the United States. This result, of course, is not consistent with a move in the United States toward an industrial policy of greater protectionism.

At this point, it is important to ask what type of protectionism can be expected. Indiscriminate protection by the United States would not only be very harmful to Mexican trade but could also be harmful to U.S. trade as well. Clearly, the "harm" done to the United States by Japanese or West European exports is not comparable to the possible "harm" caused by Mexican exports. U.S. trade policy cannot be the same toward Japan and other countries as it is toward Mexico. Other issues besides commodity flows tie Mexico and the United States: Labor migration and Mexico's foreign debt are two of these, but geopolitical considerations are also important.

Therefore, there is room to improve and amplify trade relations between the two countries. The particular form that this relationship takes, whether in a

GATT-type arrangement or through some bilateral agreement, is not the main point; the key issue is to recognize that during the 1980s Mexico will need to change substantially its volume of trade, with direct implications for trade policy in Mexico as well as for U.S. policy toward Mexico.

PROBLEMS OF ENERGY POLICY

In viewing the changes in energy policies that took place in Mexico during 1983, it appears that the practice of greatly subsidizing the use of energy in Mexico has been abandoned and changed to a policy of parity between domestic and world prices. Although the motivation for this change might have been the need to rapidly increase the revenues of the public sector, this new policy had some additional effects. In particular, the drop in the relative price of energy inputs during the 1970s had resulted in an increase in the energy/output coefficient together with a decrease of the labor/output coefficient for the economy as a whole.[2] Therefore, energy and labor appear to be substitutable inputs. An important byproduct of the changes in the relative price of energy inputs may be a greater use of labor per unit of output, which in the present circumstances is an important and positive step.

CONCLUDING REMARKS

Mexico has apparently embarked on a course of change in its energy pricing and exchange rate policies, but unfortunately, not in its trade policy. The country still needs to design a set of tariffs and related instruments that will allow it to rationalize its foreign trade, reduce the high level of protectionism, and substantially increase the profitability of production for exports. The design and implementation of such policy, of course, are no easy matter. Nevertheless, the opportunity is at hand to complement the changes already started in energy pricing and exchange rate policy, to allow again the possibility of steady growth.

NOTES

1.   Although the rate of growth of population has declined, the rate of growth of the labor force will be higher during the 1980s than the 1970s.

2.   Santiago Levy, "Cambio Tecnológico y Uso de Energía en México," Discussion Paper no. 59, Center for Latin American Development Studies, Boston University, April 1983.

Comments

Joseph Grunwald

Given the cloudy prospects for U.S.-Mexican economic relations, Sidney Weintraub's illuminating discussion of the environment for trade is highly welcome. It is especially useful because he focuses on the course of protectionism in the two countries, an important ingredient of the setting in which Mexican economic recovery can take place.

Industrial policy on both sides of the Rio Grande is Weintraub's main concern. He gives it a serious though not dispassionate review, natural for someone who is deeply convinced of the universal superiority of free trade. He leaves no doubt as to where he stands: Industrial policy targeting specific sectors is bad because it leads to protectionism. Implicit in this view is the argument that industrial policy tends to foster industries in which comparative advantage does not exist or has been lost.

The notion of targeting specific sectors originates with the image of Japan's policy. Whether or not Japan has followed a microeconomic industrial policy is still a matter of debate. Nevertheless, no matter how the system has worked, agreement seems to have been present between government and business in Japan on the directions of the country's industrial development. This kind of consensus policy, apparently deeply rooted in Japanese culture, would be difficult to transfer to the United States or Mexico.

Perhaps less subtle instruments would have to be used for industrial policy to be effective in the United States. Not only can such macroeconomic incentives as tax relief and easier access to credit be applied, but also direct expenditures can be and have been used to target industries successfully. For example, it is unlikely that the U.S. computer industry could dominate the world market today without the substantial government support (primarily from the military) for research and development begun during World

113

War II.[1] Whether through targeting or macroeconomic
incentives alone, industries with good prospects for
comparative advantage can be stimulated without trade
barriers.

Mexico's industrial policies have relied principally on protectionism. This is the common element of
import substituting industrialization (ISI). Although
Weintraub resists the temptation to directly use the
difference between U.S. and Mexican industrial policies
as an explanation of the economic welfare gap between
the two countries, the reader can hardly avoid such an
inference. Public policies may have contributed to the
huge divergence in average income levels between the
two neighbors, but Mexican underdevelopment cannot be
attributed to protectionism. Except for Britain, all
industrial countries have gone through fairly long
periods of ISI. Mexico is not unique. During the ISI
stage the public policy stances differ little from one
country to the next. Consider for example the following quotations:

> [T]he United States cannot exchange with
> Europe on equal terms; and the want of reciprocity
> would render them the victim of a system which
> would induce them to confine their views to agri-
> culture and refrain from manufactures. A constant
> and increasing necessity, on their part, for the
> commodities of Europe, and only a partial and
> occasional demand for their own, in return, could
> not but expose them to a state of impoverish-
> ment. . . .

> The most prominent circumstance of dissimili-
> tude arises from the comparative state of manu-
> facturers. . . . All the difference is lost to a
> community which, instead of manufacturing for it-
> self, procures the fabrics requisite to its supply
> from other countries. . . .

> [T]here is no other expedient than to pro-
> mote manufacturing establishments. Manufacturers,
> who constitute the most numerous class, after the
> cultivators of land, are for that reason the
> principal consumers of the surplus of their
> labor. . . .

> [A] formidable obstacle . . . to the intro-
> duction of [a] branch of industry into a country
> in which it did not before exist [is] the supe-
> riority antecedently enjoyed by nations who have
> preoccupied and perfected the same branch. . . .
> To maintain, between the recent establishment of
> one country and the long-matured establishment

of another country, a competition upon equal
terms, both as to quality and price, is in most
cases, impracticable . . . [and] must necessarily
be so considerable as to forbid a successful
rivalship, without the extraordinary aid and
protection of government. . . .

The propriety of [government] encouragement
. . . ought to be determined upon considerations
irrelative to any comparison [of immediate pro-
ductiveness]. . . .

As often as a duty upon a foreign article
makes an addition to its price, it causes an
extra expense to the community for the benefit
of the domestic manufacturer. A bounty does no
more. But it is the interest of the society, in
each case, to submit to the temporary expense--
which is more than compensated by an increase of
industry and wealth, by an augmentation of
resources and independence, and by the circumstance of eventual cheapness. . . .

Considering a monopoly of the domestic
market to its own manufactures as the reigning
policy of manufacturing nations, a similar policy,
on the part of the United States, in every proper
instance, is dictated, it might almost be said,
by the principles of distributive justice.

These quotes, of course, are from Alexander Hamilton's
Report on Manufactures of 1791.[2] Hamilton was unequi-
vocal about the need for government intervention to
achieve industrialization. He prescribed subsidies,
protective as well as prohibitive tariffs, and other
measures that today would be considered comprehensive
development planning.[3]

U.S. policy may not have followed the full force
of Hamilton's enthusiasm, but there is little doubt
that government has played a significant role throughout U.S. economic history, from the early canals to the
present-day stirrings for a new industrial policy that
are of such concern to Weintraub. It would be difficult to match in world history the successful government planning that has gone into the development of
U.S. agriculture. The Homestead Act of 120 years ago
was a comprehensive and well thought through piece of
legislation, ranging from land reform to training and
research and its dissemination. Although more recent
U.S. agricultural policies leave much to be desired,
U.S. agriculture has become the most productive in the
world.

The point is not that public policies are

efficient, but that government usually plays a role
during the earlier stages of a country's economic
development. The protection of industries has been an
essential ingredient of that role. Once high levels of
industrializations are reached, countries will
naturally become more free trade oriented. Japan
started to let go of its restrictive trade practices
only recently, well after advanced industrialization
levels had been reached. The fact that Europe, the
United States, and other industrial countries are again
turning toward protectionism may be as much a reflection of the increasing competitiveness of some developing countries as an indication of a slowing down of
economic growth.

Indeed, it can be argued that the underdevelopment
of some countries can be explained in part by an
excessive degree of laissez-faire during earlier times.
Last century's free-market policies, Latin American
economist Anibal Pinto contended, frustrated Chile's
economic development.[4] Last decade's experimentation
with such policies, some will claim again (although the
causality is still being debated), led that country to
economic disaster. Mexico's development policies seem
to have been passive until the end of the last century
when the Porfirio Díaz regime introduced some industrial measures, such as tax exemption on imported
machinery and capital goods. However, nothing then or
earlier could compare with Hamilton's industrial policy
or Gallatin's policy of internal improvements in the
United States.[5]

Although in the nineteenth century some significant industries, particularly textiles, were already
set up in Mexico, modern ISI started with the Great
Depression and World War II. No premeditated, coherent policy gave rise to it; rather it began because
of severe foreign exchange restraints resulting from
the crisis of the 1930s and because of the foreign
supply shortages due to World War II. Domestic and
later foreign (mostly U.S.) entrepreneurs took advantage of this propitious climate and started to produce
domestically what had previously been imported. The
beginning was fairly haphazard rather than a conscious
formal industrial policy. Raúl Prebisch provided the
theoretical underpinnings for the Latin American ISI
after the process had already started. Only later
could one speak of an industrial development policy as
special import barriers were erected to protect high
priority industries and special concessions were given
to imports of capital and intermediate goods needed by
the domestic plants. Public measures became more consistent though not necessarily more efficient.

Weintraub believes that Mexico is questioning
whether the government has played too large a role,

whereas the United States is questioning whether the
government has played too small a role in fostering
structural change. Neither he nor other serious
observers believe that Mexico would abandon ISI, adopt
free trade, and let the present comparative advantage
take its course. But, given the current economic depression there and the outlook for relatively slow
world economic growth for the remainder of the 1980s,
Mexico would find it difficult to effect a massive
liberalization of its economy in the foreseeable future.
Rather than stimulating an opening up of the Mexican
economy, the 1983 crisis may push the country toward
insulating itself against the major effects of external
shocks.

ISI was originally expected to save foreign
exchange and make a developing country less dependent
on industrial countries. However, import dependency
in Mexico actually increased because the new industrial
plants required substantial imports of machinery,
equipment, industrial raw materials, technology, and so
on. The debt crisis brought this higher vulnerability
of national development to the surface: After taking
care of minimum debt service obligations little is left
over to import the necessary inputs. This situation
might not appear acute in 1983 Mexico because the
serious internal depression collapsed national demand.
Nevertheless, the country probably could not halt its
economic development for long without causing social
and political strains that might be difficult to
manage.

Therefore, Mexico may try to lessen its vulnerability by minimizing the need for foreign supplies.
Thus, a second stage of ISI may be geared to produce
with small import requirements the inputs for domestic
industries. If the new import substitution is based on
local ingenuity resulting in cost-cutting innovations,
the current economic crisis may well bring positive
results. If, however, the new ISI is propped up by
fresh, uneconomic trade barriers, the long-run cost may
be large indeed.

Policies are difficult to transfer across cultures.
Just as Japan's government/private enterprise consensus
policies are probably unworkable in the United States,
the open-market policies of Singapore, Hong Kong,
Korea, and Taiwan, to which Weintraub refers, are not
likely to operate successfully in Mexico. The culture
and value system of postrevolutionary Mexico seem to be
more like those of the United States and Europe than of
the Far East. It should therefore not be surprising
that Mexico has felt more comfortable with Hamiltonian
policy prescriptions than with any lessons from the
Far East.

Many observers inside and outside the country

agree with Weintraub that Mexico has carried government
intervention too far. This combined with indigenous
waste and inefficiencies would indicate that it is time
for a change. That change, however, will not be the
adoption of Far Eastern behavior. My belief that ISI
is here to stay does not mean that some opening of the
Mexican economy will not take place; it is desirable
as well as feasible, and so is the streamlining of
government controls and regulations, and the reduction
of the excesses of public corruption.

Sidney Weintraub's discussion of Mexican assembly
industries--maquiladoras--needs to be put into proper
perspective. Weintraub indicates that the maquiladoras
in the textile industry, which he says are U.S.-owned,
are "geared for exports and [are] able to compete in
the U.S. market," whereas the Mexican-owned non-
maquiladoras are not. The export performance of
Mexican industry in general cannot be compared with
that of assembly industries as Weintraub does. By
definition a maquiladora is not only designed for
exports but its raison d'être is to be able to compete
in the U.S. market. Otherwise, why send U.S. components abroad to be assembled for the U.S. market? The
national origin of the ownership has little to do with
this. In fact, Mexican maquiladora ownership is higher
in textiles than in other branches, and Mexican output
does not seem to be less competitive than that of U.S.-
owned assembly plants.

Maquiladoras are enclave operations, with weak
links to the rest of the Mexican economy, but this
situation is not ironclad. Rather, this condition has
in large part to do with the Mexican institutional
arrangements governing assembly industries as well as
with the behavior of the U.S. firms. Various factors,
including Mexican government regulations and protectionist policies, have discouraged Mexicans from becoming involved in maquiladoras as owners and suppliers
of assembly plants and users of assembly output. The
decided preference of U.S. maquiladora operators for
U.S. over Mexican inputs has not helped. Weintraub
shares the widely held view that the maquiladora is a
dead-end activity for Mexico. Consequently, massive
investment in that sector would be an inefficient use
of resources.

There is no reason, however, why maquiladoras
cannot be better integrated into the Mexican productive
system. As of the end of 1983, Mexican government
policy appears to be moving in that direction.
Although no one would advocate concentrating Mexican
development efforts on the assembly industry, a
greater use of assembly output as inputs into Mexican
industries and an improved transfer of technology
through the maquiladora would be highly desirable.

These may well result in reducing costs in some sectors of the Mexican economy, thus improving their international competitiveness.

NOTES

1. See, for instance, Kenneth Flamm, "Technology Policy in International Perspective," in Policies for Industrial Growth in a Competitive World (Washington, D.C.: U.S. Congress, Joint Economic Committee, 1984).

2. Reprinted in Alexander Hamilton's Famous Report on Manufactures (Boston: Home Market Club, 1892), pp. 24-25, 45, 17, 22, 26-27, 13, 54, and 51 (page numbers listed in order of the quoted paragraphs).

3. For a fuller discussion of Hamilton's policies, see Joseph Grunwald, "Some Reflections on Latin American Industrialization Policy," Journal of Political Economy 78, no. 4 (July/August 1970): especially the Appendix, 848-853.

4. Anibal Pinto, Chile, in caso de desarrollo frustrado (Santiago: Editorial Universitaria, 1959).

5. See Albert Gallatin, Report of the Secretary of the Treasury on the Subject of Public Roads and Canals (Washington, 1808).

Part 3

Fluctuations and Growth

4

Economic Fluctuations in Mexico and the United States

Pasqual García-Alba
Jaime Serra Puche

INTRODUCTION

This chapter deals with the real and potential relations between economic fluctuations in Mexico and those in the United States. Rather than constructing a model of economic cycles, we discuss the constraints within which economic policy choices operate in the two countries. This approach was chosen for three reasons. First, economists widely recognize that theoretical models are usually unable to generate or replicate actual fluctuations. Traditional models contain both exogenous and endogenous variables, and any sustained cyclical behavior of the model comes about by embedding the cycle in the exogenous variables. Endogenous variables follow the exogenous ones monotonically or with dampening cycles; in the rare cases in which the model does generate a sustained endogenous cycle, it exhibits a strong regularity that does not resemble the frequency and amplitude of actual fluctuations.

Second, an analysis of economic fluctuations in Mexico and the United States, by means of an elaborate theoretical and econometric model, would have to be based on a specific business-cycle theory, but existing statistical techniques do not satisfactorily discriminate among different business theories that are essentially contradictory. For example, in causality analysis, an approach that has gained popularity in recent years (see Granger, 1969), the contemporaneous value of a variable x is estimated as a function of the lagged values of another variable y. If the relationship is significant, we conclude that y causes x. However, this method has serious limitations. Even in the extreme case in which the value of x is fully determined by the past values of y, the approach fails to correctly detect causation if the lagged polynomial in y is not long enough and if the response of x to

123

to past values of y is not stable. When analyzing
economic variables that are heavily influenced by
policy decisions, as is the case in this chapter, those
two situations are very likely to arise since government intervention affects the time structure of re-
sponses.

Third, the quality of the data, above all in the
Mexican case, prevents us from successfully fitting a
formal model. It would not be wise to fit a sophisti-
cated model to poor data that can be trusted only to
reflect very general and aggregative patterns of behavior.

The next section deals with general issues related
to the business cycle. Then we discuss anticyclical
policies and their relationship to the cycle. Next we
concentrate on issues related to the interdependence of
economic variables in Mexico and the United States,
emphasizing the behavior of real variables between 1950
and 1982, but leaving aside important financial phenomena. Finally, we conclude with long-run considerations that, in our understanding, should have priority
over very short-run, erratic fluctuations in policy
design. All these topics are analyzed from the Mexican
perspective.

THE BUSINESS CYCLE

Economists have for a long time looked for enduring and well-behaved characteristics in economic fluctuations or, in other words, for economic or business
cycles. These characteristics are practically the
same in every analytical approach: automaticity and
regularity.

Automaticity refers to the tendency of economic
variables to automatically fluctuate around their long-
run behavior, as an inherent property of the economic
system. According to this view the fluctuations can be
moderated but not avoided. Because of this automaticity the short-run fluctuations are, to some extent,
independent of long-run movements. This behavior then
translates into policy recommendations for stabilization without regard to their long-run effects, such as
growth potential. This is only a natural consequence
of the belief that short-run economic fluctuations are
independent of long-run movements.

The usefulness of the business cycle as an analytical concept depends upon the presence of regularity.
The occurrence of fluctuations in economic variables at
fixed intervals would enhance the possibilities of
successful forecasting and instrumentation of anticyclical economic policies: expansionary ones when
economic activity goes down and contractionary ones

otherwise. The use of this concept is more powerful
with the presumption that current booms and recessions
share their main features with past and future booms
and recessions.

Indeed, economic activity shows a great deal of
fluctuation. It is always possible to fit a path that
picks up some of the long-run behavior and ignores
erratic short-term fluctuations. Arbitrarily, this
path may be called the long-run tendency, and the
deviations may be used to define the cycles. The usual
procedure to find regularity is to fit different overlapping ideal and exact cycles of different amplitudes
and frequencies. This unrestricted procedure used in a
finite sample allows analysts to obtain a good statistical result. After all, the number of ideal cycles
from which to choose is infinite; some are very likely
to replicate the behavior of finite time series.[1]

The "success" of this procedure has led to the
misleading conclusion that time-series techniques,
which only consider past behavior and ignore economic
theory, are superior to sound econometric models, at
least for very short-run projections. The fact that
the behavior of economic variables responds greatly to
their own inertia, ignoring the effect of policy
variables, should be considered a serious limitation to
the use of business-cycle theory for the instrumentation of stabilization policies. This is due to the
concept of the cycle rather than the use of techniques
to detect fluctuations. The implicit automaticity of
the cycle requires countercyclical policies to have a
rather strong short-run effect on the economy. The
more automaticity in economic fluctuations, the more
valid is the concept of the cycle but the less useful
is business-cycle theory for stabilization purposes.

The usefulness of the cycle concept as a mere
predictor is not obvious either. Business-cycle techniques have not been able to predict turning points
successfully. Indeed, these techniques have consistently shown an inability to predict the duration and
magnitude of most important recessions in history.

Let us assume that there exists a well-defined
cycle or set of overlapping cycles that allows us to
predict fluctuations with great accuracy. We assume,
also, that the contradiction between well-behaved
cycles and effectiveness of short-run discretionary
policy is resolved. Now, let us ask the following
question: Can classic stabilization policies (implemented regardless of their long-run effects) be
accepted rationally?

The answer is no, for two basic reasons. First,
institutional and political constraints cannot be overlooked. Economic problems have social and political
dimensions too often ignored by economists, who

consider it possible to implement economic policies
without taking into account the institutional framework. In pure economic terms, ignoring institutional
constraints, a set of policies might be commendable,
but it might jeopardize social agreements that allow
the formulation of such policies in the first place.

Second, rigorously short-run policy instruments
are very difficult to distinguish from long-run ones.
The tendency to separate the short from the long run
theoretically has led policymakers, in most instances,
to give priority to the short run; in practice, this
conflict is also solved in favor of the short run. For
example, Mexico's international trade policy has not
been very successful because quota and tariff decisions
are usually made in response to balance-of-payments
constraints (which, in turn, are considered short-run
goals) and not in line with the rationality of long-run
resource allocation.

All this underlines the case for adopting a non-
model approach. There is one more element: Mexico-
United States relations are not new. An attempt to
change the quality of these relations while ignoring
their history could be very interesting, if based on a
pure quantitative model, but would be a complete
failure in practice. The relations between the two
countries have been shaped through time as a reaction
against major grievances, as well as by mutually satisfactory agreements.

THE BUSINESS CYCLE AND ANTICYCLICAL
POLICIES IN MEXICO AND THE UNITED STATES

There are important institutional determinants, as
we have said, of short-run policy. In the case of the
United States, it has been suggested that many economic
policy decisions are heavily influenced by political
considerations, such as the proximity of elections. In
this section, we shall analyze whether or not Mexican
policymakers follow political criteria. J. E. Koehler
(1968) has suggested that a "political" cycle can be
seen in Mexican public expenditure. This cycle,
according to the author, has fixed intervals, defined
by the six-year duration of each administration. In
the first year public administrators, who have recently
entered the administration, do not know how to spend.
As they acquire experience, public expenditure increases. By the fifth and sixth years, public officials are concerned with unfinished projects and thus
public expenditure increases above their long-run
tendency.

A detailed analysis of Mexican public expenditure[2]
indeed shows a political cycle, with a very similar

TABLE 1
Hypothetical Frequencies of the Rate of Growth of
Mexican Public Expenditures, Assuming Independence
from Administration Cycles

	Year of Administration		
	First Year	Last Year	Other Years
One of the two lowest rates during the administration	$\frac{1}{12} = 0.0833$	$\frac{1}{12} = 0.0833$	$\frac{1}{12} = 0.3333$
Other	$\frac{1}{12} = 0.0833$	$\frac{1}{12} = 0.0833$	$\frac{1}{12} = 0.3333$

six-year pattern in every administration. However,
actual behavior is very different from the widely
accepted Koehler's cycle. For public expenditure to
be independent of the administration cycle, its rate
of growth would have to follow the distribution of
Table 1.

To determine the dependence of public expenditures
on the administration cycle, we separate the first and
last years of the administration, on the assumption
that the behavior in these years is different from
that in the middle years (Koehler, 1968). Table 1 is
based on the assumption that expenditure growth is independent of the administration cycle, whereas Table 2
gives the observed pattern. The observed frequencies
are quite different from those of the neutral case,
where public expenditure is assumed to be independent
of the administration cycle. The X^2 test for independence, at confidence levels above 99.5 percent, shows
that the hypothesis of equal distributions is easily
rejected.[3] However, the observed frequencies do not
support the hypothesis that the rate of increase in
public expenditures is highest at the end of the
period. (Koehler works with levels rather than with
rates of change. The long-run tendency of real public
expenditure to grow might partially explain his
results.) Instead, the increase of public expenditure
seems to be lowest at both the beginning and the end
of the administration. This alternative hypothesis
would call for a distribution such as that shown in
Table 3.

This distribution is very similar to the observed
one (Table 2). If the observations for the years of
the first administration (1953-1958) are dropped, the

TABLE 2
Observed Frequencies of the Rate of Growth of Mexican
Public Expenditures, 1953-1982

| | Year of Administration | | |
	First Year	Last Year	Other Years
One of the two lowest rates in the administration	0.1667	0.1333	0.03333
Other	0	0.0333	0.6333

two distributions would be identical (Figure 1). The
hypothesis of equality of the two distributions cannot
be rejected at high significance levels, not even at
significance levels above 50 percent.

According to these tests, public expenditure
policy in the short run has been determined by the
administration cycle, with other considerations practically excluded. Since Mexico has not had a really
independent monetary policy, short-run policy in
general has followed the administration cycle; it
has been most expansive in the middle years of any
administration period. Thus, if expenditure policy
has followed such behavior, then short-run policies
have not been used for fine tuning or anticyclical
purposes.

One argument states that prior to 1970 public
expenditures played a compensatory role: It went up
when private expenditure (mainly investment) decreased
and vice versa (Ortíz-Mena, 1969). There has in fact
been a negative correlation between public and private
investment, but it has not been a result of compensatory policies. Rather, it has reflected an automatic
crowding out of private expenditure. During the period
an important share of public expenditure was financed
with private savings (see Solís, 1973). Moreover,
since public expenditure followed closely the administration cycle, we can rule out the possibility that
expenditure policies were used for purposes of fine-
tuning, as is implicit in a deliberate compensatory
role.

The behavior of Mexican public expenditure should
not be considered irrational because it did not follow
a stabilizing pattern. Public expenditure has been low
at the beginning of the administration because of the
inexperience of the new personnel and at the end

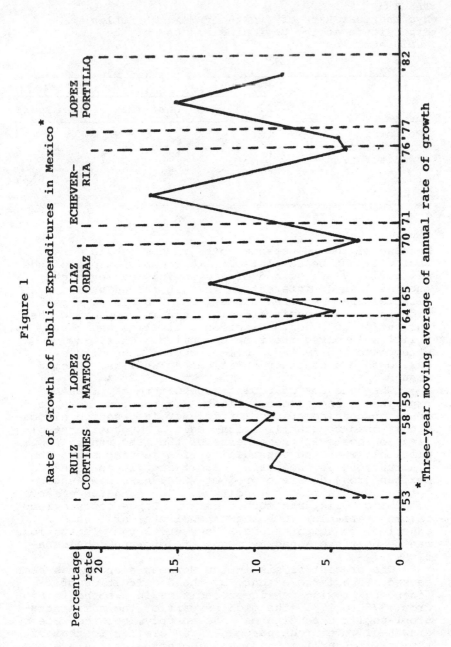

Figure 1

Rate of Growth of Public Expenditures in Mexico*

*Three-year moving average of annual rate of growth

TABLE 3
Hypothetical Rate of Growth of Mexican Public
Expenditure at the Beginning and End of the
Administration

	Year of Administration		
	First Year	Last Year	Other Years
Two lowest rates in the administration	$\frac{1}{6}$ = 0.1667	$\frac{1}{6}$ = 0.1667	0
Other	0	=	$\frac{2}{3}$ = 0.6667

because of the reluctance to begin new public works
that will not be completed. Other explanations of the
low activity at the end of the administration might
include loss of interest in the job, since public
officials become more interested in obtaining a position in the new administration than in completing their
current ("old") job. Election activities and the
politics involved are time-consuming. Thus, any
attempt to modify the cycle of public expenditure in
Mexico should consider political as well as economic
issues.

The behavior of public expenditure may thus be
explained along rational lines. It responds more to
long-run considerations (efficiency in resource allocations) than to stabilization goals. Advocating stabilization goals at the expense of the long-run is
difficult when the possibility of affecting short-run
fluctuations is uncertain. Short-run fluctuations of
Mexican gross domestic product (GDP) have been uncor-
related with public expenditure. The long-run effects
of public policy are much clearer. Large contractions
in both variables (GDP and expenditure) are, as
expected, contemporaneous. However, large fluctuations
can be best explained by means of long-run considerations.

The present crisis in the Mexican economy has been
caused, to a large extent, by the difficulties of
financing growing public expenditure in a sound fashion.
From 1978 to 1981 (the middle years of the administration) public expenditures rose sharply, but the rate of
growth of government purchases was similar to that of
the previous administrations. Nevertheless, since the
recent increase came on top of already very high
levels, public finance became more difficult to manage.

The current problems in public finance in Mexico result
from a long-run tendency of public expenditures to grow
more rapidly than public revenues could have been
expected to grow. Thus, the present crisis is more a
crisis of a development strategy than a simple cyclical
phenomenon.

The lag in the adjustment of public prices to inflation has played an important role in the rising
public deficit. The amount of subsidies reached levels
equivalent to the total deficit. Although these magnitudes are characteristic for the last years, the root
of the problem is in the long-run strategy. The
sluggishness of public prices has been a persistent
feature of the Mexican economy, and as inflation rates
increased the implicit subsidies became more important.
Other factors that contributed to the crisis, such as
developments in the terms of trade and the oil and
financial markets, cannot properly be fitted into a
business-cycle scheme, since recent experiences did not
resemble past behavior.

Other interpretations of the Mexican crisis
emphasize that in the recent past the Mexican economy
grew whereas the rest of the world was in a depression:
Mexico is in crisis because of lack of coordination
between the Mexican and the international business
cycles. However, this is not the first time that
Mexican cycles have not been coordinated; the same
situation occurred very clearly between 1954 and 1958.
In this period the average rate of growth of production
in Mexico was 6 percentage points larger than that of
the United States (between 1977 and 1981 this difference was only 4.4 percentage points). But during the
following years Mexico did not enter an economic
crisis. Rather, the economy reached its highest
historical rates of GDP growth during the first half
of the 1960s. We do not reject the hypothesis that the
lack of coordination in the cycles had a negative
impact on Mexican macroeconomic stability. We want,
however, to emphasize the importance of the long-run
performance of the economy in the explanation of fundamental economic events.

Let us now, for symmetry purposes, turn to the
United States. To an outsider, the possibility that
government can actually influence the short-run behavior of the U.S. economy seems rather uncertain. To
be sure, economic policy and especially monetary policy
have been used more often for stabilization policies
in the United States than in Mexico, where there is no
well-developed financial market. Thus, the Volcker
era has indeed made a difference. However, on the
whole, noneconomic factors have also contributed to
the design of economic policy, perhaps more than stabilization goals.

We draw attention to one noneconomic factor: the war. The behavior of U.S. public expenditure from 1935 to 1981 shows that the most relevant peaks coincide with the years of World War II, the Korean War, and the most active period of the Vietnam War. (In this latter case, the peak coincides with the Tet offensive in 1968. From then on, the rate of growth of public expenditure decreases as peace talks developed. See Figure 2.) Other fluctuations of public expenditure seem relatively unimportant. The difference in the levels of the variable in the two periods of relative peace (between Korea and Vietnam and during the 1970s) is far more significant than the very short-run fluctuations during these years. Thus, the behavior of public expenditure of the United States should be explained mainly by factors other than short-run stabilization policies, some of them of a noneconomic nature. The rationale of these policies cannot be assessed only by purely economic considerations either.

Stabilization policies have important effects on the long run. Long-run aspects of stabilization policies are, most of the time, considered as caveats of an analysis with a dominant emphasis on the short run, which is considered to be independent of secular tendencies. This view tends to disappear when the economy has poor performance for an extended time period. Let us illustrate by using Reagan's stabilization strategy, characterized by loose fiscal and tight monetary policies. As soon as inflation rates went down, this unorthodox approach gained support among experts. However, as the poor performance of the economy in other aspects became apparent and was expected to continue if short-run criteria prevailed, experts became disenchanted with the long-run implications. The longer the large public deficits are maintained, the more difficult and painful it will be to correct the disequilibria. Experts from the perspective of 1983 worry about the long-run structural changes the present policy might bring about: high interest rates and an overvalued dollar--promoted by the fiscal disequilibrium--that will depress investment and weaken the foreign sector.

However, policymakers who have become aware of the long-run consequences do not seem to have the political will to change the economic strategy. The necessary change ought to be drastic and might go beyond the realm of what traditionally is understood to be the short run. The present situation has been defined as a "tolerable second best" with bad long-run consequences.

In summary, the behavior of economic policy and, in particular, of one of its main tools (public expenditure), cannot be assessed in either Mexico or the

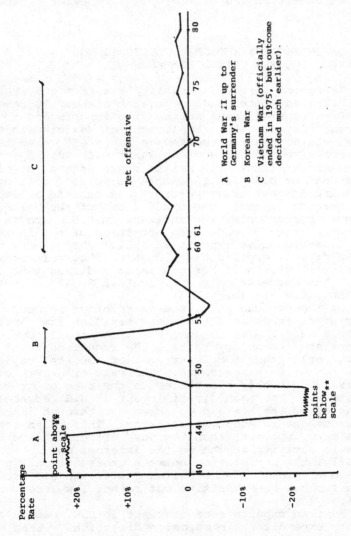

Figure 2

Rate of Growth of Federal Expenditures in the United States*

Percentage Rate

+20%

+10%

0

-10%

-20%

40 44 50 60 61 70 75 80

A World War II up to Germany's surrender

B Korean War

C Vietnam War (officially ended in 1975, but outcome decided much earlier).

Tet offensive

point above scale

points below** scale

*Three-year moving average of annual rate of growth.

**During World War II expenditure growth rates reached levels above 100%; rates after 1945 reflected an adjustment to peace.

United States by using only purely economic considerations. Institutional constraints play a major role in the explanation of this behavior. A simple economic model of the business cycle would not suffice to provide an understanding of the actual behavior of the variables.

INTERDEPENDENCE OF ECONOMIC FLUCTUATIONS
IN MEXICO AND THE UNITED STATES

In recent years, Mexican imports from and exports to the United States have represented about 70 percent and 60 percent of total merchandise imports and exports, respectively. Employment of Mexicans in the United States has represented an important valve that lets pressure off the Mexican labor markets.

Although trade with Mexico represents a relatively small part of U.S. international commerce (it is only the third largest trade partner), it has had an important marginal role in the trade flows of the United States. For example, the increase in U.S. exports to Mexico amounted to more than one-third of the increase in U.S. merchandise exports in 1981. The rate of growth of U.S. exports has been highly correlated with the rate of growth of Mexican imports during 1950 to 1982. The correlation coefficient is 70.42 percent (see Appendix 2, Table A2.3).

On the Mexican side, the correlation between imports and investment has been very high (see Appendix 2, Table A2.1). Mexico does not generate its own appropriate technology to face the requirements of the modern world; thus the importance of imported capital goods cannot be exaggerated. The rate of growth of GDP in Mexico is highly correlated to the rate of growth of investment. The main direct impact of U.S. economic variables on the Mexican economy runs through imports to investment to economic activity. This chain seems to be more important than the pure effect of external economic activity growth on the internal one. Actually, the correlation between gross national product (GNP) growth in the United States and GDP growth in Mexico has been positive but rather low (see Table A2.3).

Mexican exports seem to react to U.S. public and private expenditure in opposite directions. When public expenditures in the United States increase they tend to crowd out private expenditure (see Appendix 2, Table A2.2). This has a negative impact on Mexican exports, since the content of Mexican exportable goods is higher in U.S. private expenditures than in public ones, which have a high content of defense and services expenditures. Mexican exports have had a positive

correlation with private expenditure in the United
States (46.1 percent), whereas the correlation with
public expenditure has been negative (-47.3 percent)
(see Table A2.3).

In the foreseeable future, the performance of the
Mexican economy will depend crucially on whether a
healthy integration with the rest of the world is
achieved. This means, whether desired or not, a great
deal of integration with the United States. However,
some noneconomic obstacles to a fully healthy integration are present.

Economic theory suggests that the Mexican reticence to integrate its economy fully with the rest of
the world is irrational. (This reticence, for
instance, was shown when Mexico decided not to join the
General Agreement on Tariffs and Trade (GATT).) Custom
union theory would suggest that association with the
United States would be more favorable than association
with developing countries, since the latter would
imply a trade diversion from low-cost to high-cost
supplies. Besides, the United States can be a source
of more advanced technology than the rest of Latin
America. However, Mexican trade policy cannot be
analyzed with only pure economic arguments. Mexican
policy cannot be expected to change drastically in the
short run. Historical experience in Mexico-United
States relations leads to the conclusion that three
basic features will make up future relations.

First, in the immediate future any progress in the
relationship must be achieved on a bilateral stepwise
basis. U.S. pressures on Mexico to accept broad
arrangements or to join regional integrations including
the United States, rather than helping to ease Mexico
into a more open integration with it, would spur
opposition. Mutual confidence must be gradually
achieved against the background of an unfavorable
setting.

Second, Mexico's attitude toward its relations
with the United States cannot be judged as irrational,
since it results from a desire to seek protection
against the repetition of past grievances. The assessment, as we have said, cannot be made on purely
economic terms.

Third, any agreement should be reached on a long-
run sustainable basis. The rules of the game should
not be changed following short-run considerations
(e.g., U.S. farm pressures to impose restrictions on
Mexican exports caused by short-run fluctuations in
domestic demand and production). Of course, the same
applies to Mexico. The use of protective measures as
stabilization policy tends to damage the confidence
that should be the basis of mutually constructive
relations.

Let us now refer in more detail to the long-run impact of U.S. stabilization policies on the rest of the world--and in particular on Mexico. In pursuing short-run internal stabilization policies, the United States may jeopardize its political long-run standing in the world. If these policies continue, the odds for world integration would be slim and so would the probability of a sustained advance in Mexico-United States relations.

The judgment of the unorthodox combination of loose fiscal and tight monetary policies in the United States is usually made without regard to the long-run position of the economy. The impact of a large country's policies on the rest of the world is not the main concern of its policymakers. For example, the secretary of the Treasury of the United States has said that tax increases to cut the deficit would hurt the recovery of the U.S. economy and would damage the developing nations through a lower demand for their exports. This view ignores important aspects.

First, the persistence of large public deficits in the United States would dampen U.S. recovery. A short-lived recovery might induce instability in the world economy. In the case of Mexico, this might generate strong fluctuations and thus make it difficult to achieve the confidence necessary to improve bilateral relations.

Second, a long-run reordering of the world economies, including that of the United States, is more important than short-run recovery. The correction of internal disequilibria advocated by the United States for the rest of the world, especially for developing countries, should also apply internally. In developing countries the U.S. position is regarded as unfair, since the application of policies to secure structural corrections is asymmetric. Although the public deficit relative to GDP is substantially smaller in the United States than in most developing countries, the sheer size of the U.S. economy and its deficit have a stronger effect on the world economy.

Third, the reduction of the U.S. fiscal deficit should not be accompanied by measures to protect domestic economic activity against imports. An increase in protectionist measures would take us back to the present situation, where priority is given to short-run performance. Antiprotectionist policies could be negotiated with other developed countries in combination with a substantial drop in interest rates, following a reduction of the U.S. deficit (see Cline, 1983).

Fourth, the decrease in U.S. economic activity resulting from fiscal adjustment would be partially offset by the impact on demand for U.S. exports: The

dollar would be less overvalued, since interest rates
would go down; and the decrease of interest payments of
debtor countries would relax their foreign exchange
constraints on imports. Thus, it is not clear that the
eventual effect on demand of reducing the U.S. deficit
would be negative.

Fifth, the general impact of a reduction of
interest payments on Mexico's balance of payments would
outweigh the gain in exports associated with a mild but
short-lived recovery, supported by a continuing large
U.S. deficit (see Ortíz and Serra Puche, 1983). The
present recession of the Mexican economy is, in good
part, explained by the scarcity of imports of producer
goods; these imports have been reduced to unprecedented
levels to meet the foreign debt service that in 1982
amounted to 52 percent of the total value of merchandise exports. On the other hand, it is not clear that
a U.S. recovery, through increases in public expenditure, would benefit Mexican exports. On top of the low
content of Mexican exportables in U.S. public expenditure, non-oil exports in 1982 in Mexico made up such a
small part of total exports (22 percent) that the
short-lived recovery would not benefit Mexico in the
short or long run.

FINAL REMARK

The relation between the Mexican and U.S. economies
has had a complex history. The relationship includes
so many institutional aspects that a "pure" economic
analysis would not go far. A simple business-cycle
approach would not shed much light on the main issues
of the subject: The behavior of economic policy tools
frequently does not follow the fluctuations of the
major macroeconomic variables. Stabilization policies
that concentrate on short-run goals might end up
damaging the potential relations between the two
countries. The short-lived recovery of the U.S.
economy, without the correction of internal disequa-
libria, may damage the possibilities of a Mexican
recovery. A long-run solution should come from a more
symmetric implementation of internal corrections in
both Mexico and the United States.

138

NOTES

1. For a good description of this procedure, see T. J. Sargent (1979), pp. 254-256.

2. We analyze public expenditure data from the adjusted national accounts. Of course, these data only reflect public expenditure on final goods and services and leave aside some important components of public demand, such as transfers. However, the available data on total public expenditure prior to 1965 refer only to the federal government and are considered to be very poor. Although partial, the data from national accounts can be trusted to give a more satisfactory picture of the behavior of public expenditure. Because of scarcity of policy instruments in Mexico, decisions to increase or decrease economic activity will be reflected by changes in all kinds of expenditures, not only transfers. In the past, independent monetary policy has been practially nonexistent, in part because of the lack of a developed securities market (see Ortíz and Solís, 1978).

3. The null hypothesis is chosen in a way that avoids division by zero in all the X^2 tests.

REFERENCES

Cline, W. 1983. "Global Consequences of U.S. External and Internal Disequilibrium," mimeographed.
García-Alba, P., and J. Serra Puche. 1983. Financial Aspects of Macroeconomic Management in Mexico. Joint Research Program Series, no. 36, Institute of Developing Economics, Japan.
Granger, C. W. J. 1969. "Investigating Causal Relations by Econometric Models and Cross-Spectral Methods," Econometrica 37, no. 3, pp. 424-439.
Koehler, J. E. 1968. Economic Policy Making with Limited Information: The Process of Macro Control in Mexico, Rand Corporation, Memorandum MR-5682-RC, August 1968.
Ortíz-Mena, A. 1969. "Desarrollo Estabilizador." Document presented to the Annual Meeting of the IMF and World Bank, September 1969.
Ortíz, G., and J. Serra Puche. 1983. "A Note on the Burden of the Mexican Foreign Debt," mimeographed.
Ortíz, G., and L. Solís. 1978. "Estructura Financiera y Experiencia Cambiaria: México 1954-1977." Documento de Investigación, no. 1, Banco de México.
Sargent, T. J. 1979. Macroeconomic Theory. New York: Academic Press.
Solís, L. 1973. La Realidad Mexicana: Retrovisión y Perspectivas. 4th ed. Mexico City: Siglo XXI.

APPENDIX 1

ADJUSTMENTS TO MEXICAN DATA

For the analysis of the U.S. cycle we refer to
the data contained in the Economic Report of the
President. For Mexico, serious data problems hamper a
thorough analysis of economic fluctuations. The three
sources[1] covering the analysis period are inconsistent;
only one is now considered official and covers the
years since 1970. To make the other two sources com-
patible with the official one, we base the analysis on
the official source from 1970 onward. We then translated some disaggregated components of demand and
supply as reported in the other sources to the same
base year as the official data. The disaggregated
components of gross domestic product (GDP) were
private consumption, public consumption, investment
(which afterwards was separated into public and private), inventory accumulation, exports, and imports.
The difference in overlapping years was distributed
among the ten preceding years to eliminate jumps.

Because of variations in relative prices, the GDP
series for Mexico that results from this disaggrega-
tion procedure is very different from that obtained
directly from adjustment of the aggregated GDP series.
Elsewhere, we have illustrated the important effect
that the single change of base year has on the assessment of GDP growth in Mexico (García-Alba and Serra
Puche, 1983). If the adjustment had been made by a
more disaggregated procedure, the results would have
been different and presumably more satisfactory. However, because of the uncertainty regarding the quality
of the data before 1970, we decided that a more detailed procedure was unwarranted.

For the years for which data on public-sector
investment were unavailable, we used the authorized--
as distinct from realized--public investment, corrected
by a coefficient that tried to pick up the propor-
tional difference between authorized and realized
investment in the different years within a six-year
administration period. This coefficient was obtained
from the years for which independent information on
the two variables was available, and showed an increased ratio of realized to authorized investment
from the beginning to the end of the administration.
This coefficient per se does not imply the kind of
behavior we detected for the rate of growth of public
investment along every administration: relatively low
at the beginning and at the end of the period. We
further adjusted the public-investment series to
eliminate jumps in the overlapping years of the

TABLE A1.1
Adjusted Mexican National Accounts (in millions of 1970 pesos)

Year	GDP	Government Consumption	Private Consumption	Public Investment	Private Investment	Inventory Variation	Exports	Imports
1950	118,133.0	5,761.9	94,805.9	5,551.4	8,621.3	862.1	16,445.0	13,914.6
1951	127,888.9	5,849.0	106,331.9	6,079.2	12,365.0	1,150.2	16,151.5	17,737.5
1952	132,909.4	6,093.1	104,690.4	6,506.5	13,544.4	951.3	16,288.3	15,864.6
1953	132,861.6	6,528.6	107,811.3	4,439.1	13,260.7	1,150.7	15,234.7	15,563.5
1954	145,958.8	7,582.6	113,928.9	5,408.6	15,449.7	2,410.2	20,304.6	19,125.8
1955	158,150.8	8,341.3	120,392.2	5,944.1	17,059.2	3,564.8	23,755.0	20,905.8
1956	169,076.8	9,042.3	127,745.2	5,195.0	22,750.0	3,755.5	24,471.5	23,882.7
1957	182,529.0	9,721.5	144,003.8	6,832.9	22,888.2	1,566.3	21,590.4	24,074.1
1958	192,824.0	11,554.1	152,150.6	7,762.6	22,002.0	1,371.1	21,068.3	23,084.7
1959	197,146.9	11,967.2	155,195.8	6,432.3	22,979.1	1,164.1	20,689.9	21,281.5
1960	212,888.8	13,960.6	161,762.3	7,527.7	26,549.7	5,304.3	20,702.8	22,918.6
1961	224,389.0	14,993.4	168,627.1	11,672.0	22,952.6	6,436.3	22,395.1	22,617.5
1962	236,419.0	17,214.5	177,300.1	11,271.8	25,503.9	4,369.0	23,739.7	22,980.0
1963	256,653.3	19,396.0	188,838.9	15,759.0	25,559.9	7,311.0	24,959.5	25,171.0
1964	288,341.0	21,728.8	209,318.5	19,762.0	30,344.5	8,492.6	27,943.5	29,248.6
1965	308,458.2	22,418.8	221,537.9	14,609.9	39,581.0	12,213.9	28,458.1	30,361.4
1966	331,807.4	24,314.2	239,441.3	16,819.3	42,612.7	9,649.0	30,068.6	31,097.7
1967	355,035.8	25,881.6	257,293.1	22,519.9	45,557.2	8,063.9	29,161.8	33,441.7
1968	386,612.0	28,602.0	282,804.6	24,974.3	50,181.5	5,571.6	31,759.3	37,281.3
1969	412,874.9	29,799.0	297,149.1	27,417.9	53,868.5	7,084.6	36,957.5	39,401.7
1970	444,271.4	32,243.2	319,512.8	29,249.9	59,410.7	12,295.4	34,430.5	42,880.1
1971	462,803.8	35,671.2	336,216.2	22,451.2	64,691.0	8,899.3	35,786.5	40,911.6
1972	502,085.9	40,454.3	358,909.9	31,484.4	66,321.4	8,341.8	41,666.3	45,092.2

Year								
1973	544,306.7	44,516.3	382,715.5	43,938.2	68,289.5	10,099.0	47,365.6	52,617.6
1974	577,568.0	47,330.2	402,449.8	45,009.6	76,086.2	22,522.8	47,457.7	63,288.3
1975	609,975.8	54,018.1	425,435.7	54,732.9	77,583.2	18,534.7	43,231.5	63,560.3
1976	635,831.3	57,454.3	444,755.3	50,597.2	82,312.4	14,487.2	50,414.1	64,189.2
1977	657,221.5	56,804.2	453,822.6	47,212.4	76,774.1	22,951.1	57,803.4	57,646.3
1978	711,982.3	62,448.1	490,806.1	62,122.2	80,677.1	21,672.8	64,499.3	70,243.3
1979	777,162.6	68,443.7	534,218.5	72,853.3	98,960.9	21,704.0	72,328.8	91,236.6
1980	841,854.5	74,957.5	574,502.6	84,870.3	112,494.2	38,609.6	76,746.2	120,325.9
1981	908,764.8	82,501.2	616,706.5	98,261.8	128,165.6	46,354.6	81,499.5	144,724.4
1982	907,306.2	86,488.9	626,084.2	85,759.2	102,566.5	8,127.7	83,718.6	85,438.9

different periods.

Table Al.1 shows the adjusted national-accounts series resulting from the above procedure. We do not place much confidence in the levels of the variables indicated by this table, but we believe that they reflect the fluctuations to a degree satisfactory for our analysis.

NOTES

1. Banco de México, Cuentas Nacionales y Acervos de Capital, 1950-1967, Banco de México, Producto Interno Bruto y Gasto, 1960-1978, and Secretaría de Programmación y Presupuesto, Sistema de Cuentas Nacionales 1970-1981.

APPENDIX 2

CORRELATIONS AMONG U.S. AND MEXICAN
VARIABLES

All variables, based on Table A1.1, are considered
in the form of central three-year averages of the rate
of growth to eliminate most of the very short-run
erratic fluctuations. Table A2.1 shows correlations
among Mexican variables; Table A2.2 does the same for
U.S. variables; and Table A2.3 shows correlations
between Mexican and U.S. variables. In all three
tables the following definitions apply:

         GNP - gross national product
         GDP - gross domestic product
          GC - government consumption
          PC - private consumption
          TC - total consumption
          TI - total fixed investment
          GI - public investment
          PI - private investment
           X - exports
           M - imports
          GE - public final expenditure
          PE - private final expenditure

TABLE A2.1
Correlation Coefficients Among Mexican Variables, 1952–1981

	CT	GC	PC	TI	GI	PI	X	M	GE	PE
GDP	84.1	25.3	82.1	87.7	47.0	62.1	33.3	68.3	48.4	86.4
GC			1.1	17.5	40.0	-10.0	-3.7	9.6	61.3	-1.3
PC				68.5	35.5	50.4	-3.9	49.5	32.4	94.7
GI						-21.5*	13.0	40.6	96.6	20.2
PI							13.4	58.0	-19.6	75.3
X								47.9	11.3	2.6
M									39.6	60.3
GE										18.9

*For the 1952–1970 period this correlation reached -46.0 percent.

TABLE A2.2
Correlation Coefficients Among U.S. Variables,
1952-1981

	PC	PI	X	M	GE	PE
GNP	82.9	79.9	29.6	66.1	38.6	82.4
PC		87.2	22.1	68.1	-6.6	95.6
PI			31.3	61.1	-15.5	95.4
X				6.7	-23.7	24.1
M					23.5	63.9
GE						-16.7

TABLE A2.3
Correlations Between Mexican and U.S. Variables,
1952-1981

	GDP	X	M	GE	PE
GNP	23.3	20.3	-3.6	-3,2	15.6
X	64.9	46.3	70.4	52.3	44.9
M	28.0	17.0	-2.1	-19.4	40.3
GE	-26.8	-47.3	-19.7	-22.9	-2.0
PE	33.0	46.1	-5.3	-2.9	14.1

5

The Crisis and Thereafter: Macroeconomic Policy Problems in Mexico

Lance Taylor

Economic crises spin out from interlinked chains of events. Trying to isolate a "cause" amid the concatenation is idle: The best one can do is point to factors whose presence was required for disaster. The first part of this chapter lays the groundwork for such analysis by selectively reviewing recent developments in the Mexican economy. The second through fourth sections discuss necessary conditions for the Mexican crisis of 1982--excessive public expenditure, naive import liberalization, and touching faith in the stability of a financial system built on Mexdollars. No one of these three popular explanations is compelling. But acting together, public spending, freeing of trade, and dollar speculation greased the slide toward economy-wide collapse. Out of crisis stepped a new look for Mexico--couturier the International Monetary Fund (IMF). The fifth section is devoted to the new style, with commentary about how long it is likely to remain in fashion; doubts are expressed about the durability of the IMF model.

Finally, longer term issues are addressed--the oil syndrome, the capital market, migration, and income distribution. No economic panaceas are in sight--they never are--but some basis for guarded optimism about the future can be seen if historically proven policies plus two innovations are pursued. These innovations are internal financial reform, including capital market diversification and partial sterilization of oil revenues, and a serious attempt to control external capital flows. As a result of the crisis, some of the institutional foundations for these policy innovations already exist. But whether they will be implemented--and help forestall a second round of disaster--is another question.

TABLE 1
Components of Mexican Saving and Investment, 1978-1982
(in percentages of GDP)

	1978	1979	1980	1981	Prel. 1982
Saving					
Public sector	3.5	3.2	2.2	-0.8	-0.7
PEMEX, operating surplus	2.4	3.1	4.8	4.2	7.1
Balance	1.1	0.1	-2.6	-5.0	-7.8
Private sector plus depreciation	17.0	18.6	21.9	24.0	19.9
External	3.1	4.1	4.0	5.8	1.7
Total	23.6	25.9	28.1	29.0	20.9
Investment					
Public sector	7.2	7.8	9.5	12.9	10.3
PEMEX	2.7	3.0	2.9	3.9	3.1
Balance	4.5	4.8	6.6	9.0	7.2
Private sector and stock changes	16.4	18.1	18.6	16.1	10.6

Source: Ministries of Finance and Public Credit, and Programming and Budget; Bank of Mexico.

ROOTS OF THE CRISIS

Table 1 is a summary of the Mexican savings-investment balance over the period 1978 to 1982. The first four years were the boom during the José López Portillo administration, and the crisis played during most of 1982. Real GDP growth during the boom was 8 or 9 percent per year; it was about -0.2 percent in 1982 (according to preliminary estimates). The table shows that rapid growth was largely investment-led, as the investment share in gross domestic product (GDP) went from 23.6 to 29 percent between 1978 and 1982. The share of public-sector expenditure also rose sharply over the period (Table 3) from 22.6 percent in 1978 to 31.9 percent in 1981 and 38.3 percent in 1982. However, not all this increase represented an independent injection of demand. Current public-sector spending apart from interest payments went from 11.4 percent in 1978 to 14.8 percent in 1981, about three-fifths of the investment increase.

The saving to finance greater investment came from

the private sector. (A further breakdown of saving by firms and households is impossible to make.) The downward swing in public-sector saving during 1978 to 1981 was 4.3 percent of GDP. The share of external saving (the current account deficit) rose by only 2.7 percent, so that private saving had to rise from 17 to 24 percent of GDP. Two observations immediately follow from the rather large private marginal saving rate of one-third over the period.[1]

First, there was a concentration of nonagricultural income, presumably leading to a rise in the overall saving propensity. Employment growth was rapid but less than GDP growth during the boom--3 or 4 percent per year. At the same time, the real minimum wage fell. Precise indicators are hard to come by, but Pascual García Alba and Jaime Serra Puche (1983) showed an average decrease of 3.3 percent per year between 1977 and 1982, for example. If the whole wage bill declined proportionately (public-sector wage changes toward the end of the period suggest that such may have been the case), then a shift of several percentage points in the functional income distribution from labor to capital is implied. One likely outcome would be an increase in the overall rate of private saving. At a disaggregated level, this trend was aided by rising profits in nontraded sectors as a consequence of demand pressure from the oil boom and by government transfers benefitting private firms. In any case, forced saving via distributional shifts is an old story in Mexico.[2] There is scant reason to doubt that it occurred during the López Portillo sexenio.

Second, there had to be financial vehicles for the increased private saving. Table 2 presents rough estimates of where private assets were placed. The title of the table refers to the fact that in the years just before and during the crisis, substantial increases occurred in net private foreign assets--capital flight. The net flows in 1980 through 1982 were on the order of $10 billion; gross private outflows would of course have been larger. If the individuals and companies that placed these assets abroad--the famous saca-dolares--financed them by tapping private enterprise and public-sector tills, then they are responsible for a substantial portion of Mexico's overall debt. On the other hand, reductions took place in net foreign asset holdings in the earlier part of the period, which helped postpone the crisis.[3]

These observations suggest that the 1978-1981 period showed many signs of a classic boom, propelled by public-sector investment (principally) and current public spending (secondarily). The private marginal saving rate was one-third--shifts in the income distribution may have contributed to its high level.

TABLE 2
Three Estimates of Capital Flight in Mexico, 1978-1982
(in billion pesos)

	1978	1979	1980	1981	1982
Saving and investment					
Private saving	403	576	941	1,418	2,366
Less private investment	-383	-554	-796	-945	-982
Less change in net liability of financial system to private sector	-55	-98	-121	-326	-847
Change in net private foreign assets					
Total	-35	-76	24	147	537
Total, billion dollars[1]	-1.5	-3.3	1.0	5.6	5.6
Public sector deficit					
Foreign public-sector borrowing	59	65	110	437	352
Less current account deficit	-73	-125	-172	-341	-156
Less change in net foreign assets of financial system	-15	-27	-36	-21	+284*
Change in net private foreign assets					
Total	-29	-76	-98	75	480
Total, billion dollars[1]	-1.3	-3.3	-4.2	2.9	5.0
Balance of payments					
Errors and omissions (x-1) Dollars	0.04	-0.72	2.58	7.71	10.53
Less net private foreign borrowing Dollars	-1.04	-1.78	-6.47	-4.92	-0.36
Change in net private foreign assets					
Total	-23	-57	-91	73	981
Total, billion dollars[1]	-1.02	-2.5	-3.89	2.79	10.17

* The plus sign signals reserve losses in 1982.
[1] Converted at average annual exchange rates.
Source: Secretariat of Budget and Planning.

Initially, extra private saving was directed toward private investment, which rose at the beginning of the boom period. It later tailed off, as assets increasingly were placed abroad. Nothing looks abnormal in the timing of these events--indeed, the López Portillo economic chronology is not far different from that of his predecessor, Luis Echeverria. What special factors triggered a major crisis at the end of the López Portillo sexenio, far greater than Mexico had experienced before?

A FISCAL CRISIS OF THE MEXICAN STATE?

Some readers will recognize the title of this section as a takeoff on the title of James O'Connor's 1973 book (The Fiscal Crisis of the State). O'Connor argued that under advanced capitalism the state's capacity to guide the economic system grows steadily weaker, as it must satisfy popular claims for high spending and low taxes that help legitimize the existing political order.

For authors influenced by Marx (including Schumpeter), such ideas are hardly new.[4] What is novel is that in Mexico fiscal crisis notions have been adopted by conservatives as a central explanation for the events of 1981 and 1982. Some economists such as García-Alba and Serra Puche (1983) simply correlated fiscal deficits with many of the bad traits of macroeconomic life--high inflation, slow growth, big trade gaps. However, in a subtle paper Carlos Bazdresch (1983) put the argument squarely on the political plane:

> Nonetheless, the situation of the public finances--and their almost permanent weakness-- is no accident. The situation is, in the final reckoning, a reflection of the strength or weakness that the State possesses when confronting civil society. . . . [The crisis made evident] the inability of the government to impose on different groups a solution to social demands that would be feasible for the future, coherent, and viable. This weakness . . . is not independent of the government's political base, nor of its capacity to legitimize itself under democratic institutions. Here, perhaps, was the root of the problem. (Bazdresch [1983], pp. 46-47; my translation).

Table 3 presents information on consolidated public-sector accounts that can be used to say something about this argument in economic terms. First,

TABLE 3
Mexican Public-Sector Accounts, 1978-1983 (in percentages of GDP)

	1978	1979	1980	1981	Prel. 1982	Budget 1983
Revenue						
PEMEX operating surplus	2.4	3.1	4.8	4.2	7.1	7.1
Other	14.5	14.7	14.0	12.9	12.6	13.5
Total	16.9	17.8	18.8	17.1	19.7	20.6
Expenditure						
Current spending	13.4	14.6	16.6	17.9	20.4	19.6
Interest payments	2.0	2.0	1.9	3.1	5.7	6.0
Other	11.4	12.6	14.7	14.8	14.7	13.6
Capital spending (including transfers)	9.2	10.0	9.9	14.0	12.3	9.5
PEMEX	2.7	3.0	2.9	3.9	3.1	1.8
Other	6.5	7.0	7.0	10.0	9.2	7.7
Total	22.6	24.6	26.5	31.9	38.3	29.1
Overall deficit	5.7	6.8	7.7	14.8	18.6	
External finance	2.5	2.4	2.5	7.5	3.8	
Internal finance	3.2	4.4	5.2	7.3	14.8	
Other items						
Current account deficit	3.1	4.1	4.0	5.8	1.7	
Change in net private foreign assets						
Method 1	-1.5	-2.5	0.6	2.5	5.8	
Method 2	-1.2	-1.8	-2.3	1.3	5.2	
Method 3	-1.0	-1.9	-2.1	1.2	10.6	

Source: Secretariat of Budget and Planning.

non-oil public-sector revenue stagnated during the boom
period, dropping by about 1.5 percentage points as a
share of GDP. More detailed data show that Mexican
federal government non-oil taxes, social security
revenues, and the Federal District's own revenues held
roughly constant shares of GDP (at about 11.3, 2.5, and
0.3 percent, respectively). The major revenue decrease
took the form of higher losses by state enterprises
aside from PEMEX, which rose from 0.4 to 2.5 percent of
GDP between 1978 and 1981. The major losses were sustained by CONASUPO (the food price regulatory agency)
and state railroads and electric utilities. Including
the CONASUPO subsidy to millers and bakers, these
transfers largely benefitted private-sector producers
and helped support the rise in private-saving rate
already noted.

Second, public-sector capital spending rose
sharply in 1981, after holding steady at about 10 percent of GDP. Part of the increase was due to PEMEX.
Current spending, aside from interest payments, rose
from 11.4 to 14.8 percent between 1978 and 1981. More
detailed data show that increases in both transfers and
purchases of goods and services were involved.

Does a fiscal crisis lurk behind these numbers?
Perhaps, but it appears to have been a modest one.
Comparing the data for 1981 and 1982 to those for 1978,
we find the following changes in key shares of GDP:

	1981	1982
Nonenterprise public revenue	0.5	-0.5
PEMEX operating surplus less investment	0.6	4.0
Other public enterprise operating surpluses	-2.1	-1.5
Interest payments	1.1	3.7
Other current spending	3.4	3.3
Non-PEMEX capital spending	3.6	2.7

The oil dividend might be taken as 4 or 5 percent
of GDP, the PEMEX surplus net investment in 1982 after
the major projects for petroleum capacity were completed. A substantial part of the dividend was de-
voured by increased interest payments. Higher world
interest rates may have political causes, but these
surely transcend the Mexican arena. More telling is
the fact that Mexican policymakers allowed losses on
non-PEMEX public enterprises and current and capital
spending to increase after 1978 by between 7 and 9
percent of GDP. These extra outlays were almost
double the oil dividend and occurred before the
plataforma petrolera was fully in place. Finally,
nonenterprise public revenue was allowed to stagnate.

All this suggests imprudence in policymaking—
Mexican authorities learned nothing from the retrench-
ment that other oil exporters had to go through after
the 1973 oil shock ran down. However—increased
interest payments aside—the greater public-sector
presence in the economy could have been financed by the
oil dividend and tax increases of a few percent of GDP
that a newly enriched country could in principle
afford. Equally, the increase in state outlays should
have been delayed until the resource base was fully in
place. But unless one argues that all the oil dividend
should be transferred directly to the private sector—a
case difficult to sustain in the twentieth century—the
structural Mexican fiscal crisis appears to be of con-
trollable dimension.[5]

Turning to the finance of the public deficit, the
public sector may have been roughly in foreign exchange
balance—with PEMEX capital goods imports and interest
payments offsetting oil receipts in dollars. However,
as shown in Table 3, the public sector borrowed a substantial portion of its deficit abroad. The loans were
incurred both directly and through the banking system,
but in the 1978 to 1980 period they were less than the
external current account deficit. Increases in
reserves of the financial system were small (Table 2);
hence the private sector brought assets from abroad to
close the foreign capital account.

This happy state of affairs ended in 1981, when
confidence ebbed and the private sector started placing
assets abroad. The public sector had to borrow more
than the current account deficit (which itself was
growing rapidly) in external markets. The Mexican
state effectively transferred dollars to the private
sector to a large extent in 1981 by market interven-
tions by the Bank of Mexico to support the peso. These
transactions are the mirror image of the capital flight
documented in Table 2. The flight might have been less
had an acceptable peso-denominated asset been available
to the public. Similarly, for a given trade deficit
and accumulation of reserves, less government borrowing
or a buildup of long-term public assets abroad would
have reduced the quantity of dollars available within
the country to be a vehicle for capital flight. For a
policy of rationing dollars to be effective, of course,
restrictions on the movement of private capital would
also have been required. Capital controls were put on
the books in the wake of the crisis, but could have
been utilized before.

Finally, a word should be said about monetary
policy and inflation. As the data in Table 3 show,
the oil dividend augmented by foreign borrowing represented a substantial increase in potential absorption,
all in the form of spendable dollars. Only a fraction

of the extra income could be directly spent on imports (though mighty efforts were made in this direction). The rest for directed toward nontraded goods. As a consequence, the relative price of nontradables tended to rise, or the real exchange rate (nominal peso/dollar rate divided by a nontradable price index) to fall. Also demand shifted away from domestic tradable goods, such as industrial products. Indeed, industrial output reversed its historical tendency and grew more slowly than GDP during the boom.

Mexican authorities elected to hold the nominal exchange rate stable for at least two reasons. An increase, or devaluation, would have been inflationary since it would have driven up costs of imported inter- mediate imports that are passed along into final goods prices. Second, the financial system based on freely convertible Mexdollars required a stable nominal rate to minimize perceived exchange risk. Hence the real exchange rate had to fall (or appreciate) by increases in domestic prices.

In the first instance, the relative price change took the form of higher nontraded sector markups, con- sistent with the income redistribution noted in the first section. These profit and price increases were soon passed along into higher wages, rising costs of production, and a generalized inflationary process. Econometric studies suggest that increased interest costs on working capital also contributed to inflation toward the end of the period. Demand stimulated by the dollars transferred toward Mexico from oil and foreign borrowing was a first cause for the acceleration of inflation from 18 percent annually in 1978 to 28 per- cent in 1981. But in the overall process (especially for industrial sectors) the proximate impact of demand pressure on limited capacity in driving up prices appears to have been a secondary factor--recall that industrial demand was stagnant.[6]

Attempts at controlling inflation took the form of pegging the nominal exchange rate and increasing sub- sidies on certain final goods--foodstuffs, gasoline, the Mexico City subway, and so on. The subsidies explain the increased losses by public enterprises noted in connection with Table 3.

Monetary restriction was not pursued, largely be- cause as Bazdresch (1983) put it: "The possibility of controlling the quantity of money by the means avail- able for monetary policy was, during this period, almost nil." The two tools at hand were changes in reserve re- quirements and modifications in the structure of interest rates. But interest rates were tied to the world level through the Mexdollar deposits (which received LIBOR plus a premium), and reserve requirements by the 1970s were already high (perhaps exceeding 100 percent at the

margin) and quite flexible. Open-market operations
were not feasible because a domestic bill market did
not exist in any volume (steps toward creating one were
taken in 1982), and there was no effective rediscount
mechanism.

The authorities thus had very limited power to
affect the money stock. In flow terms, money supply
grew in pace with nominal GDP until 1980; only in 1981
and 1982 did it grow somewhat more rapidly because of
increased credit to the public sector. A simple mone-
tarist explanation of the acceleration in inflation
resulting from increased public borrowing early in the
period is ruled out by this chronology. One must look
for nonmonetary explanations for changes both in prices
and patterns of economic activity.

TRADE LIBERALIZATION

For reasons already explained, the peso appre-
ciated strongly over the boom period. Exact estimates
vary, but real appreciation between 1977 (the year of
a major devaluation) and 1981 of 30 to 40 percent is
the consensus result. At the same time, there was a
substantial liberalization of import resrictions, as a
follow-up to a stabilization program undertaken in
collaboration with the International Monetary Fund in
the first year or two (before the major oil discoveries
led to a shift in overall economic policy) of the López
Portillo sexenio. Prior permits and quotas on about
5,000 importable items were to be replaced by tariffs
giving the same approximate protection. Then a major
tariff reduction and rationalization was to follow in
1981-1982.

In practice, commodities accounting for about 40
percent of total import value were free of permits by
the end of 1980. Then, as the crisis mounted, policy
swung back the other way, with greater use of permits
and tariff increases adopted in 1981. On the export
side, a drawback scheme was dropped in 1982 after devaluation made Mexican products more competitive
abroad.

Non-oil exports were sluggish during the boom
period, with volumes in 1979 through 1982 falling
below those of 1978. Taking into account net tourism
and border transactions, their share in GDP fell from
7.9 to 3.7 percent. The decrease can be attributed to
at least three causes--the spurt in internal demand,
real exchange appreciation, and slow growth in the
United States. Allocation of importance among these
factors must necessarily be inexact. With regard to
external demand, John Eatwell and Ajit Singh (1981)
noted that in 1980 Mexican manufactured exports fell

TABLE 4
Composition of Mexican Imports

Key Import Ratios[a]	1978	1981	Elasticity
Intermediate imports / GDP	7.0	7.4	1.25
Consumer goods imports / Public + private consumption	0.8	2.2	7.70
PEMEX imports / Investment by PEMEX	63.4	36.6	
Other capital goods imports / Non-PEMEX investment	3.9	11.4	

Breakdown of Import Growth[b]					
Type of Import	Volume 1978	Change 1978-1981	Assumed Elasticity	Normal Change	Excess Change
Consumer	4.2	10.2	1.5	1.4	8.8
Intermediate	49.7	17.9	1.0	13.8	4.1
Capital goods	17.9	21.1	1.5	16.5	4.6
Other	7.2	-1.0		-1.0	0.0
Total	79.0	48.2		30.7	17.5

Source: Secretariat of Budget & Planning.

a Import ratios in percentages.
b Import volumes in billions of 1970 pesos.

by 8 percent, exactly the proportion by which total
U.S. real imports declined. A more basic contradiction
is that at the time Mexico sought to grow more rapidly
than the rest of the world, while selling a basket of
non-oil exports with an income elasticity not strik-
ingly greater than one. It is not surprising that the
share of non-oil exports in GDP fell. Real appreciation of the exchange rate did not help matters, but
the important point is that export stagnation did not
figure in the policy debate. By contrast, the big
increase in Mexican imports provoked intense controversy regarding the trade liberalization program.

Table 4 presents rough calculations of import
growth by different categories.[7] As shown in the upper
part of the table, imports of consumer goods rose
sharply as a share of total private and public consump-
tion--the relevant elasticity is almost eight. Intermediate imports show an elasticity of only 1.25 with
respect to GDP--a degree of responsiveness expected
during a boom. PEMEX imports as a share of the enterprise's investment level declined. The share of
imports in other investment rose but maintained a low
level by developing country standards.

The lower part of the table shows a decomposition
of the increase in real imports (1970 pesos) into
normal and excess changes, using assumed values of
elasticities for the ratios in the upper panel. Of an
increase of 48.2 billion pesos between 1979 and 1981,
30.7 could be considered routine and the rest excessive. Almost half the excess of 17.5 billion is
accounted for by consumer imports, and the rest in
more or less equal proportion by intermediate and
capital goods.

Can these excess changes reasonably be attributed
to price effects--35 percent real appreciation plus
the liberalization program? Plausible macro-level
price elasticities would lie between zero and minus
one, probably closer to the former figure. From the
numbers in Table 4, one can see that price changes
plus the boom might rationalize the increases in
capital and intermediate imports, but fail hopelessly
with consumer goods.

Two major factors help explain the rise in consumer imports. The first is slow growth of agricultural output, a problem that has plagued Mexico
through the 1970s. Food imports rose sharply in 1979
and 1980, following a real decline of 2 percent in
agricultural real value added in 1979. The sector
recovered in 1980 and 1981, with good weather and input subsidies from the newly created Sistema Agricul-
turo Mexicano (SAM). A new lapse in production
occurred in 1982, and rapid growth of food imports in
1983 was a nagging policy problem. For long-term

stability in the Mexican economy, structural change in
agriculture to ameliorate slow growth and supply fluctuations is required.

The other factor is the import liberalization
program. As Terry Barker and Vladimiro Brailovsky
(1983) argued, there is no reason to assume that
Mexican importers were on their demand function, under
a quota system prior to liberalization. A decomposition of the remarkable increase in consumer imports
between price effects and an upward shift in demand
(see Table 4) is simply not feasible. However, with
due importance granted to administrative slackness and
oil euphoria in stimulating consumer imports, the fact
remains that the rise in the trade deficit (especially
the consumer import contributions) was not overwhelming
in macroeconomic terms (see Table 1). Import liberalization must at best be assigned a secondary role in
provoking the crisis.

The changes in the GDP shares of major components
of the current account between 1978 and 1981 take the
following values (in percentages, with both factor
income payments and imports given a negative sign):

	Percentages
Exports	1.6
Oil	5.8
Other	-4.2
Factor income	-1.4
Public interest	-0.4
Private interest	-0.7
Other	-0.3
Imports	-2.9
Consumer	-0.9
Intermediate	-0.1
Capital	-1.6
Other	-0.3
Total	-2.7

The major shift in this decomposition is the
deterioration of non-oil exports, mostly the result of
slow U.S. growth, exchange appreciation, and elimination of policies aimed at export stimulation. Capital
goods imports rose along with the investment increase
of 5.4 percent of GDP over the period, and interest
payments also grew rapidly. The increase in the share
of consumer goods imports accounted for one-third of
the change in the current account.

These numbers suggest that creation of the
plataforma petrolera plus exchange appreciation were
the major factors influencing the current account
during the boom years. Trade liberalization may have

TABLE 5
Financial Survey of Mexico, 1978-1982
(in percentages of GDP)

	1978	1979	1980	1981	1982
Net foreign assets and SDR allocation	2.5	2.9	2.9	2.8	0.6
Credit outstanding					
Total	44.0	43.7	42.1	48.2	71.2
Pesos	31.1	31.0	30.3	30.8	36.2
Dollars	12.9	12.6	11.8	17.4	34.9
Credit to private sector					
Total	19.4	20.0	20.2	20.4	16.8
Pesos	16.9	17.0	16.7	15.6	13.0
Dollars	2.5	3.0	3.6	4.7	3.7
Credit to public sector and other					
Total	24.6	23.7	21.9	27.8	54.4
Pesos	14.2	14.1	13.7	15.1	23.2
Dollars	10.4	9.6	8.2	12.7	31.2
Money and quasi-money					
Total	29.9	30.9	30.7	33.5	35.8
Pesos	26.2	26.3	26.1	27.4	33.8
Dollars	3.7	4.6	4.5	6.1	2.0
Foreign liabilities of financial system	13.5	12.4	11.4	14.0	32.4
Other liabilities	2.7	2.8	2.7	3.2	3.0

Source: Secretariat of Budget and Planning.

played a role in the increase in consumer goods
imports, but its influence was secondary. Stagnation
of nonpetroleum exports--the classic symptom of the oil
syndrome--was the major contributor to Mexico's widen-
ing trade gap. Aggressive exchange rate policy to
support these exports may not have been in the cards
in a booming, inflationary economy; however, a well-
directed export subsidy scheme or dual exchange rates
might have been. Such policies will almost certainly
have to be pursued if another temporary oil boom
occurs in the future.

MEXDOLLARS

Table 5 shows the structure of the Mexican financial system during the boom period. As will become
more clear shortly, interpreting the numbers is tricky:
Below the first and above the penultimate lines, the
"dollar" items refer to dollar-denominated transactions
of the Mexican banking system--Mexdollars are involved,
not real ones. By contrast, the "dollar" or "external"
entries in Tables 2 and 3 refer to bona fide obligations abroad.

As can be seen from the first and next-to-last
lines, external net obligations of the financial
system were large, amounting to a third or more of
internal (peso and dollar-denominated) liabilities, and
well over 10 percent of GDP. When credit demand increased during the boom, Mexican banks at the margin
sought medium- and long-term loanable resources abroad,
since domestic deposits were highly encumbered by
reserve requirements and restrictions on priority areas
for credit allocation. About four-fifths of these
dollar obligations were lent to the public sector, but
credit was offered to the private sector as well. Some
of the foreign exchange found its way back to the
Mexican banks as dollar deposits--these were Mexdollars.
In an open capital market, the Mexdollar deposits were
always freely convertible with pesos, and both currencies were held for portfolio diversification.

In magnitude, Mexdollar stocks never amounted to
a large share of total bank liabilities, but flows
fluctuated widely. The ratio of dollar deposits to
total deposits (or the dollarization coefficient) was
taken as a sensitive policy indicator. It increased
from 5 to 25 percent after the interest rate on Mexdollars was raised to LIBOR levels in 1977. A portfolio shift was no doubt involved--recall from Table 2
that net private foreign-held assets declined during
the late 1970s. For reasons of confidence, convenience,
and yield, Mexicans brought foreign assets home.

With some justification, authorities viewed Mexdollars as a stabilizing factor in the financial
system. After the interest rate increase, for example,
two high government functionaries told us that
"capacity for managing monetary policy has improved,
with the reduction of capital movements across fron-
tiers and their conversion into portfolio changes
between pesos and dollars within the country. In this
way the financial market is more integrated with movements in the international rate of interest, but more
isolated from brusque changes in capital flows" (Solís
and Rizzo [1983], p. 375; my translation).

In the small, this justification for the Mexdollar
system was undoubtedly correct; in the large, it was

dreadfully mistaken. The reason is easy to see from
Table 5--Mexico was operating as open a capital market
as any country ever has with negligible reserve cover.
In the long run, the outcome was not surprising. To
paraphrase John Maynard Keynes, Mexdollars in 1982 became a bubble on a whirlpool of speculation. Two runs
on deposits virtually wiped out the nation's dollar
reserves, and the system collapsed.

For details, one can see from Table 5 that net
foreign assets of the financial system in (say) 1980
were 2.9 percent of GDP, compared to an import share of
13.5 percent. Reserves were on hand to finance between
two and three months' imports, a low level for transactions purposes. Effectively no cover existed for
Mexdollar deposits amounting to 4.5 percent of GDP, let
alone the financial system's foreign liabilities of
11.4 percent of GDP. From the failure of this sort of
financial system, a moral is easily drawn: In small
economies, there is no hope of maintaining open foreign
capital and commodity markets without deep reserves,
no matter how many sensitive but limited financial
buffers like Mexdollars happen to exist.[8]

THE CRISIS AND THE FUND

Blow-by-blow descriptions of the 1982 crisis are
available elsewhere, and there is no point in repeating
them here.[9] The first flurry was a 70 percent devaluation of the peso that dragged out over a week in
February 1982, before the authorities could reestablish
the market. Curiously, them seem to have made scant
provision for access to external resources (central
bank swaps and similar tactics) to support a targeted
devaluation. The same mistake was made in the second
episode of crisis in August.

Net inflows of dollars were recorded in the weeks
following the February devaluation. However, minimum
wage increases were decreed in late March, which roughly
offset the real wage decrease to be induced by pass-
through of higher import costs due to devaluation.
With the real effect of devaluation nullified by higher
wages, capital flight began again, and Mexdollar stocks
rose. A run on Mexdollars in August triggered the
second devaluation and creation of dual exchange rates.
Since reserves were exhausted and no real dollars were
left to pay off accounts, Mexdollar balances were
frozen, to be repaid in pesos at an exchange rate
below the free market. Capital controls were instituted: They probably slowed but could not stop
capital flight through exchange houses that sprang up
on the U.S. side of the border.

While these shocks followed one another through

the economy, the sexenio of José López Portillo was
ending--with a political bang from his nationalization
of the banking system. Miguel de la Madrid took the
helm in December, and his economic team immediately
instituted a line of policy laid down in a Letter of
Intent signed with the International Monetary Fund.
The main policy goals were the following:

1. Reduce the public sector deficit from 18.5
    percent of GDP in 1982 to 8.5 percent in 1983,
    5.5 percent in 1984, and 3.5 percent in 1985.
2. Consolidate two exchange rates left from the
    crisis period by the end of 1983, and follow
    with a crawling peg in 1984 to keep the real
    rate roughly constant. The final result would
    presumably be a peso stronger in real terms
    than even after the devaluation of 1977. As
    a consequence of exchange depreciation and the
    reduction in aggregate demand implicit in
    point one, the current account deficit as a
    share of GDP is supposed to fall to 2.2 per-
    cent in 1983, 1.8 percent in 1984, and 1.2
    percent in 1985.
3. Institute restrictive wage policy, aimed at
    reducing inflation from 100 percent in 1982
    to 55 percent in 1984, and 18 percent in 1985.
4. Rule out indexing of transactions; inflation
    was to be reduced steadily and erosion of out-
    standing peso claims by inflation with con-
    trolled nominal interest rates was abjured.
5. Allow continuation of some controls over
    capital movement, as well as quantity restric-
    tions and tariffs on imports.[10]

All these moves were supposed to produce zero real
GDP growth in 1983, 3 percent in 1984, and 6 percent in
1985.

By mid-1983, the current account target looked
likely to be overfulfilled, with perhaps a small surplus over the calendar year. Oil exports remained
strong, but non-oil exports were flat, presumably
gearing up to climb the J-curve created by devaluation.
The reason for the current account improvement was a
sharp fall in all types of imports except food (1982
was another bad crop year). Working out stocks of
importables built up before the crisis was no doubt
involved in the current account improvement, but the
main cause was an unprecedented decrease in real GDP,
expected to be around 5 or 6 percent over the year.
The IMF medicine was working in the usual way, improving the current account by creating massive economic
contraction.

The public-sector deficit was in the target range:

Interest payments were higher than anticipated but investment lower. The inflation target seemed likely not to be met, as firms that had been hit by the crisis sought to recover profit margins. Nominal minimum wages increased by less than half the price inflation during the first half of the year. With such a loss in wage earner's real income, consumption demand declined.

Without a full macro model of the economy, it is impossible to say whether the targets for years after 1983 can be fulfilled. There is, however, room for reasonable doubt. If the public sector respects its deficit targets and interest payments remain high, then demand injection from investment and current spending must be strictly curtailed. External interest rates are not under Mexico's control, but internal rates will depend on monetary tightness in the absence of indexing of financial instruments. There is no particular reason in the current policy regime to expect a rapid interest rate decline. Contractionary effects from reduced fiscal presence will only be made worse if inflation is underestimated, since then planned nominal levels of current spending amount to less in real terms.

Other components of final demand are unlikely to demonstrate rapid growth. The price control effort will continue to hold down real wages and consumption demand, so the only possibly dynamic element is non-oil exports. Here, the real devaluation will no doubt help performance, but much depends on the strength of the recovery in the United States. The whole program is precariously dependent on the United States' achieving fast growth with low interest rates--not a secure thread to dangle from.

With regard to inflation, much will depend on the degree of wage repression that can be sustained. Simple computations can be based on a decomposition of the growth rate of prices into growth rates of wages, profits, and import costs. (The weights in the decomposition are the initial shares of the three components of cost.) Let us assume that the profit rate is allowed to rise at 5 percent per year to stimulate the private sector and that import costs are held constant in real terms by the crawling peg. Let wages be increased once a year by a fraction (the "pass-through coefficient") of last year's inflation rate. It is easy to show that even with a pass-through coefficient of 0.6 the annual inflation rate will still be about 30 percent in 1986, well above the target. A pass-through of 80 percent leaves inflation above 60 percent in 1986. Eighty percent wage indexing has proved controversial in several countries; 60 percent may be politically impossible in the medium run. The conclusion is that effective control of inflation may well require profit cuts or abandonment of the crawling peg with consequent exchange appreciation. The prospects are not promising.

TOWARD THE FUTURE

Before leaping forward, it pays to look back. The 1983 Mexican policy package repeats many themes from the first years of the Echeverria and López Portillo administrations. Their early visions of economic progress rested on fundamental realignments of the Mexican economy. Such changes were not possible, and their initial programs failed. Given this history, it is hard to see how a third repetition of orthodox reformist policy can work out.

First, rapid appreciation of the peso took place after López Portillo's devaluation in 1977; a major cause was the unanticipated oil dividend. A more fundamental contradiction is that an undervalued exchange rate seen from outside Mexico maps into a low real wage seen from within. The real wage decrease under López Portillo was accompanied by rapid growth in output and employment while non-oil exports were stagnant. With the employment escape valve plugged by the IMF package, it is not obvious that real wages can be held down sufficiently during the 1980s to allow non-oil exports to be a major factor in growth. This conclusion becomes sharper when one recognizes that all Mexico's export competitors operate under a similar injunction to sell more abroad.

The second line of attack of current Mexican policy is on the supply side. Standard economic analysis suggests that an outward shift of the aggregate supply curve will stimulate activity at reduced inflation rates. A more daring assertion is that the shift will result from getting a myriad of micro prices right. Another important Mexican official told us that "if goods, whose relative prices have suffered serious deterioration because of price controls in recent years, acquire reasonable [price] levels, there might also be new investment to expand their production" (Gil Díaz [1983], p. 10).

In nuanced form, Jean-Baptise Say comes to Tenochtitlan. News from the north suggests that in the absence of aggressive fiscal policy, price manipulation may not work out so well. Without demand stimulation (as under Reagan), simple fiddling with prices and regulatory rules (as under Carter) will not go very far toward generating efficiency gains. A more serious look at practical policy options is required. In particular, policies aimed at economic expansion will sooner or later have to be adopted, especially if

petroleum export or credit market prospects improve.
How can they be made feasible?

The primary problem revolves around the real
exchange rate and other commercial policy tools. Any
recovery of the oil price or greater access to foreign
borrowing will create pressure for real appreciation
and (as just argued) a higher real wage. The outcomes
might be an official decision to slow the rate of the
crawling peg or an increase in the rate of inflation.
Either way, stimulus for non-oil exports would be reduced. It would seem worthwhile to have in place
mechanisms by which these exports could be supported
while overall inflationary pressures are held down.
Some sort of directed export subsidy scheme is one
possibility; multiple exchange rates are another.
Unlike devaluation, such policies do not generate
economy-wide cost pressures toward higher prices, but
act more selectively. They should be pursued in line
with overall industrial strategy.

Second, there seems scant reason to dismantle
import protection. Though liberalization did not star
in the crisis, it was an important supporting player.
Making essentially noncompetitive consumer imports very
expensive or banning them outright are policies to be
retained; they can bring immediate balance-of-payments
benefits and stimulate further import substitution in
the long run. Policy with respect to capital goods and
intermediate imports is more difficult, since one must
balance possible inducement of import substitution
against high costs for existing producers. Again, a
sensible industrial strategy must serve as a basis for
decision.

Both export stimulation and import restriction
have long been practiced in Mexico, in part to compensate for the country's wide-open capital market. The
crisis demonstrates that in the future it will be
necessary to restrain capital flows--to lock the barn
door before the horse has fled. A number of related
measures can be imagined. One is simply to retain far
higher reserves than in the past, supplemented by
appropriate swap arrangements between the Bank of
Mexico and other central banks. Since Mexico is not a
major player in world capital markets, it should begin
to force itself into the network of safety lines linking the advanced countries.

A second group of measures should make holding
foreign assets more difficult and nonmonetized domestic
assets more attractive. The carrot here would be a
deep market in peso-dominated bills and bonds, to be
established beginning at the short end of the maturity
spectrum. Steps have been taken in this direction, and
they should be pursued. The payoff would be a market
to smooth portfolio shifts in the small (as Mexdollars

used to); with such a market the monetary authorities could break away from their antiquated reliance on changes in reserve requirements to regulate the money supply.

The sticks in capital-market policy would be stiff controls over capital movements--prior interest deposits with the banking system on loans, prior permits, out-and-out prohibition of certain sorts of transactions. At the same time, the state could build up long-run dollar balances apart from monetized reserves. Partial sterilization of oil reserves in a National Stabilization fund held abroad would be an appropriate policy when the next market recovery comes; letting all the dollars into the country would simply set the stage for the sort of speculation that took place in 1981 and 1982. Finally, steps should be taken to dissuade Mexican nationals from holding large accounts in foreign currencies. Mexico is virtually the only developing country where the upper economic classes have such open capital market privileges. Along with the freedom of motorcycle police to be bribed, they are an aspect of personal liberty that could safely be curtailed in the de la Madrid government's campaign for moral renovation.

In the matter of control of inflation, an internal incomes policy has to be coordinated with demand pressures (or lack of same) coming from oil sales abroad. Inflation as a Mexican phenomenon under both Echeverria and López Portillo reacted to the overall level of aggregate demand. However, the process itself was intimately linked with foreign price increases (reduced in impact by exchange appreciation) and internal cost pressures.[11] Under the circumstances, inflation can be slowed by four sorts of income policies--wage repression, nominal exchange rate appreciation (or slower depreciation in a crawling peg), reductions in indirect tax rates, and policies aimed at reducing markup rates.

All these policies are unsatisfactory. Wage repression faces obvious political and ethical objections. Exchange appreciation creates loss of competitiveness, a particularly difficult problem in a developing country afflicted with the oil syndrome. Markups may be reduced by effective trade liberalization, which may also retard the process of import substitution. Price controls are difficult to apply administratively and always create the danger that company owners will abandon the economy through capital flight.

The final area of concern is the internal income distribution. Part of the problem of lagging agricultural supply, for example, arises from the low incomes received by traditional producers of key crops, including maize and beans. The SAM program under López

Portillo was an attempt to rectify this situation, but
it was abandoned early in the de la Madrid administration. Within a few years, something like the SAM will
probably have to be invented again.

Migration is also intimately linked with distribution. Labor flows to and from the United States
have eased adjustment on both sides of the border. In
the long run, however, the redistributional changes
necessary to moderate pressure for migration must come
from Mexico. Aggressive tax and transfer policies to
help poor people will ultimately become essential. At
the same time, such moves may undermine the business
class's faith in the system. Somehow, rentiers and
entrepreneurs must be persuaded or forced to direct
their energy toward the country, instead of toward
accumulation of bank accounts and consumer luxuries
from the north side of the Rio Bravo. If this redi-
rection of economic energies fails, not much hope can
be retained for the independent autonomous development
of Mexico.

NOTES

1. In nominal terms, private saving rose from
404 billion to 1,416 billion pesos between 1978 and
1981, and private consumption from 1,948 billion to
5,017 billion. The approximate marginal private-
saving rate of one-third follows from these numbers.
2. For a description of forced saving during
Mexico's inflationary growth period before and after
World War II, see, for example, Tannenbaum (1950).
Eatwell and Singh (1981) provide evidence regarding
distributional shifts in the boom period.
3. The estimates in Table 2 are based on the
following assumptions: (1) Public deficits are
financed only by borrowing abroad or the financial
system--there are no privately held public securities;
and (2) Private assets are held only as physical
capital or deposits with Mexican financial institutions, or are held abroad. Discrepancies among fiscal,
monetary, balance-of-payments, and national-accounts
statistics partly explain the difference between the
estimates. Especially in 1982, dollar/peso conver-
sions were affected by short-period fluctuations in
volume of flows and the exchange rate.
4. See, for example, Musgrave (1980).
5. A once-for-all structural aspect of the
public-sector deficit was refinancing of the Mexdollars
into pesos after August 1982. The federal government
absorbed the losses--to the tune of perhaps 5 percent
of GDP--and transformed them into (mostly) internal

peso liabilities.

6. A number of recent empirical analyses support the assertations in the text. See especially Ize and Salas (1984).

7. The decompositions of imports by type in Table 4 were made by applying current price shares of different types to constant price import totals. An element of error is involved, but it is not likely to change the major conclusions.

8. Just to drive the point home, consider the case of Thailand, another country whose economy has traditionally maintained open capital markets. There, commercial banks obtain 10 to 20 percent of their resources abroad but lend only in local currency. Nationals cannot hold foreign-denominated deposits and--most important--the central bank retains reserves substantially larger than the commercial banks' foreign liabilities. When faced with severe external pressure after the oil shocks, Thailand did not have a run on local foreign exchange deposits and a financial crisis. Deep dollar cover frightens speculators off.

9. Ize and Ortíz (1983) and Barker and Brailovsky (1983) are useful references with contrasting interpretations.

10. Several descriptions of the IMF/de la Madrid policy package are available. The one here follows Ros (1983).

11. See Ize and Salas (1984) or Ros (1980).

REFERENCES

Barker, Terry, and Vladimiro Brailovsky. 1983. "La Politica Economica entre 1976 y 1982 y El Plan Nacional de Desarrollo Industrial." Paper presented at a Seminar on the Mexican Economy: Current Situation and Macroeconomic Perspectives, El Colegio do México, August 8-10, 1983.

Bazdresch, Carlos. 1983. "Las Causas de la Crisis de 1982." Paper presented at a Seminar on the Mexican Economy: Current Situation and Macroeconomic Perspectives, El Colegio de México, August 8-10, 1983.

Eatwell, John, and Ajit Singh. 1981. "Is the Mexican Economy 'Overheated'? An Analysis of Short- and Medium-Term Issues in Economic Policy." Mimeographed. Faculty of Economics, University of Cambridge.

García-Alba, Pascual, and Jaime Serra Puche. 1983. "Financial Aspects of Macroeconomic Management in Mexico." Report no. 36, Institute for Developing Economies, Tokyo.

170

Gil Díaz, Francisco. 1983. "Investment and Debt: A Perspective for the Next Decade." Chapter 1 in this volume.

Ize, Alain, and Guillermo Ortiz. 1983. "Riesgo Politico, Substitucion de Activos y La Dineminca de la Tasa de Cambio." Paper presented at a Seminar on the Mexican Economy: Current Situation and Macroeconomic Perspectives, El Colegio de México, August 8-10, 1983.

Ize, Alain, and Javier Salas. 1984. "Prices and Output in the Mexican Economy: Empirical Testing of Alternative Hypotheses." Journal of Development Economics (to appear).

Musgrave, Richard A. 1980. "Theories of Fiscal Crisis: An Essay in Fiscal Sociology." In The Economics of Taxation, ed. Henry J. Aaron and Michael J. Boskin. Washington, D.C.: Brookings Institution.

O'Connor, James. 1973. The Fiscal Crisis of the State. New York: St. Martin's.

Ros, Jaime. 1980. "Pricing in the Mexican Manufacturing Sector." Cambridge Journal of Economics 4: 211-231.

Ros, Jaime. 1983. "La Politica de Estabilizacion: Problenas y Perspectivas." Paper presented at a Seminar on the Mexican Economy: Current Situation and Macroeconomic Perspectives, El Colegio de México, August 8-10, 1983.

Solís, Leopoldo, and Socrates Rizzo. 1983. "Excedentes Petroleros y Apertura Externa." In Las Relaciones Financieras Externas: Su Efecto en la Economia Latinoamericana, ed. Ricardo Ffrench-Davis. Mexico City: Fondo de Cultera Economica.

Tannenbaum, Frank. 1950. Mexico: The Struggle for Peace and Bread. New York: A. A. Knopf.

Comments

Clark W. Reynolds

Chapters 4 and 5 draw upon evidence from recent economic fluctuations in Mexico and the United States to show that although domestic politics have played a significant role in the stability of each country, increased trade, financial and labor market interdependence are becoming progressively more important. Although both chapters tended to concentrate on the implications of these findings for Mexico, they are also important for the United States. Developments in U.S. labor, product, and financial markets make Mexico's economic health of more than academic interest to this country as well. Indeed, what is happening between the United States and its neighbor may well be the harbinger of the real north-south problem, long recognized by the developing countries but only beginning to be apparent to the industrial countries. This problem is less a question of resource transfers than of growing structural interdependence in which political and economic factors play a joint role.

In Chapter 5, Lance Taylor focuses on the internal policy panorama of the López Portillo regime (1976-1982), which is weighed in the balance and found wanting, but he is also quick to question the International Monetary Fund (IMF)-endorsed adjustment policies of the succeeding president, Miguel de la Madrid. The author's recommendations, which might be called structural-dirigiste, fall somewhere in between. They call for greater controls on trade and capital movements, including export subsidies or multiple exchange rates. Taylor also favors measures to increase financial savings for domestic investment. These are not seen as alternatives but as additions to current monetary and fiscal austerity measures, severe import restraints, dual exchange rates, and incomplete convertibility of the peso. The payoff presumably would be more rapid recovery and growth with less social pain than the present program entails.

171

Observers can be pardoned a degree of skepticism,
not only because of the potential of such measures to
distort the system and create monopoly rents, but because fast-growth scenarios accompanying similar proposals were misused to support López Portillo's fast-
track program. There is the danger that such models
will be used (or abused) again to justify growth at any
price. Many Mexican policy commentators argue that
structural measures, involving controls on trade, investment, profits, wages, and interest rates, may be
substituted for more conventional fiscal, financial,
and exchange rate policies and at less social cost.
Such views, however misguided, are welcome to would-be
populist leaders who wish to maximize freedom from
economic restraints. Unfortunately, as the 1982-1983
crisis has shown, the outcome could well mean less
growth, more inflation, and greater unemployment than
a timelier application of more conventional measures.

What is needed is a way to integrate the concern
for structural reforms implicit in Taylor's analysis
with the use of equilibrating policies in fiscal,
financial, and exchange markets. In fact, this
strategy is being considered in Mexico today at the
highest levels of government; it could be the most
important contribution Mexico makes to the current
policy dilemma. Pure monetarism, in which financial
liberation is proposed without attention to the social
and political constraints on fiscal policy, or to the
potentially destabilizing role of international trade
and capital markets, is correctly seen to be naive and
unworkable in Mexico. On the other hand, a purely
structural approach carries with it the danger of
macrodisequilibrium, inflation, balance-of-payments
problems, inefficiency, and unpredictability arising
from political rather than economic market forces.
Planners in Mexico claim to be searching for a balance,
in which prices in general are permitted to seek market
equilibria but with subsidies and welfare measures
targeted to specific areas of need. Incentives rather
than direct controls are to be increasingly applied.
It remains to be seen whether such a syncretic
strategy will in fact prove workable.

Taylor's analysis deals with shares rather than
absolute levels of gross national product (GNP).
Although this approach is understandable for expository
purposes, massive changes that occurred in the level
and structure of income and product during the recent
boom make the use of absolute magnitudes more applicable. This is the case especially regarding the
analysis of alternative policies that in practice must
be applied ex ante rather than ex post. For policy
purposes one cannot target shares of gross domestic
product (GDP) but must look to real levels of spending,

even though resulting ratios (such as the ratio of deficit to GNP) are customarily adopted by institutions such as commercial banks and used by the IMF as measures of performance. The share approach makes somewhat more sense on the revenue side, but even there the pattern of receipts depends increasingly on oil, fiscal and administrative reform, and on changes in the pricing of government services. A share approach, in short, is better at revealing symptoms than causes of macroeconomic performance.

What does emerge from Taylor's look at savings and investment shares of GDP is the enormous swing in private-sector savings, up during the boom, along with foreign borrowing, and then down again, with domestic investment proving to be the main source of instability. This is perhaps the outstanding point of the chapter-- that private savings could be so volatile and so necessary to the López Portillo strategy and yet be its Achilles heel. But the lesson of the crisis does not seem to have been learned: the role of the private sector in accumulation is critical in a capitalist mixed-enterprise system. Instead, the analysis tends to regard private savings as something that policies can shift willy-nilly, whether on or off shore, when in fact they are a highly discretionary residual of other key decisions, responding in complex ways to actual and expected levels of income and wealth, wages and profit flows, prices, taxes, and exchange rates, all of which relate to expectations about the government and its treatment of the private sector.

In Chapter 5 Taylor suggests that private savings outflows should be stemmed to increase the surplus available for domestic investment and "lock the barn door before the horse has fled." Unfortunately, the horse is already out of the barn and across the border. What seem to be needed are fewer sticks and more carrots if savings are to return, and positive investment incentives if savings are to grow in the future. The author's best recommendation, in this reader's opinion, is for the United States to support Mexican stabilization policy and pursuit of an equilibrium real exchange rate by offering an extended swap arrangement by the Treasury and the Federal Reserve. (A similar recommendation was proposed in Clark W. Reynolds, "U.S. View of the Political-Economic Implications of Trade and Financial Interdependence with Mexico," presented at the United States-Mexico Project's conference on U.S.-Mexico Trade and Financial Interdependence, Stanford University, September 13-15, 1983.) This support might be supplied in the context of a bilateral agreement on trade and financial relations that would seek to avoid wide swings in policy on either side, in the interest of more stable and harmonious recovering and growth by both countries.

The statement by Taylor that "econometric evidence suggests that Mexican prices do not respond to aggregate demand or changes in the money supply" is absurd unless one adds the words "in any systematic way" to the sentence. Although much of the economy is oligopolistic, a wide range of activities are competitive and tightly linked to international prices--Taylor admits as much. The important point that "in the long run the problem of Mexico's extremely unequal income distribution cannot be evaded" is introduced but not developed in the chapter, except perhaps in the argument against wage controls and in favor of controls on capital flight. The suggestions that the dirigiste character of the economy be maintained works against evidence that dirigism in the past has gone hand in hand with sustained income concentration and political corruption. A campaign is being waged against corruption, but it probably will not increase, rather than decrease, the hold of the PRI on the political system. If that control declines and further political opening takes place, this will work against a dirigiste approach, which must of necessity rely on a strong central government. In fact, political democratization and economic decentralization and further reliance on market mechanisms are more likely to go hand in hand. The de la Madrid administration does appear to be introducing a new approach, namely the linking of macrostabilization policies with attempts at structural reform. The objective is to increase efficiency and competitiveness of the economy in terms of resource allocation in a labor-using direction, favoring exports and the potential for investment in activities that would be competitive given the structure of international prices and Mexico's comparative advantage.

Chapter 4 by García-Alba and Serra Puche goes well beyond Taylor's in looking both at internal political elements in the Mexican business cycle and at implications of links between the United States and Mexico in trade, finance, migration, and other aspects of interdependence. It begins by examining the "six-year presidential cycle" theory. This theory assigns an important role to domestic factors in economic fluctuations, as each successive administration seeks to place its stamp on the pattern of development and faces the same phasing, first of institutional constraints on planning and then of financial constraints on implementation. The evidence presented by the authors indicates the existence of a cycle, though the pattern is somewhat different from that customarily described before 1970, since in subsequent periods expenditures tended to stabilize even before the last year of each administration. This difference suggests that the growing importance of political and institutional factors behind the most recent crises (1976 and 1982) actually increased the importance of external constraints, since the capacity to borrow abroad and the burden of debt were both strongly sensitive to U.S. monetary policy. Ironically, massive increases in Mexican debt have made the U.S. financial markets increasingly sensitive to policies affecting Mexican stability, including the six-year cycle.

In their thoughtful and challenging chapter, García-Alba and Serra Puche call attention to the fact that increased interdependence goes well beyond income determination effects to the broadest aspects of structural change, affecting the developing of both countries. Migration, equity and debt flows in both directions, technology transfer, trade, and production sharing all interact, providing a challenge to conventional analysis. By raising such issues before the tools have been evolved to deal with them, much less the institutions necessary to manage interdependence, the authors pose the basic questions implicit in this book's theme. This observer can only second with considerable enthusiasm their argument that long-run ordering of economics is better than short-run recovery, and that both involve a greater degree of policy interaction than we have been accustomed to accept either north or south of the border.

Comments

Daniel M. Schydlowsky

I would like to begin my comments on the very interesting points raised in Chapters 4 and 5 by illuminating the recent historical record of Mexico's economic performance from a somewhat different perspective; then I would like to derive Mexico's apparent policy imperative for the short term; finally, I would like to address the question of U.S. economic interaction in the large and the small.

As in many other Latin American countries, one determining factor of the country's economic performance has been the structure of its exchange rate system. Again, as with many other Latin American countries, Mexico's exchange rate system has consisted of its financial exchange rate, a range of import duties and export promotion instruments, and some quantitative import restrictions. A very rough sketch of the structure of the system as it was in the mid-1970s is presented in Table 1. As shown in the table, although the financial exchange rate was uniform, the total exchange rate structure was anything but uniform. Indeed, it exhibited the usual progression from traditional exports to semimanufactures and finished goods. As a result, it provided a profit incentive for import substituting production but an implicit tax on industrial exports.[1]

With the oil boom, an additional element appeared in the exchange rate system. Mexico's sudden riches caused a dramatic increase in domestic aggregate demand. From 1978 to 1981 real government expenditure alone rose 20 to 25 percent per year. It was fueled by oil revenue and by extensive borrowing abroad. However, a substantial part of the new types of goods demanded was not available from domestic sources of supply; thus they needed to be imported. In other cases, the dramatic increase in demand exceeded domestic supply capacity, thus also leading to an increase in import demand. Yet a third category of

177

TABLE 1
Mexican Exchange Rate System, Circa 1977
(rough approximation)

	Financial Rate	Trade Policy	Total Rate
Mining and agriculture	27	-	27.00
Financial flows	27	-	27.00
Processed foods	27	20%	32.40
Semimanufactored goods	27	40%	37.80
Durable consumer goods	27	60%	43.20
Nondurable goods	27	50%	40.50

Source: See Note 1.

goods, which could be supplied from domestic installed
capacity, led to imports of raw materials and intermediate goods, thus also increasing the demand for
imports. In all these ways, Mexico's increase in
domestic aggregate demand translated itself very
quickly into a substantial increase in demand for
imports.

Since Mexico is a small buyer on world markets, a
substantial increase in Mexican demand should not
affect world prices. Thus, one would have expected
internal demand in Mexico to spill over easily onto
world markets and to have no significant inflationary
consequences. Such was not the case because Mexico's
import infrastructure was unable to accommodate so
dramatic an increase in demand in so short a time.
Ports became congested causing increased shipping
(demurrage) charges; unloading became more expensive;
spoilage and pilferage increased. The domestic rail
and trucking system became overloaded, and import trade
found its inventories depleting faster than its re-
plenishing cycle had allowed. Thus, in effect a
physical bottleneck intervened that made it impossible
for the increase in domestic demand to spill over
fully into imports; instead, the increased demand
caused a rise in prices. The foreign supply curve to
Mexico was indeed infinitely elastic, but the supply
curve of imports to the domestic market was upward
sloping in shape and contained a very inelastic portion.
As demand shifted up, the new short-run equilibrium
moved to the very inelastic part of the import supply
curve. The physical restriction, however, operated in
a way exactly analogous to that of a quantitative
restriction of imports or a tariff increase. Therefore,

for the first years of the oil boom, a fourth factor
was introduced into Mexico's exchange rate system to
reflect the selective impact of the import constraint
on different kinds of goods. This fourth factor de
facto <u>devalued</u> the total exchange rate by requiring a
greater number of pesos on the domestic market per
dollar's worth of imports.

Over time, the physical bottleneck became loosened.
Mexico expanded its importing network; short-term
bottlenecks in transportation were resolved; port
capacity was expanded and reorganized, and so on. So
over a period of a few years, the steepness of the
domestic supply curve of imports was reduced and with
it the implicit surcharge that the physical bottlenecks
imposed on the exchange rate system. As these bottlenecks lessened, the total exchange rate of Mexico was
being correspondingly revalued. At about the same time
(1979-1981), Mexico undertook a foreign-trade laborali-
zation reducing its imports duties in view of its ample
foreign exchange revenues. This step implied further
revaluation of the total exchange rate. Domestic
prices went up with the de facto devaluation caused by
the import bottlenecks but then did not come down as
these import bottlenecks and other import restrictions
were eliminated. Downward rigidity of prices in this
case was reinforced by increases in wages that had
occurred in the interim. Thus, when the total exchange
rate was revalued, domestic prices stayed up and
imports flooded in undercutting domestic producers,
worsening the balance of payments, and replacing
domestic production.

Market perceptions of the strength of the Mexican
peso and the appropriateness of its exchange rate
were not well synchronized with the movement in total
exchange rates. The market expected that the oil- and
debt-fueled boom would lead to a massive increase in
imports. This expectation was further reinforced as
domestic prices rose substantially whereas the
financial exchange rate was adjusted at less than 5
percent per year. However, import growth did not
materialize as quickly as people thought. The cause
was the physical bottleneck that de facto devalued the
total exchange rate. However, what the market perceived was only the very slowly crawling <u>financial</u>
exchange rate and a surprisingly modest surge in
imports. Thus, the market concluded that the financial
exchange rate was firm and confidence reigned. Later
on, when the physical bottlenecks were eliminated, and
the total exchange rate was revalued, capital flowed
into the country, and imports surged. By this time,
however, the markets were not particularly worried
since they had "seen" Mexico digest its previous increase in demand very well. Moreover, the market, of

course, did not notice the implicit revaluation that
had taken place. Thus, it was not alarmed at the surge
of imports nor at the displacement of domestic production that ensued from the true overvaluation of the
total exchange rate of the Mexican peso that had
occurred in the interim. Short-term capital therefore
continued to flow in to finance the ever-widening trade
gap. In late 1981, the markets began to wake up to the
facts of Mexican overvaluation, and once the perception
began to take hold, events moved very quickly, and with
the force of an economic avalanche. The capital outflow became unstoppable and forced a massive devaluation in February 1982 and another one in August 1982.

Since the demand for imports is price inelastic in
the short run, the sharp curtailment of the availability
of foreign exchange could only be accommodated by
a very substantial depression in the level of economic
activity (gross national product fell by some 4 to 5
percent in 1983). Therefore, the Mexican economy is
characterized by an aggregate level of activity well
below potential, substantial excess capacity in industry and services, and unusually high unemployment.
This recession is deliberately induced by policy.
Foreign exchange revenue, principally from oil, has
been affected by softness in the oil market. On the
other hand, the requirement of servicing the foreign
debt, at least insofar as interest payments are concerned, is substantial. With nominal interest rates
still at historically high levels, the amount of
foreign exchange available for current imports is
severely restricted. The recession is designed to
bring import demand within this cash constraint.

Mexican policy interests in this context are overwhelmingly clear: (1) export revenue must be raised;
(2) international interest rate must come down; and
less imperative but nonetheless most desirable, (3)
capital that had left Mexico during the capital flight
years should return to the country.

Increase in exports can come either from oil
exports or from non-oil exports. The increase of
revenue from oil exports is not entirely under Mexican
control. Mexico can, albeit with effort, raise the
quantity of oil that it pumps and can attempt to market
this on world markets; it takes the risk, however, that
such action will substantially affect prices. Should
it set off a price war between major oil exporters,
Mexico may well turn out to gain little if anything.
Thus, expanding foreign exchange revenue from oil
requires some international coordination. Additional
revenue from nontraditionals is much more subject to
Mexican unilateral control. In the short run, the
financial exchange rate has run far enough ahead of
domestic costs to make a wide range of Mexican

production competitive in world markets, particularly
in the market of the United States. Over the longer
run, however, it is very clear that the productivity
of Mexican agriculture and manufacturing is well below
the productivity of its oil sector. Moreover, lasting
productivity differentials are probably present within
the Mexican non-oil economy as well. Therefore, a
uniform total exchange rate system is not appropriate
for the medium term. However, differentiated total
exchange rates will imply tariffs and exports supports.
Exporting non-oil products with tax rebates or other
government supports runs the risk of countervailing
activity in the importing countries. Thus, although
Mexico can institute export-oriented trade policies,
the success of these policies depends at least in part
on the benevolence of Mexico's trading partners.

On Mexico's second major policy interest, a fall
in the international interest rate, it has relatively
little direct influence. In international markets,
Mexico is a price taker; U.S. monetary policy is the
overwhelming determinant of the course of interest
rates. Even on the matter of spreads over LIBOR or
prime, Mexico has not turned out to have a large
amount of leverage. Were it to want to bargain more
aggressively, it might need to coalesce with other
Latin American debtors. Finally, the reversal of
capital flight is subject only to limited impact by
Mexican policy alone. Not only is the capital flow
interest rate sensitive, but the view of Mexican prospects held abroad, particularly of its exchange rate,
substantially influences the speculative behavior of
Mexico's own citizens.

Given this policy context, the prospects for U.S.-
Mexican economic interaction grow directly out of
Mexico's policy needs. Such interaction can occur in
the small and in the large. Interaction in the small
is most likely to occur around Mexico's promotion of
nontraditional exports. The logical market for Mexico
is the United States: To this market it will want to
sell tourist services, vegetables, flowers, manufactured goods, and so on. Where trade in goods is concerned, some form of government fiscal or credit
support will be indispensable over the medium term.
Even if that were not the case, the quantities that
Mexico can provide to the closer U.S. markets are
considerable. Therefore, a U.S. willingness to accept
Mexican imports and not to impose countervailing
duties, quotas, or other restrictive measures is quite
essential for Mexican success in this endeavor. However, Mexico does not belong to the General Agreement
on Tariffs and Trade, nor has it made substantive
equivalent arrangements with the United States. Thus,
the interaction in the small around particular Mexican

exports is a very important aspect of U.S.-Mexican economic relations, and will become increasingly important as Mexico tries to balance its productive structure.

Interaction in the large will occur around the international interest rate and the supply of oil. Were U.S. monetary policy to become looser, and the interest rate to fall, the level of activity in the United States and the other Organization for Economic Cooperation and Development (OECD) countries would rise. This increased activity would naturally bring about an increase in the demand for oil. If this demand grew sufficiently, the market for oil would get tight and the Organization of Petroleum Exporting Countries (OPEC) would succeed in once again raising the nominal oil price. When that occurred, cost push would result throughout the developed countries, and a new inflationary spiral might well begin. Thus, unless a reduction in the interest rate is accompanied by an increase in the supply of world oil that can offset the tightness in that market resulting from higher levels of activity in the OECD countries, any fall in the interest rate will be self-nullifying. However, the Mexican interest is for the world interest rate to decline and also to increase its sale of oil. The U.S. interest is to keep the price of oil stable or inching downward while lowering the interest rate. Thus, U.S.-Mexican interests are fully complementary in the large.

In sum, a Mexican-U.S. coalition can be seen emerging around their community of interest consisting of three parallel but interactive elements: (1) a long-term preferential price/quantity arrangement on Mexican oil sales to the United States; (2) a change in the U.S. monetary policy tending toward lower interest rates buttressed by the assured increase in the availability of oil on world markets, and (3) a benign U.S. government attitude toward expanded Mexican exports of non-oil goods to the United States even with various explicit and implicit government supports.

NOTES

1. For a more detailed discussion of the consequences of this structure of the exchange rate system, see Daniel M. Schydlowsky, 1972, "Latin American Trade Policy in the 1970s: A Prospective Analysis," Quarterly Journal of Economics LXXXVI, no. 2, May 1972, pp. 263-289.

Part 4

Labor Markets

6
Mexican Migration to the United States: De Facto Rules

Jorge A. Bustamante

INTRODUCTION

Migration of Mexicans to the United States is an old phenomenon. Many of its characteristics have come to be repeated for several generations by actors who basically perform the same roles. The employer, the migrant worker, the government, and the labor recruiter, or coyote, are roles that have been played throughout the history of migration from Mexico to the United States since the nineteenth century. The behavior each player expects from the other in given situations, acting from different positions of power, has come to be converted into a set of rules that transcend personal experience and are transmitted from generation to generation.

Undocumented immigration has been acted out similarly for several decades. Today's performers may be new, but they behave in accordance with set rules derived from the practice of others who preceded them and found themselves in similar situations. In undocumented migration rules that have been ratified and transmitted--"rules of the game"--go beyond those shared by actors in otherwise similar roles.

This practice became clear to me during my experience as a participatory observer in 1969, when I passed as an undocumented alien in the agricultural fields of Texas near MacAllen, across the border from Reynosa. I went to a place where migrant laborers gathered to be recruited by farmers for work on their farms and mingled among a group of some twenty-five workers. Soon a truck arrived and signaled us to board. We rode to a ranch some five kilometers from San Juan, Texas; on arrival we climbed down from the back of the truck and the farmer climbed up. From this impromptu platform he told us, "There's a lot of you. I don't need as many. Let's see who wants to work for a dollar an hour, raise your hand."

Almost all of us raised our hands, to which the farmer responded, "No, still too many. Raise your hand, whoever wants to work for 75 cents an hour." This time the number of raised hands was reduced by almost half. This response produced a curious reaction. Those who had not raised their hands reacted with anger toward those who had, directing a string of insults at us. Among the gentlest words were, "starving creeps."

The farmer meanwhile took on the attitude of Pilate, as he kept up this type of auction of employment to the lowest bidder. He continued in a bored voice, "No, still too many. Whoever wants to work for 50 cents an hour, raise your hand." Again the number of raised hands was drastically reduced; only six of us were left. Then the farmer told everyone, "Those that don't want to work can go now. I'll give you five minutes to get off the ranch, and if I see you around here after that, I'll call the police so they can pick you up for trespassing on private property."

Turning to the six of us, he told us, getting down from the truck, "Let's see, you; get in line and show me your hands." I did as the rest, showing the palms of my hands in a scene reminiscent of a horse trader examining the animal's mouth to know how much he's going to pay. Upon seeing my hands, the farmer told me, "You can go with the others. I don't need you." My hands did not show the calluses that indicated the field experience he was looking for at the lowest possible price.

Without further discussion, the farmer left, leading the five who had obtained work by means of a negotiation that was certainly abusive but clearly understood by all the participants. This process had followed clear, de facto rules of a game practiced by many before those whom I happened to see in a real-life performance. As the farmer walked away, followed by his five workers, I asked myself about the economic and social significance of what I had just seen. Just as one may leave the theater wondering about the play's message, I had not seen the complete play of Mexican migration to the United States, only a fragment that involved just part of the cast.

Other factors also have a recurrent role in the immigration scenario. To understand the context of the roles of the governments of Mexico and the United States in shaping the de facto rules, by action and omission, it is necessary to consider the following conceptual background.

IMMIGRATION AND SOVEREIGNTY

One argument that supports the unilateral focus
of the United States on immigration from Mexico is
the "recovery of national control over its borders."
If this concept rests upon the sovereign right of a
country to control which foreigners may enter and under
what conditions, current U.S. immigration law has distorted this universally valid principle by expressly
permitting labor contracting of those who have entered
the country in violation of that law. The United
States is indeed the only country in the world whose
immigration law permits employers to hire those who
have entered its territory in violation of the regulations of the immigration laws.

This juridical incongruence results from a law
that on the one hand exercises sovereign right by prohibiting aliens who have entered the country without
appropriate migratory documentation from working and
that on the other hand concedes to a sector of its
population, the employers, the right to take advantage
of that violation by aliens who offer their labor.
Thus the immigration law operates as a labor law for
aliens. By permitting the hiring of persons who
violate it, the immigration law distorts its own juridical basis and at the same time creates the structural
conditions for the labor relations between the undocumented migrant worker and the employer. The employer
who hires an undocumented migrant has the legal power
to modify substantially the migratory situation of the
alien worker.

By an act of will, the employer in the United
States can decide when an alien is a worker with
certain rights and obligations and when he is a
criminal. If the employer wishes to exercise the power
that the immigration law vests in him, he need only
call the immigration police and denounce the undocumented alien. Of course, all employers in the United
States do not actually exercise this power. This power
also determines the position of the employer vis-à-vis
that of the undocumented migrant within the context of
a labor market. This power accordingly surpasses the
normative frame that defines the rights and obligations
of other workers in the United States. In this way the
power of negotiation that the employer can exercise
against an undocumented alien deprives the alien of the
minimal rights that U.S. laws concede to workers in
general. It thus distorts the juridical nature of a
country's sovereign right to determine who can or cannot enter, and at the same time to establish the bases
upon which the labor market for undocumented aliens
will operate. This incongruency reduces the validity
of the unilateral focus on immigration from Mexico

that is claimed by the United States.

CONCEPTUAL FRAMEWORK OF UNDOCUMENTED MIGRATION FROM MEXICO TO THE UNITED STATES

The old phenomenon of the migration of Mexican workers to the United States should be understood as the result of the interaction of factors located on both sides of the border. These factors are the offer of and the demand for a labor force in the context of an international market in which, historically, the offer from Mexico has been as real as the demand from the United States.

A very important part of the problem that the two countries encounter when confronting undocumented migration stems from substantial differences in how the underlying concept is viewed. The predominant view in the United States is that Mexican immigration is a crime-related phenomenon. But if indeed an undocumented migrant is technically a delinquent under U.S. immigration laws, this represents only a formal characteristic. It overlooks the real context in which the presence of the undocumented Mexican migrant in the United States responds to an economic relation that has costs and benefits for both the country of origin and the country of destination in the migratory process. The process is not one of delinquency comparable to a criminal misdemeanor, but one of labor relations that transcends the border between the two countries. Focusing on the undocumented migration from Mexico as a crime is to criminalize the presence of alien workers, workers who are taken advantage of legally by employers and in the context of work relations that yield benefits to the economy and society of the United States. The criminalization of the presence of undocumented Mexican workers in the United States is equivalent to an act of power in which the asymmetry of relations between Mexico and the United States is taken advantage of. It imposes on Mexico a juridical-labor framework for the treatment of undocumented aliens in the United States. Criminalization of the alien migratory workers thus involves an act of sheer power, given the fact that a demand for foreign workers exists in the United States.

Dealing with the most industrialized country in the world, it is paradoxical that this demand for alien workers concerns unskilled labor. Traditionally that demand had originated in the agricultural activities within the United States. In the last ten years this demand has been enormously diversified, and a growing preponderance has developed in the area of services, which has compensated for a reduction in the U.S.

demand for agricultural labor. The U.S. economy requires unskilled labor; nevertheless, its society is
not prepared to produce unskilled labor. The educational system in the United States is based on values
and aspirations that make certain jobs undesirable.
Thus even with the high levels of unemployment in the
United States and even though some U.S. citizens have
no or very slight labor skills, they do not attempt to
satisfy the market demands to which the Mexican worker
is ready to respond. In this way, the United States
acquires a factor of production that is in insufficient
supply, and therefore must be imported from abroad.
Such need for factors of production that can be found
abroad is resolved generally by agreement between the
country of origin and the country of destination.

However, the supply of unskilled workers originating in Mexico and required by the United States is not
only obtained without the country of origin's participation but is criminalized by both. Thus the United
States imposes a juridical framework on the presence
of needed Mexican labor supply, a framework that does
not correspond to the underlying situation. This
criminalization is an act of power because it occurs
in place of a bilateral plan for discussion and negotiation with full participation of the two countries
involved.

Another difference in the conceptualization with
respect to undocumented immigration from Mexico to the
United States is expressed in the reasoning that the
sovereign right of the United States to legislate in
immigration matters cannot be designed specifically
with reference to one country, but should refer universally and without distinction to all nationals involved in undocumented immigration. This argument
proves fallacious on two counts. First, the U.S.
Federal Census Bureau has affirmed that approximately
50 percent of the total undocumented aliens in the
United States are Mexican citizens; the other 50 percent are citizens from the rest of the world. This
percentage indicates the preponderantly bilateral
nature of the relationship. Second, and even more
important, is that over the 1970s and early 1980s 90
percent of the undocumented aliens arrested by the U.S.
immigration authorities were Mexicans. The difference
between the 50 percent and more than 90 percent has at
least two meanings: (1) Police activity has been
directed specifically toward the presence of undocumented Mexicans; and (2) this distinction in enforcement policy can only be explained as discrimination
against Mexicans, a policy that departs from the
principle that policing activities should be exercised
against all undocumented persons without distinction
of national origin.

Mexico participates in undocumented migration in a predominant and particular way. Special treatment of Mexico in the bilateral context of undocumented migration would therefore not have to be viewed as a privilege or concession to Mexico but rather as a real and discriminatory practice. During several decades this practice has been a most visible and pernicious source of irritation and disagreement in bilateral relations.

Although the United States government persists in a selective policing policy--a policy that results in nearly all arrests being Mexicans-- it is common to hear in Washington that the United States cannot enter into bilateral negotiations with Mexico because the immigration of undocumented workers involves many countries. Yet the results of this contradiction are used as one more justification for the unilateral focus that the United States has imposed on Mexico.

FROM CARTER TO REAGAN

The unilateral focus of the United States with respect to Mexican migration has undergone some twists more related to internal political affairs than to relations between the two countries. In this section a historical examination of some of these twists will be attempted, beginning with the administration of President Jimmy Carter.

President Carter had proposed to deal with the question of undocumented migration in the context of growing unemployment during his presidential term. President Carter's proposals for legislative reform, presented on August 4, 1977, consisted fundamentally of the following points:

1. Penalization of employers who hire undocumented aliens.
2. Increased and reinforced control over the entrance of undocumented persons on the Mexican border.
3. Regularization of the migratory status of those undocumented persons who had remained without interruption in the United States since before 1970.
4. Granting of temporary work permits to those undocumented persons who had entered before January 1, 1977, with exclusion of the rights to (a) gain public assistance, (b) bring relatives, (c) obtain permanent migratory status, (d) obtain citizenship, and (e) secure political rights.
5. Economic assistance to the undocumented persons' countries of origin.

Point 1 expresses the old demand of the American Federation of Labor and Congress of Industrial Organizations (AFL-CIO). The lobbying by this important labor union has been reflected in immigration reform bills introduced on several occasions by Congressman Peter Rodino (D-N.J.). It was not surprising that a state with a strong labor constituency should present these AFL-CIO supported bills. Nevertheless, this influence was not sufficient to counteract the power of Senator James O. Eastland (D-Miss.), president of the Senate Committee on Immigration for several decades. On several occasions Rodino's bills were approved by the House of Representatives, only to be later frozen in the Senate, thanks to the parliamentary ability of Senator Eastland, responding to the interests of the agricultural entrepreneurs of his state.

Although the state legislatures have exclusive domain in labor matters, the federal Constitution of the United States places immigration matters in the federal domain. Under this distinction, more than a dozen states in that country have already promulgated decrees that prohibit the hiring of undocumented workers by employers, even before President Carter's immigration bill was presented to Congress in 1977. These decrees contained in the laws of numerous states did not subsequently receive employer support for their implementation. This lack of enforcement demonstrates that such legislation was designed to pacify unions that viewed undocumented immigration as one of the principal factors in growing unemployment. This view of foreign immigration as the cause of unemployment is the old scapegoat syndrome that appears cyclically in the United States each time a crisis in employment occurs.

President Carter found himself pressured by groups supported by the AFL-CIO within the Democratic party to create more restrictive immigration legislation. He failed resoundingly with his bill for reforms in the Immigration and Naturalization Law, basically because it contained proposals that tried to please groups with not only diverse but also contradictory interests. He tried to please the labor contingent of the Democratic party with the proposal to punish the employers who hired undocumented workers. To this proposal were opposed the agricultural contractors headed by Senator Eastland. On the other hand, he tried to please groups of Mexican origin and liberal organizations with his proposal to regularize the situation of undocumented persons and with a proposal for economic assistance to the migrants' countries of origin. These proposals were opposed not only by the AFL-CIO but also by a strange combination of liberal groups from conservationists in the Sierra Club to restrictionists loaded with ethnic and racial prejudice such as the Zero Population Growth group and the Federation for American Immigration Reform (FAIR), both created to combat immigration. In still another direction, President Carter attempted to please the agricultural interests with a proposal for temporary visas--a proposal vehemently opposed by unions, particularly the AFL-CIO and restrictionist groups.

President Carter could not find a common denominator that would permit him to advance his legislative plan. He had intended to gain the support of the Mexican government for his plan on immigration. In June 1977, the Carter plan on immigration was presented before the Mexican government in Mexico City. This meeting of a bilateral work group was called "consultative." Nevertheless, this term was but a euphemism for advanced notification that President Carter's plan would be converted into a formal legislative proposal to the U.S. Congress on August 4, 1977.

During this same August, the working group met a second time with its central theme once again the Carter plan on undocumented persons. In this second meeting, the Mexican group was much better prepared than before, when it was surprised by the presentation of the Carter plan, and the tone of the Mexican representatives changed. Members of the working group presented the position of the government of Mexico on the Carter plan in a document that definitively rejected this plan. Now the U.S. group was surprised to hear the Mexican government's frank disagreement with the official U.S. reform proposal. In this meeting the Mexican government expressed a conceptual disagreement regarding the domineering tendencies of the U.S. government. This disagreement can be summed up in two contrasting views: The Mexican opinion explains the migration to the United States as a response in an international labor market in which U.S. demand for labor attracts Mexican workers. The U.S. view, on the other hand, sees the same immigration as a delinquency problem, which calls for solution by internal police enforcement. The disagreement in this August meeting was so profound that the enthusiasm with which the bilateral advisory group had been formed was significantly cooled off. For nearly ten months, the group on social affairs did not meet again.

The failure of President Carter's plan for the reform of immigration laws gave place to a new strategy. This consisted of the creation of a presidential commission for the study of immigration and the refugee question.

THE LOPEZ PORTILLO-CARTER MEETING OF 1978

U.S. Secretary of State Cyrus Vance went to Mexico
to make arrangements for the visit of President Carter.
Part of these arrangements dealt with the president's
agenda on undocumented Mexican workers. State Department experts on Mexico had become eager to promulgate
an agreement for guest-workers, a proposal that had
already been presented by President Carter and turned
down by the government of Mexico. This agreement was
to be presented in response to a suggestion, made by
the Mexican ambassador in Washington, that the bracero
pacts, which had been in force during World War II, be
renewed. The Mexican ambassador's view, however, contrasted sharply with the points made by the Mexican
chancellery in the August 1977 meeting.

This contrast led the State Department to think
that it could successfully insist upon an arrangement,
thus allowing President Carter to save political face
after the failure of his legislative proposal. The
viewpoint of the Mexican ambassador in Washington was
not backed by the Mexican secretary of Foreign Affairs.
This in turn considerably cooled the enthusiasm of
Secretary Vance, who had to deny publicly that a renegotiation of the bracero pact was under discussion.
It seemed evident in Mexico that the necessary conditions for bridging the gap between the Mexican and U.S.
perspectives on the migration problem did not exist.
This enabled President López Portillo to remove the
question of undocumented persons from the agenda for
his meeting with President Carter in February 1978.

Studies on migration to the United States, conducted at El Colegio de México, had carefully analyzed
the monthly statistical reports compiled by the Immigration and Naturalization Service. "Monthly Reports
of Deportable Aliens Found in the United States" were
carefully explored. These forms included statistical
data on the multiple categories into which undocumented
persons arrested by the Immigration and Naturalization
Service are classified. The information contained in
these forms is not considered confidential but neither
is it published in its totality; however, the entire
monthly reports for January 1972 to December 1977 were
obtained. Working together with Professor Roberto Han
of El Colegio de México, I found that beginning with
February 1977, the number of women and children de-
tained by the Immigration and Naturalization Service
increased abruptly. Beginning with 1,100 detentees
in February, the rate culminated at 10,200 in June.
This increase was interpreted as reflecting a campaign
by the Immigration and Naturalization Service to
selectively expel undocumented Mexican women and
children on a massive scale. This campaign, initiated

a month after the visit of President López Portillo in Washington and without previous warning, appeared to directly contradict President Carter's campaign in favor of human rights. President López Portillo presented this statistical analysis in a graph to President Carter, asking for an explanation. President Carter did not know how to reply and thereafter was hesitant to discuss the undocumented aliens issue for the remainder of his visit. Nevertheless, President López Portillo personally expounded to President Carter the principal points of Mexican policy with regard to migration as follows:

1. The emigration of undocumented workers from Mexico corresponds to a bilateral labor market phenomenon.
2. The complexity of the migratory phenomenon requires a bilateral focus by both governments. The government of Mexico therefore rejects the unilateral approach that has characterized U.S. policy.
3. To obtain the conditions necessary for a rational and bilateral approach, both governments need information, heretofore not forthcoming, to specify the quantitative dimensions and the principal effects of undocumented migration on each country. The government of Mexico had made an unprecedented effort to obtain that information through a project undertaken by CENIET for the Mexican Department of Labor.
4. The government of Mexico is ready to exchange this information for that which might be available to the U.S. government, to initiate the bilateral analysis.
5. The government of Mexico would not be willing to accept the treatment of undocumented persons as criminals, nor a violation of their human and labor rights as has been shown to occur according to the documented data.
6. There would be no trade of undocumented persons for oil.

At the meeting of Presidents López Portillo and Carter in February 1978, President Carter announced the creation of a select commission dealing with the U.S. government's policies on immigration and refugees. President Carter had named the exgovernor from Florida, Reuben Askew, to preside over this commission. A few months later, Askew was named to a totally different position and he was replaced by the president of Notre Dame University, Theodore Hesburgh. The select committee came to be known later as the Hesburgh Commission.

After the 1978 presidential meeting, President
Carter began losing the initiative on U.S. immigration
policy, which at the same time was increasingly passed
to the Congress. Although several legislative committees initiated public hearings to discuss the various
plans for immigration legislation, as 1979 advanced the
importance with which legislators viewed the subject of
immigration appeared to diminish. The consensus in
Washington toward the middle of the year was that
designing a more adequate policy would have to await
the outcome of the investigation by the Select Committee on Immigration and Refugees.

The Mexican position on undocumented migration, on
the contrary, acquired greater urgency, following a
declaration by Secretary Jorge Castaneda at the second
press conference at the Foreign Relations Secretariat,
in June 1977. On that occasion, Castaneda said,
"Mexico cannot, either constitutionally or politically,
juridically or morally, impede the movement of Mexicans
within or outside its territory." This declaration had
particular importance in the context of a suggestion
from the United States that the Mexican government
should assist the United States in detaining the flow
of undocumented migrants within Mexican territory.
This "cooperation" had been suggested with differing
degrees of subtlety in exchange for the establishment
of an annual quota of braceros along the lines of the
bracero agreement in effect until 1964.

THE END OF CARTER'S PRESIDENCY AND THE
BEGINNING OF REAGAN'S

The relations between the president of Mexico and
the president of the United States cooled considerably
after the 1978 meeting in Mexico. Many observers saw
that a mutual antipathy had emerged between López
Portillo and Carter. At each meeting fewer signs of
understanding and more signs of coolness appeared,
particularly during the visit of President López
Portillo to Washington that same year. Because of the
impossibility of making progress in mutual understanding between both governments, Secretary of Foreign
Relations Jorge Castaneda proposed that the discussion
be changed from a bilateral to a multilateral basis.
Ambassador Antonne Gonzalez de Leon was charged with
implementing the new focus at the United Nations. A
long procedure was initiated in the Civil Rights
Commission to develop a multilateral statement on the
rights of migrants, in particular those workers in an
international context.

In 1980 the electoral campaign was in progress in
the United States, and as the year advanced, the

economic situation deteriorated and unemployment increased. In an effort to gain the vote of the Mexican
population in the United States, President Carter named
Dr. Julian Nava as U.S. ambassador to Mexico. This
appointment, however, had very little to do with U.S.
policy toward Mexico; it was only to serve President
Carter's ethnic policies toward voters of Mexican or
Latin-American origin. President Carter wished to send
a message to the ethnic minority of Mexican origin that
was acquiring major importance in Texas and California,
hoping to improve his election prospects. The subsequent appointment of Nava as ambassador did not have a
significant effect on cooling off the dialogue on the
question of Mexican migrant workers.

Interparliamentary Meeting in Washington

The twentieth Mexico-United States interparliamentary meeting took place in Washington in early May
1980. These meetings do not involve official repre-
sentation of U.S. legislators; rather, they consist of
a gathering of members of the federal legislative
congresses of both countries. The Mexican delegation
is given official sanction by the concerned committees
of the Chamber of Senators and the Chamber of Deputies,
and one of their respective presidents usually takes a
turn in heading it. The U.S. delegation, on the contrary, is made up of senators and congressmen who
volunteer to meet with the Mexican delegation on previously agreed topics. The members of the U.S. parliamentary delegation, therefore, do not speak in an
official capacity; their comments, proposals, or reso-
lutions carry no obligation for the legislative organs
of which they are members.
The U.S. delegation to the interparliamentary
meetings has been composed nearly always of persons
who, because of their ethnic origins or the geographical proximity of their districts to Mexico, have a
personal political interest in these meetings. On
occasion, it has been difficult to find a sufficient
number of volunteers in the U.S. Congress to attend.
This was the case in the preparations for the meeting
that took place in Hermosillo, Sonora, in 1979, though
not in 1980 when the petroleum euphoria was at its
peak in Mexico. The representatives of the twentieth
interparliamentary meeting were then received in
Washington in a manner similar to that customarily
bestowed on representatives from the Gulf emirates.
I do not wish to say, with the preceding comments,
that the interparliamentary meetings lack importance.
However, they have not had the importance that their
participants have frequently attributed to them, for

they have not offered a formal mechanism for negotiations, nor a basis for internal or external political
obligation. Their importance consists of the fact that
these meetings are agreed-upon forums where political
messages may be given, and that they receive press
coverage. This coverage in the U.S. press is usually
slight compared to the newspaper space and time given
in Mexico.

THE REAGAN ERA

On January 5, 1981, President-elect Ronald Reagan
met with President Jose López Portillo in Ciudad
Juarez. The principal message that President Reagan
proposed to convey to President López Portillo was that
a new agreement toward Mexico was going to be inaugu-
rated. This new agreement was characterized by one of
Reagan's advisers who prepared the atmosphere for this
reunion with these words: "All the technical, financial help and openings for migratory workers that
Mexico needs to send to the United States will be given
in exchange for aligning itself with the United States
in its foreign policy against communism." A consensus
among the observers in this meeting was that a personal
empathy had been forged between the two dignitaries.
This sense of a new attitude toward Mexico was reinforced in an interview with President Reagan by
Walter Cronkite of the CBS broadcasting system on
March 3, 1981.
In that interview, President Reagan said, "I am
intrigued with a program suggested by the governors of
the United States border states and their counterparts,
the state governors from the other side of the border.
They have met to discuss this problem with each other."
Then he referred to Mexico as a neighboring and
friendly nation with a tremendous unemployment problem
and a corresponding need to count on an escape valve
to maintain its political stability. Immediately he
again repeated that he was intrigued by the program
proposed by the governors on both sides of the border,
a program that would allow the border to be a two-way
street for all our people. Visas would be granted to
whoever had a job offer in the United States, the
migratory workers would pay taxes, and the abuse of
undocumented persons would be avoided.
In Mexico a lot of publicity was given to the
notion of an "open border" to which President Reagan
made reference in that interview. This concept was
interpreted with immeasurable optimism in Mexico as
promise of an imminent regularization of the undocumented workers and of an unlimited handout of visas to
all Mexicans who might want to work in the United

States. The day after the interview, some Mexican
newspapers printed a clarification by President
Reagan's press secretary to the effect that the visas
to which the President had referred on television were
only for entering in the morning to work, while returning at the end of the day to Mexico. A little later
it became evident that President Reagan's words on
March 3 not only contained no specific proposal but
also reflected no final political decision.

It became known that President Reagan had created
his own committee for a study of immigration, presided
over by Frank Hodson, a White House functionary. The
decision to create this committee in the first weeks
of the president's administration had been made only a
few hours before the Select Commission on Immigration
and Refugee Policies created by President Carter was to
render its final report to the U.S. Congress and to
President Reagan himself. The creation of President
Reagan's committee was interpreted in Washington as a
clear indication that he would not feel obliged nor
compromised to follow the recommendations of the select
commission created by his predecessor and that these
would soon drown in the Reagan administration's indif-
ference and disdain for everything originating in
President Carter's administration.

Events in April 1981 began to demonstrate that the
administration of President Reagan was drawing quickly
away from the optimistic notion of the open border. On
April 10, 1981, the chief of the Border Patrol in El
Paso, Texas, Richard P. Staily, informed the public
communications media of a 285 percent increase in the
border police force in his district alone. This spec-
tacular increase was the result of an agreement signed
in Washington the effects of which would be felt in
early April, in line with Chief Staily's announcement.
The heavy hand of future immigration policy began to
be apparent. Not long before, a renowned member of the
Republican party, exdirector of the Central Intelligence
Agency William Colby, had stated publicly that in the
future, Mexican immigration held a greater threat for
the United States than the Soviet Union did. Around
this time Senator Allan Simpson began to appear on the
immigration scene.

When the Republican party obtained the majority
of seats in the U.S. Senate, Senator Simpson (R-Wyo.)
became the president of the Senate Subcommittee on
Immigration and Refugees, replacing Senator Edward
Kennedy, who in his time had replaced Senator James
Eastland. Senator Simpson had made contact with the
topic of immigration during his service as a member of
the Hesburgh Commission. Since the topic of undocumented immigration and refugees had not been important
in Wyoming state politics, Senator Simpson proved the

ideal politician to head the legislative campaign for a
new immigration law, a law that would respond to the
needs of the political situation.

From the start, Senator Simpson demonstrated great
skill and dedication as the new leader of immigration
politics at the national level. His idea was to find a
Democratic legislator in the House of Representatives
with whom he would jointly produce a bill that would be
presented to the U.S. public as "not a party proposal,
but representative of the national interest."

Under this strategy, Congressman Romano Mazzoli
(D-Ky.), representing a state where the immigration
topic is likewise not politically important, entered
the scene. With Senator Simpson the leader of the
pair, the Simpson-Mazzoli combination turned out to be
so effective politically in forming a new immigration
law that President Reagan decided to withdraw his own
initiative, giving free reign to what would later be
known as the Simpson-Mazzoli bill.

The Simpson Mazzoli Bill

The principal propositions in the Simpson-Mazzoli
bill are the following:

1. Sanctions against employers who hire undocumented workers. This proposal was neither new nor
original with the authors of the bill. Sanctions were
contained previously in the famous Rodino bill, which
was discussed on four different occasions since 1971
but never approved. No mention was made of the sanctions previously provided by the labor laws of twelve
states in the American union. Nor was it mentioned
that such legal dispositions have never been complied
with, nor generated any claims against employers, in-
dicating the lack of political intent to implement
these sanctions in practice. The best known antecedent
in the labor field, which in the United States is within state jurisdiction, was the famous Dixon-Arnett
bill, whose constitutionality was attacked successfully
before the State Superior Court of California. The
Superior Court's decision was then modified by the
U.S. Supreme Court in a decision that expressly authorized the states to introduce sanctions against
employers who hired undocumented immigrant workers.
The U.S. Supreme Court in that decision viewed such
sanctions not exclusively an immigration matter, which
belongs constitutionally within federal jurisdiction,
but as an issue in labor relations.

2. Creation of an identity card for all
foreigners who should be allowed to work in the United
States, making presentation of said identity card

demandable by the employer before hiring.

3. Establishment of special treatment for alien
migratory workers requiring them to pay taxes and
Social Security contributions, but without entitling
them to public assistance, a right that in accordance
with U.S. law derives from the obligation to pay taxes
and Social Security contributions.

4. Consideration and evaluation of visa requests
to the United States on an individual basis for each
applicant, thereby practically excluding the possibility
of family reunification. Each member of the
immigrant's family would have to be judged indepen-
dently of the family relationship.

5. An extraordinary tightening of the criminal
status of offenses against the immigration law. These
increased penalties on undocumented immigrants in turn
would have a direct impact on the market conditions
under which Mexican migratory workers operate and
cheapen their labor. This increased vulnerability of
the immigrant, while designed for internal political
consumption, stands in flagrant contradiction to
measures designed to maintain the flow of migratory
workers, such as the proposal for special temporary
work visas (visas H-2) and the program for regularizing
undocumented migrants.

Criminalization of the undocumented migration is
central to the creation of labor market conditions that
cheapen the services of foreign labor, even though such
labor is needed by the U.S. economy. This permits payment of a less than fair wage and a wage less than that
which would emerge from international negotiation.

6. Establishment of a program for the regularization of undocumented migrants by means of permanent
or temporary resident visas, depending upon the
seniority of the undocumented migrant's stay in the
United States. This measure is presented to the U.S.
public as a humanitarian service, when in reality it
responds to their own economic interests to maintain
the cheap labor supply from abroad, a labor supply that
then receives discriminatory treatment as compared to
other U.S. workers.

The number of workers who would benefit from this
regularization has been exaggerated as has been the
volume of undocumented immigration. Given the traditionally temporary character of Mexican immigration
into the United States, this measure would benefit
from 200 thousand to 500 thousand Mexican immigrant
workers, and only after these workers have been able
to escape the police actions proposed in the Simpson-
Mazzoli bill prior to regularization.

Senator Simpson initiated an intense campaign of
public hearings in support of his bill. This campaign

involved visits to Mexico, including an audience with
President López Portillo and interviews with various
cabinet members. The intuitive response of President
López Portillo to Senator Simpson's visit to Mexico
was similar to that given in Washington--to listen
without response. The Mexican reaction, however, was
distorted by Senator Simpson upon his return to the
United States, where he publicly reported that the
government of Mexico had offered no objection to his
plan.

Although this report might have been formally
correct, the Mexican government had in fact meant to
send a message of disagreement with the unilateral
U.S. approach to the immigration question. Mexico's
lack of response to the Simpson-Mazzoli bill was completely misinterpreted. The message that the government of Mexico had wanted to send to the United States
by not responding to the Simpson-Mazzoli plan was (1)
not to get involved in a legislative process that by
definition was an internal matter; (2) to record disagreement with the unilateral U.S. approach to the
question of undocumented immigration from Mexico; and
(3) to indicate that the government of Mexico would
react officially and openly only to a proposal for bilateral negotiation.

The U.S. interpretation of the lack of Mexican
response to the Simpson-Mazzoli bill was (1) that the
government of Mexico wished to maintain an escape valve
for its unemployed and therefore wished to maintain the
status quo on undocumented immigration; and (2) that
lack of response to the Simpson-Mazzoli bill represented a tacit acceptance of its postulates as a
"solution."

Resultant confusion was fueled by the fact that
the bill's proponents had no common interest to
initiate or propitiate a bilateral focus on the immigration question; on the contrary, the political purpose of the Simpson-Mazzoli bill can only be understood
within the internal context of the United States.

U.S. policy on restricting immigration follows a
cyclical pattern in response to economic crises and in
particular to unemployment. An analysis of the
economic crises of this century supports this view.
The author has analyzed the periods of economic crises
since that of 1907 when the first massive deportation
of Mexicans occurred. In the 1907 crisis the growth
of unemployment was blamed on foreign immigration,
making it the scapegoat for the crisis. This pattern
was repeated in the economic crisis of 1921. In that
year, the anti-immigrant and anti-Mexican xenophobia
in the principal cities of the southwestern United
States assumed a definite shading of racism; signs
could be found on the streets of San Antonio that said,

"No Mexicans or dogs allowed." The use of immigration as a scapegoat in the unemployment crisis was accompanied by the emergence of anti-Mexican ethnic and racial appeals. These appeals, at the beginning of the 1920s, marked one of the worst episodes of anti-Mexican racism in the present century. In those years everything occurred from the lynching of Mexicans, in the worst style of racial oppression of blacks in the U.S. South, to the massive deportation of thousands of Mexicans from Houston, San Antonio, El Paso, Tucson, San Diego, and Los Angeles.

The great crisis that began in 1929 and ended in about 1935 again marked an epoch of immigrant restriction, with particular emphasis on Mexicans, including the most intense massive deportations. The history of these deportations in the United States has been registered and documented by North American (Hoffman, 1974) and Mexican investigators (de Valazco). The pattern of economic crises and increased unemployment followed by xenophobic and anti-immigrant attitudes reemerged in 1954. It was followed by immigration restrictions and/or massive deportation of Mexicans that culminated in the infamous wet-back operation, resulting in more than a million expulsions of Mexicans from the United States. The next economic crisis in unemployment occurred in 1974, in which year the previously mentioned patterns once more were repeated with surprising consistency.

The Simpson-Mazzoli bill can be interpreted as cyclical response to the unemployment crisis that began in the last months of the Carter administration and that continued to grow during the first two years of the Reagan administration. Since the second quarter of 1983 the unemployment rate has begun to subside, and the most commonly used economic indicators point toward a relatively rapid economic recovery. Political pressure originating in the increase of unemployment thus is beginning to give way in the United States. Traditionally a lessening of unemployment has preceded reduction in the pressure for a restrictive immigration policy. If the tendency toward reduced unemployment is maintained, the support of the Simpson-Mazzoli bill may thus diminish and new conditions may emerge that would permit a bilateral focus on the problems posed by the immigration of Mexican workers to the United States.

The Message from the Mexican Senate
to the Senate of the United States
on December 15, 1982

The Population Office of the United Nations together with other international organizations dealing

with demographic phenomena initiated a meeting of representatives of the legislatures on the American continent. This meeting took place in Brasilia from
December 2 to 5, 1982. The objective of this meeting
was to bring population problems to the attention of
legislators from the Western Hemisphere. To this end
the international organizations invited experts on
different population topics to work with them. The
legislative bodies of Mexico and the United States were
represented in that meeting. One of the population
themes dealt with was the international migration of
workers.

Upon analyzing the different aspects of the topic,
especially that of undocumented migration, the consensus emerged that the legislatures represented there
should discourage restrictions of these problems by
means of unilateral decisions. On the basis of this
consensus, the representatives unanimously resolved
(including the vote of the U.S. representatives) that
the parliaments there represented should discourage
legal initiatives that involve a unilateral focus in
the international migration of workers. It was recommended, on the other hand, that bilateral or multilateral negotiation be stimulated and propitiated as
the most rational and appropriate approach to resolving
problems that are international by definition.

The unanimous resolution of this forum of representatives from the parliaments of the whole continent
was made on December 5, 1982. With this as foundation
and in accordance with this resolution, the Senate of
the Mexican Republic agreed to send a message to the
U.S. Senate expressing the feeling of Mexico's Chamber
of Senators that there existed an incompatibility between the Simpson-Mazzoli bill and the agreements and
recommendations of the interparliamentary meeting in
Brasilia.

This message from the Mexican Senate was not the
expression of a unilateral initiative but was based on
the resolution of an interparliamentary forum where the
U.S. Congress was represented and where its delegates
also voted in favor of the resolution. It was thus not
an act of interference in the internal affairs of the
United States, nor an act that might set a precedent
for intervention by a parliamentary organ in the legislative process of another. Nevertheless, Senator
Simpson publicly criticized the Mexican Senate for
interfering in the internal legislative process of the
United States, setting "a grave precedence" in the
relations between both countries. Unfortunately, this
totally unfounded criticism, which distorted the nature
and origin of the message of December 15, 1982, was
picked up and responded to by some representatives of
the Mexican government. These informal commentaries

provoked a certain amount of confusion within the
government of Mexico. It is important to clarify the
legitimacy of the message of December 15, a message
that for the first time stated in an explicit fashion
what previously had been communicated to the U.S.
government only in an indirect form, for the first time
since President Reagan's immigration bill was presented
during the oft-cited 1981 Washington meeting between
President López Portillo and the President of the
United States.

TOWARD A BILATERAL FOCUS

The probability that the Simpson-Mazzoli bill will
be voted upon by the full House of Representatives is
very slight. Nevertheless, if it should happen, the
government of Mexico should actively promote an initiative for a bilateral program of discussion among
representatives of the principal actors in the phenomenon of migration from Mexico to the United States,
that is, the employers, the workers, and the state.
These discussions, which would follow a tripartite
scheme similar to that of the International Labor
Organization, would seek to arrive at solutions acceptable to the representatives of the three groups. These
solutions might then serve as the basis for the formal
negotiation of an international agreement, an agreement
that should radically distance itself from a revival of
the bracero pacts in use from 1942 to 1964.

Unfortunately, the disinterest expressed by the
government of Mexico in the renovation of the bracero
pacts has been confused with a lack of interest in
negotiating an international agreement. Solution
mechanisms ought to be sought that reflect the reality
of the migratory phenomenon that has changed radically
on both the supply and demand sides of the international labor market, the market in terms of which the
nature of this phenomenon is to be commonly understood.
Such a scheme of discussion and tripartite negotiation
would yield a result that was never achieved during the
epoch of the bracero pacts, that is, disappearance of
undocumented immigration, based on cooperation by the
three principal actors.   •

Once the international migration from Mexico to
the United States is accepted as basically a labor
market phenomenon, it becomes evident that a rational
solution cannot be obtained without the participation
of immigrant workers' representatives. Otherwise,
there can only be unrealistic solutions, tending to
perpetuate the abuse and exploitation of migrants or
creating a protective paternalism, a paternalism that
would impede the exercise of labor rights as something

owed by the protective framework established by the
host states. Any solution that does not include that
participation and whose obligations are not shared by
the employers, workers, and state will retain international migration as a focus of irritation and disagreement rather than utilize its potential as an area
of international cooperation between two countries
whose geography obliges them to learn to live together.

REFERENCES

Carreros de Valazco, <u>Los Mexicans Que Devolvio La
     Crisis</u>.
Hoffman, A. 1974. <u>Unwanted Americans in the Great
     Depression: Deportation Pressures, 1929-39</u>.
     Tucson: University of Arizona Press.

7
Mexican Immigrants: The Labor Market Issue

Richard Mines
Michael Kaufman

The debate in Congress in the early 1980s over the reform of immigration laws has focused sharply on the impact of undocumented immigration on the labor market. Proponents of immigration restriction claim that undocumented immigration is a primary cause for the high levels of unemployment suffered by U.S. workers. In addition, they argue, easily exploited immigrant workers are responsible for the deterioration of working conditions and the declines in union power that have taken place in recent years. Commentators opposed to immigration restriction note that the availability of inexpensive immigrant labor has permitted the survival of certain industries in the United States that might otherwise fold or be forced to migrate overseas. Additionally, they point out, the employment of low-skill immigrant labor creates complementary higher-skill employment opportunities for domestic workers.

Unfortunately, no simple, trustworthy method exists for evaluating the net labor market impact of immigration. Anecdotal accounts both for and against expanded immigration appear frequently in the press. Political officials, union leaders, and community activists each present overly simplistic accounts of the immigration phenomenon in order to advance their particular political views. Complicating the matter, the immigration debate is conducted in an emotionally charged environment in which statements are often misinterpreted as being racist on the one hand or ethnocentric on the other. The question of what impact immigration has on the labor market is extremely complex and resists facile, clear-cut conclusions.

This chapter attempts to introduce hard evidence into a debate too frequently carried out on the level of polemics and conjecture. In recent decades, Mexican immigrants have become prominent in the California economy, first as agricultural field laborers and later in urban labor markets. We examine why the demand for

Mexican labor has increased in California over the last thirty years, why there has been a concurrent decline in the power of U.S. wage workers relative to that of their employers, and what connections, if any, exist between these two phenomena. After discussing some macrolevel trends in the evolution of the U.S. labor market, we turn to several local labor market case studies designed to move the analysis to a more empirical context.

MACRO TRENDS

In brief, our argument is that an understanding of the impact of Mexican immigration on California's labor markets requires a more careful characterization of the immigration process than has been previously considered.

Distinctive Features of Mexican Immigration

By viewing Mexican immigrants as an undifferentiated mass of low-skill labor, policymakers have overlooked the precise fashion in which immigration alters labor market dynamics. A more accurate portrait of California's Mexican immigrant working population reveals the existence of two broad categories of immigrant workers--permanent settler migrants and less established newcomers. The first group of migrants have lived and worked in the United States for many years, during which they have adopted U.S. standards of living and have become familiar with U.S. labor laws. These migrants are frequently members of unions and are willing to struggle in defense of their rights as workers.

The newcomer immigrants, by contrast, are unfamiliar with U.S. society and economy and are therefore more easily exploited. As a consequence, employers are able to use the newcomers as components of cost-cutting strategies whose ultimate results are the reduction of wage levels, the degradation of working conditions, and the weakening of unions. The principal victims of this immigrant-induced labor market degradation are not U.S. citizens, as is often claimed, but the long-term settler immigrants. Restrictive immigration proposals currently under consideration fail to take into account the distinctive groupings within the Mexican immigrant population and are therefore likely to prove both ineffective and counterproductive.

It is important to note that certain features of Mexican immigration, though also present in the immigration experiences of other groups, are much more pronounced among Mexicans. These distinctive characteristics are essential to an understanding of the role played by Mexican immigrants in California labor markets.

First, Mexican immigrants have an unusually low level of education and few, perhaps less than 20 percent, have ever worked outside their native towns and villages prior to migrating to the United States.[1] The proximity of the U.S. border and the relatively small expense required for a typical immigrant to travel from the populous Central Highlands to almost any job market in California increase the attractiveness and ease of northward migration.

Second, unlike other immigrant groups, Mexican immigrants exhibit high turnover. Among the pool of Mexicans who come to the United States, a large group does not come every year or is coming for the first time in a given year. As a consequence, many new faces enter the Mexican immigrant community each year. Indeed, one-third of the Spanish speakers in California speak no English, whereas only one-sixth of the speakers of other foreign languages are non-English-speakers.[2]

Third, Mexican immigrants are usually members of migratory social networks that regulate the way in which they move and work. The life-cycle patterns of these networks and the individuals within them help to explain the role of Mexicans in U.S. labor markets. In the majority of cases, these networks are male-led and based on the pioneering efforts of unaccompanied young men from a given sending community. After the pioneers establish job contacts and find places to live, they form settlement colonies that other migrants from their area then use as safe havens. If a network matures and becomes rooted north of the border, women and children are brought across. But many immigrant networks do not mature and continue to consist largely of unaccompanied male migrants. The members of these immature networks rarely develop good job contacts in the United States and often are unable to find steady work. These men usually do not develop the U.S. standards of living nor do they learn to complain about violations of labor laws. Frequently they alternate between temporary jobs in the United States and intermittent employment in their home towns.

These networks have become more important to the success of Mexican workers in the United States than their legal status. An experienced migrant from a well-established network can feel very secure in the United States even if he is undocumented and must occasionally reenter the country after being deported.

Mexicans in the U.S. Labor Market

We can begin to evaluate the impact of Mexican immigration on the labor market by looking carefully at the types of jobs held by Mexican immigrants. For this purpose it is useful to view the U.S. wage labor market as comprising four hierarchically arranged segments.[3] At the top is the independent primary segment where we find nurses, teachers, social workers, and engineers. These workers are highly paid, enjoy a large degree of occupational mobility and employment security, and hold college-level degrees or equivalent amounts of experience. Next is the high-wage manual labor segment[4] that is occupied by highly-paid factory operatives, skilled craftsmen, truck and bus drivers, and mechanics. These positions are frequently unionized, offer moderate incomes and employment security, but also suffer from limited opportunities for occupational mobility and little independence. Still further down we find the secondary segment where workers hold jobs as low-wage factory operatives, unskilled laborers, service workers, stockers, and fast-food workers. These positions are predominantly non-unionized, pay low wages, and offer little job security or opportunity for upward mobility. Finally, at the bottom of the job market, we find the immigrant-dominated depressed secondary segment where employers rely on low-wage, high-turnover labor forces to perform highly routinized tasks. In these markets, violations of labor law are common; workers are frequently required to work volunteer hours without pay, receive no wage premium for overtime hours, and are subject to harsh supervision. These depressed secondary labor markets are found in agricultural, service, manufacturing (especially subcontracted manufacturing), and construction industries.

Mexicans from immature networks usually work in the depressed secondary segment. As these workers gain more experience and become established in the United States, they may move up to higher segments. Settled immigrants, for example, often can be found in the high-wage, manual labor segment.[5]

Declining Position of U.S. Labor

Given this placement of Mexican workers in the U.S. labor market, why have their numbers increased in recent years, and what has been the impact of their presence on the ability and willingness of workers to defend themselves in the work place?

If we examine the economic and demographic changes of recent decades and the response of the U.S. labor

movement to these changes, we can obtain a historical
perspective on macrolevel developments in the labor
market. In the period from 1945 to 1970 when the
United States was the predominant producer of consumer
goods worldwide, U.S. manufacturing, transportation,
and mining workers made considerable gains in their
standards of living. They did so with the help of a
strong and politically powerful union movement. The
differential between the wages of skilled and unskilled
workers narrowed generally through these years. Even
in peripheral industries, subject to cyclical booms and
busts, progress was made by workers and their unions.[6]
For example, the labor movement was able to win the
extension of minimum-wage coverage to workers in the
service industries in the 1960s and to farm workers in
the 1970s.

These favorable macroeconomic conditions had
changed dramatically by the late 1960s. International
competition from Western Europe, Japan, and the Third
World intensified. Energy costs skyrocketed. Employers
reacted to the changing international economic environment with efforts to reduce their production costs.
Labor costs became a prime target for reductions.
Since the early 1970s, workers have suffered a series
of setbacks. The median real spendable income for
workers has stagnated since 1973, and by 1981 wages had
fallen to the levels of the 1961-1962 period.[7]
Accidents reported for workers in the high-wage manual
labor segment rose during the 1970s after declining in
the postwar years.[8] The enforcement of fair labor
standards and occupational safety and health standards
have received less attention in recent years. In
addition, since 1968 many corporations have moved large
portions of their operations from the highly unionized
Northeast, to the South and Southwest, regions with
historically weak union movements.[9] Industrial reloca-
tion has made it more difficult for workers to organize
to protect their labor rights.

Compounding the problems of working people has
been the anti-union shift in public attitudes. In the
immediate postwar years, labor unions were respected
institutions and the U.S. public could be relied on to
honor work stoppages and picket lines. Company
managers could not count on an abundant supply of
strikebreakers with which to soften union demands. But
as recent strikes in transportation, mining, and agriculture demonstrate, employers now have the real option
of permanently changing their labor forces to defeat
striking workers.[10]

Most important, since the early 1970s, the labor
movement has lost strength among working people.
Nationwide, the portion of the labor force claiming
union affiliation fell from 31 percent in 1970 to 25

percent in 1980.[11] In California the percentage of
production workers represented by unions fell from a
high of 69 percent in 1951 to 60 percent in 1970. By
1981 the figure had fallen to a mere 41 percent--a
decline of one-third in just one decade![12]

Demographic and Job Quality Changes

Apart from this general decline in the power of
wage workers, important changes have taken place in the
kinds of jobs generated by the U.S. economy and in the
demographic makeup of the working population. The
shift from production line jobs to service jobs has
been well publicized and requires little comment here.
Many of the new jobs in services are "good jobs" in the
sense that they are highly skilled positions requiring
specialized training and knowledge. The service industries, for example, require a high percentage of professional and managerial workers. But most jobs
created in the services are not highly skilled. Many
positions have been created for bookkeepers, auditors,
engineers, and managers, but even more jobs are being
created for janitors, gardeners, stockers, security
guards, kitchen helpers, laborers, and other unskilled
workers.

The Bureau of Labor Statistics predicts that
between 1978 and 1990 150,000 new jobs will be created
for computer programmers and 200,000 new jobs for
system analysts, but it also forecasts 600,000 new
positions for janitors and 300,000 new openings for
kitchen helpers and fast-food workers.[13]

This trend toward an increasing number of "bad
jobs" was less noticeable in the period between 1950
and 1975 because many of these positions were filled
by new entrants into the labor market. Young people,
women, and blacks all dramatically increased their
numbers in the labor market during these years. However, rising educational levels among women and blacks
have reduced their willingness to hold these low paying
jobs. The rising quantities of public assistance
received by both these groups means that fewer im-
poverished individuals are actually forced to accept
"bad jobs." Meanwhile, the number of young people
entering the work force is declining with the aging of
the baby-boom generation, and the rate of increase of
female labor force participation has leveled off since
the late 1970s. Thus, although workers willing to hold
poor-paying "bad jobs" are increasingly in demand,
fewer domestic workers are interested in such jobs.
This disparity has created the conditions under which
networks of Mexican immigrants have discovered abundant
employment opportunities in California's labor markets.

At the same time, unions have not concentrated
their energies on the fast-growth job segments where
most Mexican immigrants congregate. One important
reason for this lack of interest has been the language
and cultural barriers that separate white union leaders
from the immigrant rank and file workers. Instead,
unions have directed their efforts toward organizing
highly paid primary segment workers such as nurses,
public employees, social workers, and teachers. In
abandoning some of the more depressed sectors of the
job market, unions have focused on areas where they see
greater opportunities for success.

The Role of Mexicans

This historical sketch shows how the demand for
Mexican workers came into being, but it does not answer
our central questions: Are Mexican workers directly
responsible for degrading U.S. wage levels and working
conditions? Are they displacing U.S. workers? Are
they responsible for the observed decline in the power
of labor unions?

At first glance we are tempted to answer yes. In
many industries where Mexicans are numerous, union
strength is declining. For example, in California's
eating, drinking, and lodging establishments, where
employment has grown by at least one-quarter in the
last few years, union membership dropped by 19 percent
between 1975 and 1981. Similarly, in apparel manufacturing, union membership fell by one-fifth between 1975
and 1981 whereas employment rose by one-fifth. In construction, more union workers were employed in 1965
than are today despite enormous growth in the industry.
In 1965, practically all construction workers in
California were unionized; today less than three-
fourths are.[14]

But we should not generalize too hastily. Union
strength is declining in many industries, not solely
those in which Mexicans work. In addition, foreign
competition, demographic shifts, union policies and
outlook, the activities of large corporations, and the
actions of governmental regulatory bodies have all
played important roles in the decline of the U.S. labor
movement. Furthermore, the role of Mexicans in labor
markets is extremely diverse. To discover whether
Mexicans are responsible for the loss of worker
strength, we must narrow our discussion to specific
groups of Mexicans, in particular labor markets.

It is easy to understand that employers can use
Mexican workers as a tool with which to reduce their
labor costs and weaken unions. For example, unionized
employers can subcontract portions of their production

work to nonunion firms that rely entirely on low-wage,
immigrant workers. They can stratify their work forces
by race and familiarity with U.S. labor laws in order
to cultivate work force divisions and weaken union
strength. They can use the threat of competition from
nonunion firms employing low-wage immigrant labor to
wring concessions from their own work forces. These
cost-cutting strategies involving immigrants are potentially available to employers. The real question is
how and when are they used and who suffers because of
their use--domestic workers, other Mexicans, or no one?

CASE STUDIES

It would be nice if we could deduce in general
terms how these potential cost-cutting strategies have
affected the U.S. labor market. But to be accurate, we
must look at concrete examples from local labor markets
where Mexicans work. From these, we can derive general
conclusions about how and when employers have used
these strategies and about the effects of their use.
For at bottom this issue is not theoretical, but
empirical. In this section we will review developments
in seven California labor markets that reveal the diverse roles played by Mexican workers.

Construction Clean-up Workers in Orange County

In Orange County, California, the construction
industry grew rapidly during the 1970s, particularly
among residential construction contractors.[15] Employment, for example, shot up by more than 84 percent
during the decade.[16]
The industry was heavily unionized. Three-fourths
of the area's construction workers were members of
unions in 1978, but as we shall see, this membership
did not guarantee protection of their labor rights.
Within the construction industry specialized clean-up
firms are contracted to remove the debris at a construction site after skilled craftsmen have completed
their work. In the 1970s, this segment of the industry
was dominated by several medium-sized firms.
During the 1960s and early 1970s, clean-up work,
which was relatively plentiful and well-paid, was performed mostly by settled Mexican immigrants. But wage
and working conditions underwent disturbing changes
during the 1970s. In the 1970-1975 period, the union
pay scale for construction clean-up work was the same
as that for general labor. By the end of the decade,
however, general laborers were officially earning 28
percent more than clean-up workers. More important,

clean-up contractors had begun to systematically under-report hours by as much as one-half. As a result, workers actually received as little as $3 to $4 per hour and were denied many fringe benefits.

What had happened? Clean-up contractors had gradually turned to groups of recently immigrated, short-term Mexican migrants to staff their work crews. These workers readily accepted the low-wage jobs offered them and worked without complaining about the blatant violations of the labor contract. The veteran Mexican workers soon found these degraded working conditions unacceptable and began to abandon the construction industry for more lucrative factory employment.

Orange County's construction industry is a clear example of how employers can switch from mature immigrant networks to immature ones and thereby degrade wages and working conditions without having to formally abrogate their union contracts.

Ventura County Citrus Pickers

During the 1960s and early 1970s, progressive citrus packers in Ventura County, California, made efforts to stabilize a previously migrant Mexican labor force.[17] Packing house managers, the dominant figures in the citrus industry, suffered a rude shock in 1965 when the bracero program of contract Mexican labor was discontinued. The packing houses, which had developed a nearly total dependence on imported Mexican labor, soon found themselves unable to find domestic replacements for the 3,000 braceros they lost.

Citrus picking is relatively stable work owing to its long harvest season and the stable demand for citrus fruit that results from federal regulation of citrus marketing. As a result, progressive elements in the packing houses determined that operating with a permanent, year-round work force would be cost-effective, and they began to institute a series of changes aimed at stabilizing their Mexican labor crews: (1) they legalized a large number of the exbraceros and their children; (2) they encouraged the Mexicans to settle and to bring their families to the United States; and (3) they offered their pickers fringe benefits packages as well as attractive piece-rate wages.

By the early 1970s, a corps of professional Mexican citrus pickers was in place. As the group settled, adopted U.S. consumption patterns, and learned about U.S. labor laws, it began to pressure the packing houses for new gains. Union activity increased as a consequence. At just about the same time, a new

force--the farm labor contractor--emerged in the county.
On the one hand, the United Farm Workers (UFW) launched
a very successful organizing drive among the settled
immigrants; by 1979, perhaps 70 percent of the county's
citrus pickers were under UFW contract. On the other
hand, aggressive farm labor contractors (FLCs), many of
them exforemen with the unionized employers, turned to
new networks of recently immigrated Mexicans to fill
their picking crews.

What resulted was a competitive situation in which
rival labor management systems vied for the right to
harvest the county's citrus fruit. Though the FLCs
paid piece rates comparable to those offered at
unionized work sites, they saved money by providing
their workers with fewer benefits: the contractors
offered less health insurance, no reimbursements for
travel time, less equipment, and less transportation
to work sites. In addition, recently immigrated
workers made few demands on unemployment insurance and
workmen's compensation programs that reduced the FLCs
premiums to these funds. Although the technology of
the pick and the resulting product were identical for
both groups, the differences in benefits expenditures
and other services amounted to a 20 percent labor cost
savings for firms utilizing the work crews of the FLCs.

Over the past five years, the farm labor contractors have enlarged their share of the market to about
50 percent of the citrus crews in Ventura County. As
many as one-half of these crews are composed of recently arrived immigrants who are members of immature
networks. For those older farm workers who have
remained citrus pickers under the FLCs, the presence
of newly arrived immigrants has resulted in a decline
in standards of living. Ventura County's citrus industry represents a clear example of how employers can
cut the fringe benefits of settled immigrants and reduce their labor costs by tapping into immature immigrant networks.

Pole Tomato Workers in San Diego County

At peak season, approximately 5,000 Mexican
workers are employed in San Diego County's tomato
industry, which produces about one-third of California's
fresh market tomatoes.[18] The tomato farms are relatively large-sized operations though they continue to
be run as family businesses. In northern San Diego
County, the land used for tomato farming is quite
valuable and will eventually be developed for real
estate purposes. Tomato farmers operate in a boom-bust
environment; if the demand for tomatoes in the spring
is high and the crop is healthy, they can realize

substantial profits. However, high rents and cultiva-
tion costs mean that their investments are not risk-
free. To minimize their potential losses, north county
farmers have cut their labor costs to an absolute
minimum.

In the early 1970s, most pole tomatoes were grown
in the southern section of the county. There the work
force consisted of commuter Mexican workers who lived
in Tijuana and legally crossed the border each day. By
the mid-1970s, some of these farms operated under UFW
contracts. But by the late 1970s, four-fifths of the industry had moved to northern San Diego County. There,
employers turned to a relatively immature network of
Mexican immigrants who could more easily be exploited.
Oaxacan migrants, who speak native American languages
and come from one of the poorest regions in southern
Mexico, became the industry's new labor force. The
Oaxacans live in open fields where they work in perhaps
the worst conditions anywhere in the United States.
They are paid minimum wages and are sometimes asked to
work volunteer hours without pay. Those failing to meet
standards of productivity are quickly replaced from
among scores of workers who wait patiently nearby.
Social security payments are deducted from their checks
but are frequently credited to bogus accounts. At the
same time, the employers systematically exclude the
previously employed legal commuter Mexican work force
from the north county fields. Few commuters would
tolerate these working conditions in any case.

The example of San Diego County tomato growers
demonstrates that employers can abandon a well-
established immigrant network for an entirely new and
easily exploited group. It also reveals that employers
rely on the tendency of recent arrivals not to complain
in order to violate various housing, occupational
health, and labor standards.

Melon Packers in the Imperial
and San Joaquin Valleys

Until last year, about fifteen packing sheds, split
evenly between the Imperial and San Joaquin Valleys,
packed almost all the melons grown in California.[19]
Several hundred workers were employed in the industry.
Many melon workers spent their winter months in the
Imperial Valley and migrated northward during the
summer season to work in the San Joaquin Valley area
west of Fresno. Traditionally, the core worker group
in the sheds has been the white "fruit tramps," originally migrants from the northwestern United States
and from Oklahoma. In the postwar period, this group
of workers struggled to unionize the melon packing

industry and by the late 1950s had managed to win contracts in all the state's packing sheds. In recent
years, the white fruit tramps have been joined by a
smaller contingent of Chicano workers.

In 1983, the shed owners, who usually bargain
jointly with the union, split into three factions. One
group signed a contract with the union; a second group
closed their packing sheds and switched to a field pack
operation (in which the produce is packed in the field
itself) that relies on Mexican immigrant labor; a third
group refused to sign with the union, challenging their
employees to strike. This last group of firms managed
to finish the season with U.S.-born strikebreakers
hired from the local population. There is reason to
believe that these shed owners view the domestic
strikebreakers as a transitional labor force to be used
only until the field pack process is perfected.

At present, technological factors prevent some
firms from making the field pack a profitable venture.
Under current conditions, the inexpensiveness of field
labor seems to operate as the balancing factor in
determining a firm's ability to shift packing operations to the field. In the sheds, unionized workers
earn between $9 and $20 an hour depending upon the
particular task performed. In the fields, in contrast,
Mexican laborers earn about $4 per hour. Owners can
therefore employ a large work force in the field to
compensate for the current inefficiencies in the field
pack process. Furthermore, packing firm owners know
that they can rely on the continued availability of
low-wage immigrant field packers regardless of the
passage of restrictive immigration legislation owing
to the probable exemption of field labor.

The switch from melon shed packing to field pack
operation offers an example of how employers can use
technological innovations to lower the skill level of
work tasks and to shift from a unionized domestic work
force to a nonunion Mexican immigrant one.

Building Maintenance Workers in
Santa Clara County

In the Santa Clara Valley, sixty miles south of
San Francisco, the demand for building maintenance
workers has grown tremendously over the past two
decades with the valley's emergence as a leading center
for high-technology industries.[20] Between 1960 and
1982, the number of janitors expanded fivefold to its
current level of 11,000. Most of these janitors are
employed by small, nonunion, family-run businesses.
Most of the largest and most lucrative maintenance
contracts, however, are held by larger, unionized

firms. For many years Mexicans have been the predominant ethnic group among maintenance workers whereas other immigrant groups--notably Filipino and Portuguese workers--have been present in smaller numbers.

The most significant development to occur in the industry in recent years has been the emergence of a group of aggressive, nonunion contractors who have begun to compete with the larger union firms for the most lucrative accounts. These firms, like the farm labor contractors of Ventura County, are managed by exforemen from the unionized firms. Similarly, the nonunion firms have been able to underbid the union firms as a result of their lower labor costs. Nonunion janitors earn between $4 and $5 an hour and receive no health insurance and few other benefits. Union janitors, in contrast, earn between $5 and $7 hourly, are covered by health insurance and a pension program, and receive paid vacations and sick leave.

In the 1978-1983 period, many client firms switched their maintenance contracts to the newer nonunion firms. In addition, the janitors' union has been forced to adopt several important concessionary measures to impede the erosion of its membership base. In 1982, the union instituted a four-year new member advancement program that established a lower pay scale for newly hired workers, thus enabling unionized firms to compete with cheaper nonunion shops. The union has also been forced to accept the increased use of part-time workers who earn less and are not eligible for fringe benefits. Most important, the union's effectiveness in bargaining with management has been sapped by the implicit understanding that client firms can swiftly shift their accounts to nonunion firms if the union's demands are deemed excessive.

Interviews with South Bay janitors reveal that the labor forces of both union and nonunion firms are composed overwhelmingly of first generation Mexican immigrants. In the union firms, however, workers tend to be long-term settlers or have close relatives who are. In addition, scattered legal resident immigrants and U.S. citizens are present at the union firms. At the nonunion companies, in contrast, employers have tapped into networks of immigrants who have only recently arrived in the United States and therefore have poor job contacts.

Lower labor costs are not the only factor contributing to the growth of the nonunion segment in this labor market. The 1979-1983 recession pressured client firms to adopt cost-cutting measures, and maintenance services became a prime area for savings. The rapid expansion of the maintenance market may have caught the union short-handed. Union inefficiency may also have been a contributing factor. Still, the case of Santa

Clara Valley building maintenance workers demonstrates that nonunion employers can use the presence of a high-turnover, recently immigrated labor force to cut costs, win contracts away from union firms, and pressure unions to agree to concessions in wages, benefits, and work rules.

Poultry Processors in Sonoma County

Immigrant workers have historically made up the bulk of the production labor force of the poultry processing industry in Sonoma County, California.[21] During the 1950s, Italian immigrants were the predominant ethnic group, but by the late 1960s they had been replaced by Mexican immigrants, many of them former farm workers in the area's wine industry.

The poultry processing industry has expanded enormously in the decades from the 1950s through the 1970s, fueled by consumer attraction to poultry's low relative prices and its supposed dietary advantages. The industry has become geographically concentrated in the southeastern United States; California is actually a net importer of poultry. Poultry production shifted to the Southeast because of the area's lower taxes and lower feed and land costs, and because of the availability of a low-wage labor force there. The nonunion workers of Arkansas, Georgia, and Alabama, most of whom are U.S.-born, are paid close to the minimum wage. By contrast, the unionized Mexican labor force of Sonoma County earns close to $7 hourly and receives a full complement of fringe benefits.

In spite of these relatively high wages, Sonoma County's Mexican poultry workers have saved the local processing industry from extinction. No other workers in the area are willing to perform the arduous and dirty tasks involved in defeathering and preparing the birds for market. This fact became most apparent in 1983 when workers at one firm went on strike, eventually winning a wage increase in spite of management's claim that higher labor costs would drive it into bankruptcy. The firm's managers attempted to defeat the strike by recruiting strikebreakers, but few applicants materialized.

The case of Sonoma County poultry workers shows that Mexican immigrants, even undocumented immigrants, do not weaken unions. Settled undocumented workers were among the most militant union activists during the 1983 strike. This case study also demonstrates that domestic workers often refuse to accept the jobs held by Mexican workers. In Sonoma County, this fact proved true even though its poultry workers were the highest paid in the nation. Access to a Mexican labor

force has so far saved the local poultry industry from
extinction and in so doing has preserved the jobs of
domestic workers employed in managerial and administrative positions at the poultry plant.

Luxury Hotel Workers in San Francisco

In the early 1970s, the hotel industry entered a
slump nationwide from which it is just beginning to
recover in the early 1980s. In San Francisco, one of
the premier vacation spots in the nation, the industry
managed to maintain an optimistic outlook throughout
this slump as reflected by the construction of three
new grand hotels.[22]

Historically, hotel work has been among the
poorest paid urban work, though wage levels have risen
somewhat in recent years. Immigrants dominated the
hotel trade in San Francisco prior to 1925, but between
1925 and 1965 U.S.-born workers were predominant.
Since then, Mexicans, Central Americans, and Asians
have taken over the lowest paying jobs; of the approximately 16,000 wage employees in San Francisco's major
hotels, 40 percent are Asian and Latino immigrants.

Despite the increased presence of immigrant
workers, wages relative to other industries are much
higher now than they were in 1960 when U.S.-born
workers were more prevalent. This improvement in wages
is closely related to the success of the union movement
among the workers in the major San Francisco hotels.
Despite cultural and language barriers between the
Latin workers and the union leadership, Spanish
speakers have emerged as some of the most militant
union supporters. Latin caucuses have been formed and
have won important concessions from union leaders.
Spanish translations of the union contract have been
made available. The union has provided assistance to
workers apprehended during Immigration and Naturalization Service (INS) raids, and others have been warned
of impending raids.

In 1980, San Francisco hotel workers launched an
extremely hard-fought strike. Forty-six arrests were
made during a three-week period before an agreement was
finally reached. Again in 1983, workers were preparing
to strike when management settled. On both occasions,
Latin workers, particularly female maids, were among
the strongest advocates of the strike.

In spite of these victories, employers have been
successful in obtaining labor contract provisions that
enable them to exploit the Bay Area's immigrant labor
surplus. For example, hotel managers have pushed
through a new worker apprenticeship program that allows
them to retain workers at wage levels below union scale

during a four-month trial period. At the conclusion of this period, employers may simply replace these workers with new recruits, thus avoiding having to provide any worker full union protection. In addition, managers have abused the on-call system whereby hotels are permitted to hire nonunion workers in emergency situations. These on-call workers have been required to work extra hours at unusually high levels of productivity.

The case of San Francisco's hotel workers highlights the conflicts that can emerge between settled immigrants and more recent arrivals. The settled immigrants, though they may be undocumented, are extremely militant in defense of what is probably the best union hotel contract in the nation. But just outside the hotels' doors await the newly arrived workers who employers can use to cut labor costs and to undermine union gains.

CONCLUSIONS

To summarize, the foregoing case studies reveal that employers have utilized Mexican immigrant workers as components in several cost-reducing strategies:

1. Employers have been able to cut wages and degrade working conditions by abandoning a group of settled immigrant workers for a newly arrived network of immigrants (in the San Diego County tomato industry).
2. Employers have been able to cut wages and degrade working conditions without breaking their union contracts by tapping into immature immigrant networks (in Orange County's construction clean-up industry).
3. Client firms have been able to reduce their labor costs without directly confronting the unions involved by shifting their contracts to nonunion employers that rely more heavily on recently immigrated workers (in the Santa Clara Valley building maintenance and Ventura County citrus industries).
4. Employers have used immigrant workers to enable them to implement technological changes in their production processes (in the melon packing industry).
5. Employers have used settled Mexican immigrants to preserve an industry when domestic workers refused to hold undesirable jobs (in Sonoma County's poultry industry).
6. Employers have used the availability of newcomer immigrants to abuse certain provisions

in their labor contracts (in San Francisco's
luxury hotel industry).

From these empirical findings we can draw three
general conclusions. First, employers that can tap
into networks of recently immigrated Mexican workers
can use a set of cost-cutting strategies unavailable
to those who must rely on more established labor
forces. Second, the workers most often displaced by
employers who switch to networks of recently immigrated
workers are not domestic workers, as is frequently
claimed, but the more settled Mexican immigrants: The
primary victims of immigrant induced displacement are
other immigrants. Finally, the crucial factor in
determining how easily Mexicans will tolerate exploi-
tive labor conditions is not primarily their legal
status, but rather the strength of their migratory network, the length of time they have spent in the United
States, and whether their nuclear family is present.
These conclusions suggest that the major threat to U.S.
workers and their unions is not immigration per se but
the ability of employers to turn continually to new
networks of recently immigrated Mexicans.

What would happen if the supply of high-turnover
new immigrants could somehow be limited? Employers
would be forced either to employ larger numbers of
settled immigrants or domestic workers, to shut down
their operations or relocate elsewhere, or to become
distributors of foreign-produced goods. In the case
studies, the restriction on new entrants would probably
have the following effects: Janitors, citrus pickers,
and construction workers would be increasingly drawn
from the settled immigrant population; the melon packing sheds would be forced to postpone their move to the
field pack until its technology had been perfected; the
tomato growers might be forced to close down since they
compete directly with Mexican growers just south of the
border who utilize an identical work force; finally,
the hotel and poultry industries already rely on
settled work forces and would thus experience few
changes.

Restricting the Flow of Mexican Immigrants

Is it realistic to assume that the influx of high-
turnover, recently immigrated workers can be slowed by
pursuing the immigration reform measures currently
under consideration? These measures include reliance
on factory or job-site raids and employer sanctions.

Job-site raids, or factory surveys, as they are
called by the Immigration and Naturalization Service
(INS), have proved ineffective as a means of permanently

removing undocumented workers from the U.S. labor
market. Journalistic reports by the Los Angeles Times,
the Wall Street Journal, and the Chicago Tribune have
reached a common conclusion that most undocumented
workers apprehended during job-site raids quickly
return to the area in which they were seized and are
often rehired at the very firms from which they were
removed. These findings are corroborated by the data
we collected in several local California labor markets.
Moreover, the vacancies created by INS raids, when not
immediately filled by returning deportees, are most
often filled by other immigrant workers.

The job sectors in which most recently immigrated
workers congregate--the depressed secondary segment--
have experienced secular deteriorations of wage scales
and working conditions, the result of their historical
linkage with immigrant labor. For years, recruitment
networks anchored in the immigrant community have
channeled a steady supply of low-wage labor to
employers operating in these segments. Working conditions in these firms have deteriorated to the point at
which jobs are no longer attractive to domestic
workers. Merely creating a job vacancy in these
sectors will not change their character as immigrant
jobs. To remove these positions from the immigrant-
dominated secondary segment would require that they be
upgraded in terms of wages, working conditions, opportunities for advancement, and methods of supervision.
It is unclear in many cases whether employers will be
willing or able to endure the resulting labor cost
increases.

In addition, job-site raids fail to distinguish
between the newcomer immigrant and the more permanent
settler migrants. Often companies lose long-time, key
personnel during INS raids, crippling their operations.
These permanent settlers--documented or not--will
return because their lives have become rooted north
of the border.[23]

Nor can the problem be resolved by imposing
employer sanctions. The fining of employers found to
be knowingly hiring undocumented workers--the so-called
employer sanctions scheme--has been proved ineffective
by several studies.[24] More important, it is extremely
unlikely that the federal government will, in this era
of massive budget deficits, be willing to allocate the
resources necessary to see that sanctions are uniformly
enforced. Similar to the pattern of compliance with
Occupational Safety and Health Administration (OSHA)
regulations, the document review requirements of
employer sanctions are likely to be carried out by the
largest, well-established firms that possess the
administrative resources to support the increased
paper-work load. Smaller firms, lacking administrative

personnel, will have greater incentive to attempt to
evade the law. The result will not be to control the
supply of recent immigrants, but to crowd these immigrants into the smaller firms where depressed secondary
segment conditions are more likely to prevail. There
their vulnerability will be heightened by their
employers' knowledge that they have few alternate
employment options.

Moreover, occupational mobility for the settler undocumented immigrant will be made much more difficult as
the gap between small and large firms grows. Employer
sanctions will serve to harden the divisions between
the depressed secondary segment and the higher strata
of the job market, creating a permanent underclass of
immigrant workers concentrated in the poorest paying,
dead-end jobs. In the case of employer sanctions, an
incompletely enforced law will be worse than no law
at all.

Requirements for a Solution

The problems created by the continued influx of
high-turnover, newcomer Mexican immigrants will not be
solved by piecemeal actions that fail to take into
consideration the complexity of the interaction between
Mexican immigration and U.S. labor markets. We believe
that the solution to the labor market issue will have
to be found in structural changes in the U.S. and
Mexican economics and societies. In particular, we
envision five changes that would have to be considered
if a thorough debate on the immigration issue is to
take place.

First, an adequate number of decent jobs in the
United States need to be created that would be attractive to current and future domestic participants in
the labor market. Second, adequate amounts of development resources need to be focused on the source regions
in Mexico that send most migrants to the United States.
Next the United States should grant a generous amnesty
to those Mexicans now working in the United States or
who have worked here repeatedly. Also, the United
States must recognize that for historical reasons,
Mexicans should receive a large share of the permanent
immigration slots open for prospective legal immigrants. Finally, a method would have to be devised
for controlling the entry of high-turnover, short-term
migrants or of channeling Mexican workers into permanent as opposed to temporary migration.

NOTES

1. See Carlos Zazueta, "Mexican Workers in the United States: Some Initial Results and Methodological Considerations of the National Household Survey of Emigration (ENEFNEU), Mexican Department of Labor (CENIET)," paper prepared for the Working Group on Mexican Migrants and U.S. Responsibility, Center for Philosophy and Public Policy, University of Maryland, 1980.

2. Annual Planning Information, California, 1983-84, Employment Development Department, State of California, 1983.

3. For an overview of theories of labor market segmentation, see Irvin Sobel, "Human Capital and Institutional Theories of the Labor Market: Rivals or Complements?" Journal of Economics Issues, March 1982, pp. 255-272. Michael J. Piore's Birds of Passage: Migrant Labor and Industrial Societies (Cambridge: Cambridge University Press, 1979), relates the issue of immigration to segmented labor market theory.

4. This phrase was coined by Jeffrey Avina, research associate of the Center for U.S.-Mexican Studies, University of California at San Diego.

5. For example, Hispanics represented 14.6 percent of the skilled craftspeople in California in 1980, but they made up only 13.4 percent of the state's total labor force. See "Manpower Information for Affirmative Action Reports," Employment Development Department, State of California, 1980.

6. See David Gordon, Richard Edwards, and Michael Reich, Segmented Work, Divided Workers: The Historical Transformations of Labor in the U.S. (Cambridge: Cambridge University Press, 1982), pp. 188, 197, 218. Also see Bennett Harrison and Barry Bluestone, The Deindustrialization of America (New York: Basic Books, 1982), pp. 133-139.

7. See Gordon et al., Segmented Work, p. 168, and U.S. Department of Labor, Monthly Labor Review, July 1981, table 20.

8. Ibid., p. 216.

9. Ibid., p. 218, and Harrison and Bluestone, Deindustrialization of America, pp. 82-92.

10. Among the more highly publicized strikes in these industries have been the PATCO strike, the Phelps Dodge Copper Mine strike, and the Greyhound strike.

11. U.S. Bureau of the Census, Statistical Abstract of the U.S. 1984 (Washington, D.C.: Government Printing Office, 1984), p. 440.

12. "Union Labor in California, 1977, 1979, 1981," Division of Labor Statistics and Research, Department

of Industrial Relations, State of California, December 1982.

13.   See Henry M. Levin and Russell W. Rumberger, "The Educational Implications of High Technology," Institute for Research on Educational Finance and Governance, School of Education, Stanford University, p. 5.

14.   "Union Labor in California." In the construction industry, government statistics severely underreport small nonunion firms, many of which employ immigrant workers. Thus official estimates of the nonunion share of the construction market are likely to be smaller than the actual figure.

15.   Richard Mines, "The Development of a Community Tradition of Migration," Monograph no. 3, Center for U.S.-Mexican Studies, University of California at San Diego, February 1981, p. 141.

16.   Employment in construction has fallen precipitously in the 1980s in Orange County. See "Annual Planning Information, 1983-84, Anaheim-Santa Ana-Garden Grove," Employment Development Department, State of California, 1984.

17.   See Richard Mines and Ricardo Anzaldua, "New Migrants vs. Old Migrants," Monograph no. 9, Center for U.S.-Mexican Studies, University of California at San Diego, 1982.

18.   See Mines and Anzaldua, "New Migrants vs. Old Migrants," and Joe Nalvan and C. Frederickson, "The Employers' View: Implications for a Guest Worker Program," Community Research Associates, Inc., 1982.

19.   This case study is based on data obtained from journalistic accounts in local newspapers, interviews with officials of California's Employment Development Department in Los Banos, and discussions with Keith Jones, union official with the Fruit and Vegetable Workers Union, Local 78-b.

20.   This case study is based on interviews and research by Michael Kaufman, research associate of the Center for U.S.-Mexican Studies, University of California at San Diego.

21.   This case study is based on interviews and research by Michael Kaufman, research associate of the Center for U.S.-Mexican Studies, University of California at San Diego.

22.   This case study is based on interviews and research by Hector Ramos, research associate of the Center for U.S.-Mexican Studies, University of California at San Diego.

23.   These settled workers often hold jobs attractive to domestic workers. But it is clearly futile to deport workers in whom employers have invested years of training and who often have built up considerable assets in the United States.

24. For a sampling of the literature on the failure of employer sanctions legislation, see Mark J. Miller and Philip Martin, <u>Administering Foreign-Worker Programs: Lessons From Europe</u> (Lexington, Mass.: Lexington Books, 1982), and "Information on the Enforcement of Laws Regarding Employment of Aliens in Selected Countries," Report to Congress, Government Accounting Office, August 1982.

Comments

Alan Richards

Four problems beset the study of international migration: (1) data limitations, (2) analytical difficulties, (3) ethical conundrums, and (4) political quandaries. The mobility of all migrants and the illegality of some lead to serious data deficiencies; for example, we do not know how many Mexican citizens work in the United States, much less how many are employed in specific industries and states. Even when reasonable estimates are constructed, analysts must also disentangle supply from demand effects and assess the importance of general rather than partial equilibrium impacts to understand the impact of immigration on U.S. labor markets.

Because of such data and analytical difficulties, it is hardly surprising that the study of migration generates so much controversy. Ethical and political dilemmas make matters worse. Only a Pangloss could argue that migration harms <u>no one</u>. Whatever one thinks about the long-run, overall, social impacts, it is undeniable that some U.S. workers are adversely affected in the short run; further, these workers are poor (by U.S. standards). At the same time, of course, other poor Americans, and certainly even poorer Mexicans, gain from the process. Consequently, <u>any</u> migration policy implies that <u>some</u> poor people lose.

This ethical problem contributes to the bizarre political coalitions that migration debates engender. Open borders are promoted by civil rights groups, some Mexican-American political leaders--and large Southwestern growers and sweat-shop operators. Immigration restriction is advocated by some Black groups, by trade unions--and by Anglo racists. Such coalitions make people uncomfortable and offer numerous guilt-by-association temptations to opponents of any policy.

These four problems ensure that migration questions have no easy answers. The best that can be done is to try to establish a framework for analysis that

recognizes these issues. Optimal policies do not
exist; categorical assertions ring hollow. Whatever
is done, poor people will lose. Negotiation and compromise are essential. One of the best characteristics
of both these chapters is that they seem to have been
written in this spirit.

Clearly, the causes and consequences of migration
on both sides of the border should be studied. Unfortunately, the chapters neglect the impacts on Mexican
development. This omission is a pity, especially since
both authors have done pioneering work on this very
subject.[1] The chapters focus exclusively on the pull
(demand) factors in the United States and on the impact
on U.S. labor markets. Although such issues are important, the forces underlying Mexican migration and the
impacts on Mexico should receive equal attention.

In Chapter 6, Jorge Bustamante places great stress
on the need for a bilateral approach to migration
policy. Given the (unmentioned) impacts on Mexico, I
agree with this perspective. However, his insistence
that the Mexican constitution forbids the government to
interfere in any way with the movements of its citizens
seems inconsistent with a bilateral approach. If bilateral negotiations are to mean anything, then both
sides must be willing to compromise: The United States
must let in perhaps more Mexicans than it might at
first wish, whereas Mexico must send rather fewer than
it desires. Only if this constitutional argument is
the opening gambit in a negotiation is it consistent
with Bustamante's desire for a bilateral solution to
migration problems.[2]

Bustamante also points to several (allegedly) new
features of migration. He argues that Mexican inflation and the devaluation of the peso are reducing
migration by making it prohibitively expensive. No
doubt the costs have gone up; the benefits have increased as well, of course, and I suspect that inter-
mediaries will be found to extend the larger amount of
credit that may now be necessary for emigration. He
points to a complex pattern of labor shortages combined with labor surpluses that Mexican emigration
creates in the sending areas. This scheme is highly
plausible and is confirmed by research on other labor-
exporting countries, such as Turkey and Egypt.[3]
Different kinds of labor are highly imperfect substitutes for each other, on both sides of the border.
He stresses that employers in the Silicon Valley have
launched explicit campaigns to recruit immigrant
workers. This is also consistent with a large amount
of literature that stresses that migration-for-work
streams are almost invariably employer initiated; in
the United States the tradition dates back to the
Civil War.[4]

The demise of the Simpson-Mazzoli bill, which Bustamante mentions, illustrates the analytical problems facing migration researchers. It is not obvious that changes in the U.S. unemployment rate are the key to the bill's failure. As we would expect, both supporters and opponents of the bill were quite diverse. The interplay of these complex coalitions, which were using the bill's progress through the House for other purposes (e.g., Democrats versus the Republican president), generated the outcome. Changes in unemployment may or may not have played an important role. The point must be demonstrated, not just asserted.

Finally, Bustamante stresses the U.S. need for unskilled labor. He is hardly alone in such a view.[5] Such arguments typically rely on an aggregate analysis of the whole U.S. economy (e.g., Clark Reynolds used a Cobb-Douglass production function, with one kind of labor input). These models conceal as much as they reveal because they assume that all types of labor are perfect substitutes. But analysis of specific labor markets, such as that by Richard Mines and Michael Kaufman, shows that the impacts of migration are highly concentrated both geographically and occupationally. Most Mexican immigrants find work at the lower end of job hierarchies, particularly in California and more generally in the Southwest.

Microlevel studies of the impact of migration on specific labor markets, on the other hand, often suffer from a different problem: They fail to disentangle supply and demand effects. Debates on the impact of migration on U.S. workers have too often simply compared regional unemployment rates with known immigration. Fluctuations in demand for the different product mixes of different regions have been neglected. Much more detailed, disaggregated research that isolates geographical and industry variables from immigration itself is badly needed.

It is interesting that Mines and Kaufman do not argue that there is direct labor displacement. The issue is the stagnation, even the fall, of wages and working conditions at the low end of the U.S. labor market. Most participants in the migration debate agree that shortages of labor in the United States in the medium to long run are at the lower end of the labor market. Since there is little evidence of such shortages at the upper end of the labor market, ceteris paribus, this would reduce inequality of earnings in the United States.

The problem, of course, is that the ceteris are not paribus: Changes in technology, industrial plant location, government welfare policies, and so forth may undercut such an equalizing tendency as readily as

continued Mexican immigration. Migration is only one
of many forces shaping the distribution of earnings in
the United States. The "second best" problem for
policy is acute.

Mines and Kaufman's stress on the importance of
new immigrants for U.S. labor markets seems valid and
important. The use of illegal, newly arrived Mexican
immigrants as strikebreakers or union deflectors fits
into a long pattern in U.S. labor history. In the late
1870s, anthracite coal mine owners used newly recruited
South and East European peasants to break strikes of
Irish workers. Henry Frick's agents actively recruited
new immigrants to help break the Homestead Steel strike
in 1892. Blacks were extensively recruited for the
same purpose during World War I and the 1920s. Such a
pattern, of course, both feeds upon and reinforces the
racism of domestic workers, who may ignore and in
earlier periods exclude minority workers from unions,
making the new recruits more willing to act as strikebreakers, leading in turn to more racism, and so on.
One can only hope that such a vicious circle will be
avoided as increasing numbers of Mexicans enter the
U.S. labor market; the historical record, however, is
disquieting.

Mines and Kaufman argue that the example of the
San Francisco hotel workers shows that the length of
residence in the United States, not ethnic origin,
explains immigrant workers' trade union activity. The
history of U.S. labor from 1907 to 1912 supports this
view. This period witnessed a sharp upsurge in strikes
by immigrants, most of whom were first-generation immigrants, but who had been in the United States long
enough (in this case, roughly six to seven years) to
become accustomed to U.S. wages and working conditions.
Of course, again one must scrutinize a whole array of
demand factors, as well as any factors other than immigration that might affect the elasticity of labor
supply, before one can arrive at firm conclusions on
the role of immigration in trade union success or
failure. However, U.S. labor history does indicate the
difficulty of having "trade unionism in one country."[6]

Some analysts of immigration believe that the
impact of recent immigrants on wages and working conditions delays technological changes in the United
States.[7] In California agriculture, for example, they
argue that immigration has merely delayed the inevitable mechanization of certain crops. This is possible,
but again, numerous additional factors must be considered. Some kinds of technological change have been
adopted while switching to (more docile) new immigrants; that was a principal reason for their recruitment by Homestead Steel in 1892. New technologies
often create new, highly monotonous and unappealing

jobs.[8] The impacts of immigration on U.S. labor markets
require detailed empirical research into all the forces
shaping the demand and supply of labor. Mines and
Kaufman's study is an important beginning, but clearly
a great deal more research needs to be done to sort out
these issues.

None of this discussion implies that immigration
should necessarily be restricted, still less that this
be done unilaterally. The point is that there are costs
to some U.S. citizens, and these costs need much closer
study. However, I doubt very much that such costs will
be explained away. At the same time, there are undoubtedly benefits to Mexicans and to Mexico, and
obvious benefits to U.S. consumers, employers, and some
workers from the process. And there are certainly costs
to Mexico as well, as Bustamante mentions. Bilateral
negotiations may be an appropriate approach to regulat-
ing the migration flows.

I tend to think that any agreement will be only a
stopgap, to be undermined nearly as soon as it is signed.
The stark reality is that it is most unlikely that migration on any politically feasible scale will narrow
substantially the wage gap between Mexico and the
United States. Although migration is in some ways the
most politically salient aspect of U.S.-Mexican relations, it is derivative. The long-run economic issues
most germane to Mexican emigration are those of the
wage gap and especially the problems of agriculture in
the sending areas. How can the income of poor Mexicans
be raised? What Mexican policies can best to this?
What political constraints face such policies? How can
U.S. policies help or hinder the implementation of such
policies? These real questions face migration policy.

Readers will notice that the chapters that follow
entirely ignore the agricultural sector, neglect issues
of income distribution, and evade regional economic
issues inside Mexico. These omissions are fairly typical
of discussion of the Mexican economy these days. The
emphasis seems to be exclusively on reviving the rate
of growth of the economy. Although this is a worthy
goal, if such growth resembles that of the recent past,
the forces stimulating migration will not be affected.
For nearly thirty years, Mexican gross domestic product
(GDP) growth has been very respectable by international
standards. Yet the wage gap has not narrowed, the main
sending areas of the northcentral plateau remain poor
(by Mexican standards), and, of course, peasant rain-
fed agriculture is in a serious crisis. Policies and
issues discussed elsewhere in this book will probably
have little effect on migration. The problems that
stimulated these two very interesting chapters are
likely to be with us for a very long time indeed.

234

NOTES

1. For example, Jorge Bustamante, "Undocumented Immigration from Mexico: Research Report," _International Migration Review_ 11, no. 2 (1979): 149-177; and Richard Mines, "Developing a Community Tradition of Migration: A Field Study in Rural Zacateca, Mexico, and California Settlement Areas," Monograph no. 3, Center for U.S.-Mexican Studies, University of California at San Diego, February 1981.

2. Stressing that Mexican migration to the United States is primarily a labor market phenomenon rather than a criminal issue is surely breaking down an open door for any audience of social scientists.

3. See, for example, N. Abadan-Unat et al., _Migration and Development_ (Amsterdam: Nijshoff, 1976); Alan Richards and Philip L. Martin, eds., _Migration, Mechanization, and Agricultural Labor Markets in Egypt_ (Boulder, Colo.: Westview Press, 1983); and Bent Hansen and Samir Radwan, _Employment Opportunities and Equity in Egypt_ (Geneva: International Labor Organization, 1982).

4. Specifically, to the Act to Encourage Immigration of 1864.

5. See, for example, Clark Reynolds, "Labor Market Projections for the United States and Mexico and Current Migration Controversies," _Food Research Institute Studies_ 17, no. 2 (1979): 121-156.

6. Michael Piore argued that the cessation of immigration, combined with the entry of second-generation immigrants into the industrial work force, played an important role in the rise of the Congress of Industrial Organizations (CIO) in the 1930s. See _Birds of Passage: Migrant Labor in Industrial Societies_ (Cambridge: Cambridge University Press, 1979).

7. For example, Philip L. Martin, "Labor-Intensive Agriculture," _Scientific American_ 249, no. 4 (October 1983): 54-59.

8. See the example of the mechanical lettuce harvester described in William Friedland, Amy Barton, and Robert Thomas, _Manufacturing Green Gold_ (Cambridge: Cambridge University Press, 1980).

Part 5

General Assessment

8
Mexico's Integration into the World Economy

Albert Fishlow

It is difficult to do justice to all the issues raised in this book. One must necessarily try to adopt one of two strategies. One may be comprehensive and cover all the points made, or one may provide a summary on the assumption that the essential points must have been touched upon. I will adopt a strategy that may appear to be the latter but that is based on precisely the stimulation of the preceding chapters.

I shall divide my remarks into three categories: (1) the nature of the current crisis; (2) the question of alternative strategies to deal with it; and (3) the implications for United States-Mexico relations.

THE CURRENT CRISIS

One of the central issues that emerges from several of the chapters is how the crisis should be characterized. I believe that it is erroneous to speak about the present crisis solely in terms of a scarcity of foreign exchange or of a foreign exchange gap. First, on any comparative standard, Mexico clearly was affected relatively little by the oil price crisis of 1973, as it was not a significant net importer at that time. And conversely, it was very favorably affected by the increase in price in 1979. Thus the Mexican debt problem is mischaracterized if viewed as sharing all the traits of the problems of other Latin American countries or of other oil-importing countries in general. Indeed, Mexico was least affected in 1973 among all the newly industrialized countries; and of course the effect in Mexico was highly positive in the 1979 period.

The second reason why it seems to me incorrect to characterize the current crisis as one of foreign exchange is that the present situation has continued since the beginning of the 1970s, when it could be

widely recognized that the model of stabilizing growth
was no longer a satisfactory guideline for Mexican
policy. And the present crisis can be viewed as a
continuation of the crises characteristic of all the
recent administrations. Luis Echeverria had a crisis,
and so did José López Portillo. Miguel de la Madrid
is initially seeking to deal with the problems that he
inherited, but it is premature to assume that his
administration will not also face a crisis. To
appraise the outlook, we must seek a deeper understanding of the nature of the problem.

The key to the debt problem is that the style of
Mexican integration into the world economy, which
characterized the period after 1954 with its devaluation, became progressively less satisfactory over the
course of the 1960s. A different mechanism for integration was therefore sought. The weakness of that
integration was precisely the classic fixed exchange
rate mechanism that opened Mexico to capital inflow.
As a result, the Mexican economy became progressively
more dependent upon external debt. This tendency was
apparent already in the late 1960s--I remind you that
Echeverria's strategy aimed at reducing the financial
dependence of Mexican development on the external
sector. This strategy included a fiscal reform as well
as an attempt to redistribute income to make domestic
demand consistent with smaller import requirements,
hoping in this way to deal with Mexico's excessive
demand for capital imports.

Mexico's integration into the international
economy was essentially averted by a series of exogenous circumstances. These circumstances made it
possible for successive administrations to avoid the
internal structure realignment required to change the
nature of external integration. For the Echeverria
administration, the particular deus ex machina was the
rapid expansion of Eurocurrency markets in the wake of
the rise in the price of petroleum. This price rise
made it possible to shift the supply curve of capital
in a favorable fashion, thereby financing a continuing
Mexican deficit in 1973, 1974, and into 1975 until the
crisis peaked.

For the López Portillo regime, the deus ex machina
was the extraordinary willingness of capital markets to
finance Mexican expansion on the basis of future petroleum revenues, a response that permitted Mexico to recover very quickly from the International Monetary Fund
(IMF) stabilization program. The IMF stabilization
program in Mexico in 1976 was the shortest on record,
not because it was successful in terms of internal realignment or because the particular change in relative
prices had been successful in altering the relationship between tradables and nontradables in the Mexican

economy. Rather, it was the shortest because no sooner
had limitations been imposed on Mexican borrowing than
PEMEX was able to go to the external market and borrow
on extraordinarily favorable terms. And this was
followed in 1979 by the windfall gains associated with
revaluation of Mexican petroleum.

Therefore, to see the problem in its short-term
foreign exchange dimension is to define it inadequately.
Such a perspective ignores some of the difficulties
that must be faced in finding a solution to the crisis.
These difficulties also tend to be obscured by projections, some of which indicate that with reasonable
assumptions about oil prices, imports, and exports, the
Mexican economy will arrive at a lower degree of debt
relative to exports by the end of the 1980s, with a
declining debt-service ratio, and will travel on a
trajectory of growth without external limitations.

Such projections, it seems to me, suffer from two
characteristics. First, I have never seen publicly
released projections made by a commercial bank that
indicate that the problem gets worse rather than
better. Assumptions are selected so as to yield the
result that one wishes.

Second, emphasis upon the external side of the
projections ignores the question of realignment of
domestic production and the nature of the internal
incentives needed to change the productive structure.
Especially in Mexico and to some extent in other Latin
American countries, central focus on the debt crisis
limits the range of potential policy and may put the
problem in a wrong perspective. One may be led to
ignore the need for internal realignment that is the
counterpart of the external indebtedness, as well as
the need for import substitution and export promotion
as a part of investment strategy and for reassessment
of the relative role of the public and private sector.

As I see it, the Mexican situation and the 1983
crisis render it more important to focus on the role
of the public sector than on the foreign exchange
shortage.

ALTERNATIVE STRATEGIES TO DEAL WITH CRISIS

If we in fact redefine the crisis as a progressive
crisis of the public sector, not merely in terms of the
deficit that has been one of its manifestations, but
more generally in terms of the question of internal
incentives offered to the private sector to respond,
we will be able to understand the issue of alternative
strategies.

One strategy proposed by the de la Madrid government is to focus very clearly on the public sector.

This strategy argues that if one can get aggregate policy right in reducing the weight of the public sector, it will then become possible to generate the internal savings required to ensure a high level of sustainable growth.

This strategy also argues that getting the public sector right is to get prices right. That is to say, an important part of the breakdown of the public sector results from the fact that it has allowed the state enterprise sector to get out of control and has failed to adopt an appropriate set of pricing rules that would permit enterprise revenues to match their investment requirements, as well as to generate a surplus over and beyond current expenditures for reinvestment.

The second side of the de la Madrid public-sector strategy is continued integration in the world economy. Such integration is predicated on getting prices right, that is, getting the exchange rate right so that one can engage in a policy of promotion of non-oil exports, and getting interest rates right, so that one can rely upon a continuing inflow of private capital, undisturbed by discrepancies between the internal rate and rates prevailing in world markets.

The third, though unspoken, strategy is to get real wages right to permit reduction in the high rate of inflation and to provide an incentive for private investment as a basis for recovery.

Implicit in reducing the public sector and in not making it the leading aspect of a new wave of development is the need to encourage the private sector. Private sectors must experience some relative assurance of profitability. If one does not want to use the exchange rate, explicit subsidies of commercial policy, or credit policy to provide those incentives, then one is back to the classic remedy of checking real wages. This remedy involves a setting in which the continuing pressures from the excess supply of Mexican labor reflect themselves in internal labor markets, rather than being neutralized by spilling over into migration or being hidden by policies that expand public-sector employment and wages for those sufficiently fortunate to find public employment jobs.

Such a strategy has worked well in the context of the short-term stabilization problem. And in part it has worked well because the diagnosis of excess aggregate demand in the period after 1979 was correct. What we have heard of the relative inefficiency of the public sector, as recounted in some chapters, is of course characteristic of any economy, private or public, in which one accelerates growth, and in particular accelerates imports and investment. In that kind of circumstance one creates bottlenecks, which in turn engender inflationary pressures. In the short

run these pressures do not increase supply or even re-
allocate resources, but simply set in motion forces
that reinforce inflation by creating additional wage
demands, uncertainty about relative prices, and tendencies to pass through those wage demands in favored
sectors.

Stabilization that responds well to an excess
demand situation, therefore, is likely to be relatively
successful. This, I submit, is why IMF intervention in
the Mexican case has been so much more successful than
in the case of Argentina or Brazil, where that particular situation was much less prevalent, not to speak
of the Chilean circumstance with its 33 percent unemployment.

The relative success in pursuing the fundamental
objective of short-term stabilization was due to the
decision to reduce inflation rather than to index. The
Mexican economy at the beginning of the de la Madrid
administration was confronted with a polar choice.
With rates of inflation of 100 percent and potentially
more, it could either go through a scheme of indexing
as a mechanism providing reliable rules that would
sustain some degree of private-sector activity as well
as reduce a potential eruption of social pressures from
the laboring class, or go to a situation in which in a
relatively short time one might reverse expectations
and bring inflation rates down to the point where
indexing would no longer be necessary and one could
still use administered rules as a mechanism of adjustment rather than automaticity.

I would argue, however, that the relative
success--because I think it has been a relative
success--of the de la Madrid administration in opting
for that first alternative should not obscure the
questions associated with the medium-term strategy.
Those questions are threefold: The first question is
whether the international economy into which Mexico
must integrate will expand sufficiently to give the
Mexican economy a positive stimulus rather than apply
a break on internal development; in other words, what
will be the relative demands for petroleum and therefore what real windfall benefits will this particular
sector receive in the future as compared to the past.
The second question is what opportunities will Mexico
have for competition in non-oil exports at a time when
a variety of other countries--in particular Latin
American countries--are seeking to enter into world
markets to increase their export shares. The third
question is what will be the access to and the possibility
of resumption of private capital flows in response
to high domestic interest rates in creditor countries,
given the general reluctance of banks to continue
foreign investment abroad and uncertainty regarding

the return of private capital following the extensive capital flight.

Certainly it will be extraordinarily difficult for a Mexican government to resume Mexdollars within the near future. After all, once a Mexdollar has turned out not to be a dollar but a currency that may be turned into a peso at the government's convenience, it becomes difficult to persuade people that the government will not again act in this fashion. That new arbitrariness, introduced into the financial structure, is relatively significant--and whether it can be overcome by getting prices right is a question that must be evaluated. Although the desire for export promotion and efficient import substitution is not new, it remains to be seen whether the circumstances are less favorable now than they were in the past.

It is also important to ask why this strategy, which has been in effect since the early 1970s, has not been successful. Has there simply been a policy failure, caused by a technocracy unable to calculate shadow prices? Or have economists suddenly become gifted, struck on the road to Damascus with a true image of how the Mexican economy should function, whereas in the past they were blind to the realities? I think not. I think such an interpretation of past failure to get prices right obscures a second problem-- getting policy right. Getting prices right has significant redistributional implications within the Mexican economy; it operates to the advantage and disadvantage of different groups whose relative power remains a significant factor in determining what policies are taken. After all, López Portillo, who left office vilified for his nationalization of the banks, had barely three years earlier been the great Mexican president who understood the importance of entering the General Agreement on Tariffs and Trade (GATT), and who was going to lead Mexico into a period of liberalization. To understand the characteristics of the reversal, it is absolutely essential to understand the setting of the Mexican economy and the potential limits of the strategy now presented.

Part of that problem, I suggest, emerges from the internal realignment of forces necessary to get prices right. The income distribution problem is serious in a labor-abundant economy, and has been compounded by the expectations associated with petroleum. The effect of the windfall gains that the Mexican economy enjoyed and the rapid rate of growth experienced has set in motion a notion of opportunity. And that, of course, is reflected in the import statistics. One has only to look at the import statistics for 1978, 1979, and 1980 to understand the nature of the problem. Increases of imports on an order of 30 or 40 percent a

year created the notion of an opportunity of increased
employment and improved standards of living for the
middle class and became part of the perception that
governs the political economy of Mexico into the
future. I submit that this notion will not be easy to
deal with.

A first important factor is migration. Migration
has served as an important balance wheel in the process. It has been important not as a cyclical adjustment to the Mexican economy whatever the relative
changes may be in flows, nor (and I differ here with
Jorge Bustamante's opinion in Chapter 6) is it a response to a particular U.S. demand condition. Rather
it has been a source of a continuing opportunity for
labor to spill over; it has been a source of remit-
tances; it has absorbed a relatively significant part
of Mexican labor supply; and no relative rate of growth
of the Mexican economy over the last decades of the
century will change these facts.

In that sense, when one talks about migration
policy, one is talking about more fundamental factors
than demand or supply conditions in the U.S. market or
whether one is not taking jobs away from Americans.
In a fundamental sense, there are of course general
equilibrium effects. The seven cases that Richard
Mines and Michael Kaufman described in Chapter 7 and
the particular setting of each is of course only part
of the story. While one looks at particular cases--
whether one was able to unionize or not--an additional
chain of events in fact always occurs. Elasticities
of substitution in the labor market are large or small
in particular circumstances, but general equilibrium
effects always exist. The importance of migration, I
suggest, is something that from a Mexican perspective
very importantly has to be left to the market. This
includes the question of whether to maintain the
present migration situation, to go to a guest-worker
scheme, or to adopt some other mechanism, bilateral or
not, to regulate migration. Migration should be permitted to respond to market forces because it has to
serve as the ultimate balance wheel in a market-
oriented strategy. Much of the discussion about migration misses its role in the scheme of things and in the
internal logic of that strategy.

Second, we have to recognize that reorganization
and reform of the whole Mexican political system are
at the heart of the matter. In one way or another,
what lies behind the current Mexican strategy is some
image of an incomes policy, an image of persuading
labor that although nominal wages may not go up substantially, it is part of a positive sum game; that
there will be real rewards in the future if only one
avoids the attempt to increase nominal wages now and

set in motion an inflationary spiral whose only effect
would be a continuing liability to raise real wages in
the future.

Implicit in this strategy is the notion that there
can be an incomes policy concerned with finding a way
in which the Mexican labor movement can have a different type of voice than it now enjoys. And this
again points to the essential role of government in
using its public-sector policy to ensure that real
wages of key groups are less affected than those of
other groups. The control of particular prices--the
mechanism by which one wants to target policy in a
specific way--is and has to be just as much a part of
the de la Madrid strategy as it was of the Echeverria
and López Portillo strategy. Such is the case despite
all the proclamations of efficiency, despite all the
proclamations of getting prices right, despite all the
proclamations of eliminating subsidies and managing to
run the economy right.

In the last analysis, then, one comes down to precisely how to reconstruct the public sector with some
degree of political support, not by getting prices
right but by getting policies right--an important
distinction. To the degree that the de la Madrid
administration accepts the shibboleth of getting prices
right as a substitute for getting policies right, it
will lose out on the internal support that is indispensable for coming to grips with the internal problems
that have characterized Mexican development over the
1970s. These problems are selecting priorities in
terms of sectors, ensuring a sufficient rate of capital
accumulation, and ensuring the reallocation of resources between tradable and nontradable products.

U.S.-MEXICAN RELATIONS

In this distinctive environment, the question of
U.S.-Mexican relations takes on a particular significance. It takes on such a significance, first, for
the obvious reason that Mexico is more closely integrated with the United States than it is with any other
economy with which it has a relationship, and second,
because there is no other developing economy, with the
exception of a few very small ones in the Caribbean,
that is as closely integrated with the United States.

One of the salutory features of many of the
chapters and in particular Chapter 3 by Sidney
Weintraub was the emphasis on an independent U.S.
dynamic. This feature is very important to understand,
compared with the more naive views of integration that
presume that somehow U.S. perceptions will be shaped
dominantly by what goes on in Mexico rather than by the

relationship of the United States with the Soviet
Union, or with Japan, or with Europe. One can speak in
eloquent terms about the fact that Mexico is the third
largest purchaser of U.S. goods, and one can note that
exports have gone down as a consequence of the debt
crisis, but these assertions miss the fundamental existence of the dynamic of other U.S. priorities that must
be taken as givens.

One of these givens, and I think this is obviously
important, is a certain conception of the importance of
reducing the domestic rate of inflation. That priority
is shared in the United States by not only those who
profess Reaganomics or those at the conservative end of
the spectrum, but also by a much wider support group.
This commitment to a lower inflation rate makes
Mexico's problem of integration with the United States
economy much more difficult because it removes external
international inflation as a way of writing off
Mexico's foreign debt and because it reduces the freedom of domestic policy to deviate significantly from
the U.S. rate of inflation. The critical decision is
to slow down U.S. inflation, rather than the decision
about interest rates, which follow rather than precede
and cause inflation. And it is important to understand
the priority in those terms, rather than to blame the
interest rates as such.

U.S. priorities are obviously significant to the
Mexican economy, not merely in the area of global
trade in the context of industrial policy, but also
with regard to its domestic target of inflation. The
same applies very clearly to migration. We see here
the conflict in very blatant fashion. We see it in
the pressures to avoid excessive Mexican competition
from workers coming across the border and competing
with U.S. labor, and we see it in the trade dimension
as well. We see it in the desire not to have Mexican
labor compete in Mexico either. We see it in the
pressures for protection and its use to resolve U.S.
internal political difficulties. Because of the degree
to which we rely on liberal trade within the United
States, the administration is denied an instrument
needed to achieve satisfactory political coalitions and
to implement its own objectives, which may be a social
welfare platform or a platform of cutting public
expenditures.

The immigration problem is complicated further
because it pits newly arriving Mexicans against those
who have been in the United States for a longer period.
And it pits those Mexicans who come for temporary
periods against those who may in fact stay for longer
periods. So the issues begin to be blurred.

I raise these points because I think it is important not to praise the positive sum-ness of this

close U.S.-Mexico relationship in terms that cannot be
sustained. And I think that there is considerable
rhetorical danger when the case is put in terms of how
the United States will benefit, as Secretary of the
Treasury Donald Regan argued before the Congress--if
the United States only gets an IMF quota, then of
course it will send more exports to Mexico. What the
secretary of the Treasury does not say is that for the
IMF program to be successful Mexico must sell more to
the United States than the United States can export to
Mexico. This net import requirement associated with
the strategy goes against the mercantilist grain used
to sell the idea of a closer relationship.

I would argue, in addition, that one should not
overstate the positive sum-ness of the particular
relationship from the standpoint of the uniformity of
the benefits. Too frequently the arguments are made
in terms of the United States and in terms of Mexico,
and in terms of the fact that the two can benefit. Of
course, one wants to consider this aggregate, but any
set of interrelationships involving the two countries
that favors a particular allocation of resources and
a particular set of factor prices will favor some
groups in one country and some groups in the other.
They will not be uniform in their particular impact.
And it is precisely the absence of that uniformity
that must be understood when talking about the nature
of integration.

A final point in talking about positive sum-ness
is the differentiation between the formal relationship
and the market relationship. Whole sets of integrations that escape any kind of control, regulations,
and decisions made in Washington and Mexico City occur
along the border every day. And because they occur
along the border every day, they present constraints
on Mexican decision-making in its internal policy to a
much greater degree than they do on the United States.
But even in the United States, the frequency with
which President Reagan visits the border areas and
promotes special programs to assist those who are hurt
by changes in exchange rates is a direct function of
the proximity to the fall of 1984. The political
cycle is not something unique in a Mexican environment.

A final observation about the United States-
Mexico relationship is the importance of not presuming
that this relationship is ideally bilateral rather than
multilateral, simply because the two countries are integrated and interact. The particular nature of any
solution to the debt problem, for example, will emerge
in a multilateral rather than a bilateral context.
Banks cannot give Mexico special arrangements on
interest rates without being force to extend them to
Brazil and Argentina and a variety of other countries.

Mexican success and astuteness in renegotiating the
debt came because it cleverly announced it was bankrupt
and therefore could not manage its affairs, whereas
Brazil tried to prove that it was efficient and that
competent technicians could deal with the situation.
By saying how incompetent it was, Mexico secured a renegotiation through 1983 and 1984 postponing any payments, whereas Brazil had to come back, day after day,
month after month, in a constant attempt to renego-
tiate. Mexican shrewdness in assessing its situation,
rather than the bilateral quality of the relationship,
was important in that negotiation.

I believe that the great danger that Mexico and
the United States run in trying to secure bilateral
trade agreements is that they are unlikely to be
entirely satisfactory or enduring. The degree to which
the relationship becomes bilateral rather than multilateral clearly places a considerably greater public
presence and weight on the official relationship between the two countries and puts a great deal more
constraint upon the Mexican political system in dealing
with the United States. It becomes much harder for any
Mexican president to follow a policy, such as the one
proposed--getting prices right and integrating into the
world economy--if this occurs in a bilateral negotiating framework rather than in a multilateral one.

So the worst possible U.S. policy step toward
Mexico would be to cause it to be integrated into the
U.S. market on the basis of a special and unique
relationship--a relationship that would cause the
internal efforts to get the Mexican prices right to
fail--because it would operate in guaranteed markets
and in special circumstances. Thus this policy would
offer a deus ex machina for avoiding the internal
questions of Mexican development and for coming to
grips with its internal problems.

I want to conclude on a final point, the question
of linkages and great negotiations. There is a myth
that if U.S. and Mexican representatives would sit
down with good will on both sides and talk over the
broad agenda encompassing the range of interests that
these two countries have in common, they could work out
an agreement that would incorporate all the ways in
which the two countries impinge upon each other, and
assign a set of benefits to each in a fashion that
would make the entire arrangement enduring and beneficial. I think that it is fair to attribute this
ultimate vision to Clark Reynolds, also a contributor
to this volume, the vision of positive sum opportunities that exist for superswaps, supermigrant flows,
supertrade, and superpersons. This particular image
of the great negotiation and the opportunity of depending upon all these linkages--linkages in which the

United States receives guaranteed supplies of oil
cheaply, Mexican workers get good jobs in the United
States, Mexican manufactured products come into the
United States without encountering protectionist
barriers, joint projects are set up, foreign investment
goes to Mexico to create efficient import substitution
and export promotion--is to me not a sign of great
imagination but of lack of realism. An attempt to
establish these linkages by negotiation would only
provide an opportunity to shore up what should have to
stand on its own weight. It would create a vastly
complicated structure that attempted to equilibrate the
variety of benefits and costs on both sides. By the
very nature of the relationship between the countries,
operating in the political and institutional reality,
for the great linkages in fact to occur would require
nothing less than for Mexico to accept a U.S. proconsul
sitting in Mexico City by the side of the Mexican
president and for the United States to surrender the
state of Texas.

9
Changing Strategies

Francisco Gil Díaz

Albert Fishlow has concluded his excellent
summary and synthesis with rather dramatic overtones,
which lead me to start with the narration of the drama
that explains some of the important policy decisions.
I shall intersperse my assessment with comments on the
ideas provided by some participants on the recent
macroexperience of Mexico.

The players in this drama have been there since
the end of the 1940s, although a longer perspective
would probably show a permanent historical thread. In
Mexican economic literature and in the main Latin
American economic journals, a continuing argument has
been waged between what could be called the fiscal
conservatives and the fiscal expansionists. The argument has appeared in diverse forms, schools, and
ideologies. The fiscal conservatives range from representatives of the political Right to those of the Left,
including an important leader of the Communist party,
and in general, the group encompasses orthodox
Marxists. Why the fiscal conservatives were not necessarily all free marketeers than and now is part of the
political story Lance Taylor has discussed in Chapter
5. The struggle was one between sound budgetary
policies and so-called expansionary measures.

Fishlow mentioned the period christened "stabilizing development" (SD). This is a strange name, as if
development could happen otherwise. The consistent
budgetary policies that characterize stabilizing
development can be dated from about 1954 to 1972, a
period about which many people now feel nostalgic.

The fiscal conservatives held the top economic-
policy positions. This was perhaps the main reason
why the line on excessive budgetary expansion was held,
despite the pressures for social expenditures in a
country with so many needs and so many poor people.
The results of their policies were price and exchange-
rate stability combined with rapid growth, which, in

turn, supported political stability.

The end of this period was influenced by the
social turmoil created by the student movement of
1968--a movement of multifarious nature, similar to
the ones that took place all over the world--but it
made some people in Mexico believe the system was in a
critical situation, so that considerable debate and
thinking in the presidential campaign of Luis
Echeverria was dedicated to the causes of the 1968
unrest and what to do about it.

The policy variables, their relationships, and the
objectives sought throughout this period are contained
in a famous document by then Finance Secretary Ortiz-
Mena. This document was instrumental in christening
the period with the name <u>stabilizing development</u>, and
it provided a timely target for the proponents of other
policies. In the document, the beginning of stabilizing development is dated from 1959, but a common policy
can be detected since 1954. In fact, if a personal
common denominator can be found for the epoch, it is
the quiet, influential, and able stewardship of the
central bank by Don Rodrigo Gómez, who was its director
from 1953 to 1970.

At any rate, it will be useful to outline the
characteristics of the 1954-1972 period to clear up
the considerable misunderstandings that arose from the
SD document and from the undocumented criticism of it
by its adversaries. This chore is important because
the misunderstandings that arose from this episode are
partly responsible for some of the policy mistakes made
in the 1972-1982 decade. One way to outline this
period is to review the main arguments of the SD
document.

Tax policy was described in it as designed to
favor investment and to foster savings. The intent of
commercial policy was to protect private enterprise so
that domestic firms would be created or expanded.
Budgetary policy was directed to keep inflation low and
the nominal exchange rate fixed, while foreign credit
was to play a complementary role to domestic savings.
Interest rates were set at the level at which they
would maintain savings inside the country, thereby
providing a positive real rate of return to savers, and
subsidies were incorporated to promote investment.

Opponents of a sound budgetary strategy who had
criticized the government's policies since the early
1950s took advantage of the Ortiz-Mena document and
blamed the strategy it outlined for the 1968 turmoil.
They pointed to the lack of improvement in income distribution, to the many miserable people, and to the
alleged policy of favoring the wealthy. They also
pointed out the low tax load to promote investment,
which they said created an illusion of growth. Another

alleged sin was excessive reliance on foreign credit,
which put the country "in hock." But, so they argued,
there had been no true development: Growth had not
trickled down, and the position of the masses had not
improved.

Such was the analysis some of the critics made of
the period, but now let us look at the facts. Foreign
credit had been relied upon, but it had remained a
reasonable and basically constant fraction of gross
domestic product (GDP) for about nineteen years. The
trade deficit had also remained a moderate and constant
fraction of GDP, so that it presented no threat.
Economic policy had established an equilibrium and a
coherent steady-state set of relationships.

How about the argument that the tax load was kept
very low? Again, the numbers speak for themselves. An
examination of the different components of the Mexican
tax structure shows that taxes were low on consumption,
with excise plus sales taxes a comparatively low proportion of GDP. But even at that time, corporate
income taxes as a fraction of GDP were higher than in
many developed countries and higher than in most developing countries. The personal income tax could
perhaps have been somewhat higher, but the personal
income tax to GDP ratio has usually been low in developing countries, and the Mexican performance was not
much out of line with what one observes elsewhere.

The nominal tax on financial interest income was
low, but not so the tax on the real interest rate
earned by savers. In fact, the total tax--considering
the inflation tax as a tax on nominal-interest income--
was higher than the highest marginal rate in the
personal-income schedule for most of those years. So
taxation might have been increased--probably through
increasing excise and sales taxes--but the realistic
picture is certainly not that of an extremely low level
of taxation or one that could have been easily increased. Nor does it show the privileged treatment of
high incomes that has been portrayed.

Let us now look at the story concerning subsidies.
A lot of subsidies were placed on the books, but many
of them were not implemented. Some critics of the
period have written about the tremendous giveaway
through accelerated depreciation. Accelerated depreciation was in the tax code, but nobody ever made use
of it--a fact that has not been pointed out. It was
not made use of because the law required that this
treatment be demanded by an entire industry, and the
Treasury never authorized a whole industry's petition
to apply accelerated depreciation.

One policy in the SD paper, however, is borne out
by the facts: the protection given to inward-oriented
production through commercial policy, and the intended

stimulus to investment and production through subsidized prices for public goods. The inward orientation of commercial policy started at the end of the 1950s. At the end of the 1950s and the start of the 1960s, there was a tremendous rise in the percentage of imports subject to prior permits. Such imports eventually rose to 60 percent of the total and have never come down from that figure. This has been the basic commercial tool for protecting industry in Mexico, and it has resulted in very high rates of effective and sometimes implicit protection. But also,.protection through prior permits is an unerring device for the creation of monopoly profits when domestic producers have some market power. This has converted some elements of the private sector into enthusiastic supporters of protection through quotas, preferably zero quotas, instead of protection through tariffs.

At the same time that the real prices of public-sector firms had started to deteriorate, the budget was kept under control. The element that gave in-- because something had to give--was public investment, since current expenditures were not reduced. And it was mostly public investment in agriculture and education. Despite many years of spending on education, the figures show that the population has an average schooling of less than four years. Other figures are also striking: The percentage of workers who have either no education or less than six years of primary education is lower--and it is significantly lower--in the early 1980s than it was thirty or forty years ago. Needless to say, the educational level of agricultural workers is also quite insufficient to allow them to improve their productivity. The level and distribution of education very probably explain the unequal distribution among the population of the ability to generate income.

The end of stabilizing development coincides with the start of the Echeverria administration. Echeverria actually continued with the policies of stabilizing development in his first year. As Jaime Serra Puche and Pascual García-Alba have shown, the last years of an administration are usually characterized by excess demand pressures, whereas the first years are characterized by the need to correct those excess demands. The Echeverria administration was no exception. It was confronted initially with such pressures, and an adjustment was made in the administration's first-year budget. The effect of the adjustment was a fall in the rate of growth sharper than had been anticipated or projected by policymakers. As happens to most economists, their predictions were not exact.

But Echeverria had brought into high government positions advocates of expansionary budgets, and the

events of his first year in office led to his lending
an increasingly receptive ear to their arguments. The
good angels were persuasive and the president followed
their advice; the results, however, were not as good
as had been promised or expected, and he became
worried. He was confronted with the trauma created by
the 1968 movement and with the apparent evidence that
the strategy adopted was not producing the desired
results. So at the end of 1971, the decision to change
course 180 degrees was taken. The year 1972 thus marks
the start of the new period.

But was there really a need, as was insistently
argued at the time, to change strategy? I believe
there was, since some of the criticism of the earlier
strategy was, in my view, correct; the problem was that
the things that were changed were not the ones that had
been rightly criticized, and those areas in which
economic policy had been at fault were made worse. One
area that had been criticized--the tax structure--had
room for change. There was an increase in sales and
excise taxes, and the percentage of GDP collected
through taxation increased 4 percentage points during
the Echeverria administration. This is a remarkable
achievement, considering that it had taken from 1940
to 1970 to achieve that same increase, and that the
additional 4-percentage-point gain occurred in only
four years. But, although the change was in the right
direction--since indirect taxes had contributed a comparatively low share to total tax revenue by international standards--tax gains were offset by considerable
erosion in the real income of government firms.

There were other changes. The import substitution
and the excessive protection given to Mexican industry
had been criticized in the strategy followed by stabilizing development. But the balance-of-payments
problems that resulted from excessive budgetary expansion led to a strengthening of protection.

To analyze trade policy in Mexico, its unique
geographical situation has to be taken into account.
Mexico shares a "leaky" border with the most advanced
and diversified consumers' market in the world, which
in addition is dotted with in-bond stores with goods
at prices often even lower than in the United States.
Many Mexican citizens feel comfortable going to a San
Antonio store and ordering a two-door refrigerator to
be delivered to their home one week later. The
delivery of smuggled goods is sometimes even faster
than ordering homemade goods through a Mexican re-
tailer; the quality is often better, and the price--
with the exception of some goods when the Mexican
exchange rate is undervalued--is substantially lower.

So when analyzing trade policy, one has to recognize that the amount of market integration between the

two countries is enormous. Some people, neglecting this fact, look at the size of the Mexican economy and consider it a good case for protection. But once protection sets in, the true openness of the economy makes the manufacturer end up with a small and inefficient scale of production. Recently, an even more worrisome trend has been to protect capital inputs. To the extent that internal, inefficient production of capital goods comes about because of protection, the opportunities Mexican manufacturers have to export will become even more limited. Since protection is achieved through border closings, exporters will have to buy some capital inputs from national producers operating on an even smaller scale and at incredibly high costs.

So, however questionable the merits for protection or closed markets in other economies may be, the geographical nearness of Mexico to the U.S. market must be considered when designing Mexico's trade policy and when interpreting its effects. The consequences of continued and increased protection have been the fostering of monopoly profits, the rising costs of internal production, and an increase in the capital intensity of production, thus requiring greater amounts of savings and creating greater reliance on foreign credit for the private sector while progressively squeezing the export capability.

After this brief portrayal of the main actors and the scenario, we can turn to the closing climactic chapter of this drama, which took place since the early 1970s.

One of the consequences of the change in economic strategy was the loss of price stability. Some of the authors in this book discussed whether inflation in Mexico has been of the cost-push or demand-pull variety. I believe evidence supports the hypothesis that Mexican inflation has been the cost-push type, if cost-inflation is identified with the pressures of international prices, whether that international inflation comes from a raising of the peso-foreign currency exchange rate or from higher prices of world goods. To be sure, demand policies may have had some effect. In those situations in which the budget had created a tremendous amount of excess demand and the exchange rate was no longer defensible, we ended up with an overvalued exchange rate. This happened in 1975 and 1981.

But, even in these two years in which the exchange rate became overvalued, it is not entirely clear whether the reason was excessive demand or the drastic increase in production that took place in those same two years to futilely prevent a worsening in the balance of payments. Once the balance of payments was beyond repair, the nominal exchange rate had to be

abandoned, and the higher nominal exchange rate created
additional inflation, as did the devaluations of 1976
and 1982. But looking at the real exchange rate and
its movement over a long time, one can see that, except
for the two years mentioned, it was practically constant after it lost the undervaluation it acquired from
the 1954 devaluation.

The experience with the real exchange rate, therefore, is consistent with characterizing the internal
inflation as the outside variety, despite the vagaries
in aggregate demand that began in 1972. Furthermore,
the data show no evidence that the end of the stabilizing development period was characterized by an overvalued exchange rate.

One of the objectives of the new strategy was to
decrease Mexico's external dependence. This goal
sounds tragicomic now, looking at the results; Mexico
has never been more dependent on the outside world.
I disagree with Albert Fishlow's view of the nature of
the crisis--whether it comes from a lack of foreign
exchange or from a more basic macroeconomic policy.
The crisis was of a macropolicy nature, and even though
we cannot minimize the fact that there was a foreign-
exchange or external-credit-suspension problem, this
latter is intimately related to the former.

To tell the complete story after the 1976 devaluation, one should mention that in the second half of
1977 the government fixed the exchange rate. It had
not done so until then, and it did not fix it in the
sense that it had been fixed during the stabilizing
development period. However, it did fix it for practical purposes by establishing a system of coverage of
foreign debts by the central bank. This system allowed
firms to get foreign credit and to use it at a cost
equal to the domestic interest rate. The moment this
program was announced it was in great demand by private
firms. As the central bank was in the process of
registering these requests, capital inflow increased,
even before the increases in oil prices. Mexico was
already exporting oil, but the sharp improvement in
the terms of trade had not as yet taken place.

Availability of these freshly contracted loans and
some repatriation of capital were a reflection of the
greater confidence that was created, because the
nominal exchange rate was considered to be stable as
a result of the coverage commitment acquired by the
central bank. Confidence in the peso was gained.
Private investment began to increase in the last
quarter of 1977 and continued through 1978, before the
large increase in public spending took place. So one
of the reasons for the speed with which the IMF program
was abandoned and for the recovery that took place was
this restoration of confidence--one of the main

ingredients that must again occur for the next recovery
to take place. Without confidence, there is no way the
balance of payments can be managed and growth resumed.

As noted by Lance Taylor, exchange controls do not
work. He proposes some of them nevertheless, but they
do not work except to prevent the entry of capital.
One of the largest capital flights Mexico has had took
place from September to November of 1982, when absolute
foreign exchange and trading restrictions were imposed,
limiting or prohibiting what people could do with
dollars, gold, or whatever. Foreign currency just did
not come in. And what happened to the money from
Mexican exports? It was taken to a new peso market in
the United States. Without confidence, people will not
save at home; their behavior will exert continuous
pressure on the exchange rate, on inflation, and on
exports to exceed imports to finance capital flight.
All this in turn continually depresses the prospects
for resumption in the growth of the economy. Thus,
many of the measures that have been implemented are
aimed at the restoration of confidence, which unhappily
is much harder now because of what happened in 1982.

I would like to end with some comments on the
instruments and policies that should be followed to
generate the recovery. As I see it, the whole story
suggests a basis for optimism. The story of bad
decisions on public investments is not the basis for
excessive self-criticism; it provides, rather, some
hope and some optimism, since there is so much cloth
to cut. Much of what has been said in the other
chapters supports this optimism. The savings potential
obtained through project evaluation and through honest
management of resources is enormous. The numbers are
staggering, and the argument applies as well to many
public enterprises. The low level of investments now
taking place reflects a tremendous amount of used
capacity and indicates that people are no longer spending just for the sake of spending.

Now that provides some room for future policy.
The situation would be quite different if we needed a
lot of fresh credit to sustain an increasing rate of
investment, as we did in the 1977 recovery, when a
large gap separated the actual and the needed or desired stock of capital.

There are other elements in the story. Inflation
is being brought down for reasons already discussed,
and this drop has permitted a substantial fall in
nominal interest rates. Nominal interest rates have
fallen more than 15 percentage points from their peak
in 1983, and they are continuing to fall. This continuation is very important, because I agree with
Fishlow that we had to make a critical choice in 1982
between controlling inflation or indexing. Since

Mexico correctly decided not to index, we are now faced
with the problem of high nominal interest rates. These
high rates, when there is no indexing, generate a very
quick amortization of payments, thereby crowding out
mortgage credit and other long-term credits desired by
long-term investors. Through the same reasoning, the
reduction in nominal interest rates expected for 1984
will also give the government room for adjusting its
finances and will encourage private investment in durables and investment goods.

I am not as pessimistic as others about the trade
sector. To be sure, once the real exchange rate becomes aligned more nearly with its historical level,
problems are going to arise in the exports of some
manufactured goods. The real exchange rate may not go
up to what it had been for so many years, considering
the slack in demand, but it will go up. The peso is
still substantially undervalued. Although return of
the real exchange rate to historical or near-historical
levels will create difficulties for a few exports--
which were probably transitory exports anyway--consi-
derable room can be found for growth exports by
efficient manufacturers and for import substitution,
which has already taken place to a substantial degree.
Import substitution can be a useful and efficient tool
to reduce imports and to expand domestic markets, if it
results from correct aggregate-demand policies and the
right relative prices. For these reasons I think there
is room for a resumption of growth, provided public
finances continue on their straightening path, and the
needed microstructural adjustments are carried through.

Contributors

Jorge A. Bustamante, General Director, Centro de Estudios Fronterizos del Norte de Mexico

Albert Fishlow, Professor of Economics, University of California, Berkeley

Kenneth Flamm, Senior Fellow, The Brookings Institution

Pasqual García-Alba, El Colegio de Mexico

Francisco Gil Díaz, Subdirector de Investigacion Economica, Banco de Mexico

Joseph Grunwald, Senior Fellow, The Brookings Institution

Santiago Levy, Center for Latin American Studies, Boston University

Richard Mines, University of California, Davis

Clark W. Reynolds, The Food Research Institute, Stanford University

Alan Richards, Associate Professor of Economics, University of California, Santa Cruz

Daniel M. Schydlowsky, Professor of Economics, Center for Latin American Development Studies, Boston University

Jaime Serra Puche, El Colegio de Mexico

Lance Taylor, Professor of Economics, Massachusetts Institute of Technology

Thomas J. Trebat, Vice-President, Bankers Trust Company, New York

Sidney Weintraub, Dean Rusk Professor of International Affairs, University of Texas, Austin

Index